Formal Methods Fact File

VDM and Z

Andrew Harry

JOHN WILEY & SONS
Chichester • New York • Brisbane • Toronto • Singapore

Published in 1996 by John Wiley & Sons
Baffins Lane, Chichester,
West Sussex PO19 1UD, England

National 01243 779777
International (+44) 1243 779777

e-mail (for orders and customer service enquiries): cs-books@wiley.co.uk
Visit our Home Page on http://www.wiley.co.uk or http://www.wiley.com

Other Wiley Editorial Offices

John Wiley & Sons, Inc., 605 Third Avenue,
New York, NY 10158-0012, USA

Jacaranda Wiley Ltd, 33 Park Road, Milton,
Queensland 4064, Australia

John Wiley & Sons (Canada) Ltd, 22 Worcester Road,
Rexdale, Ontario M9W 1L1, Canada

John Wiley & Sons (Asia) Pte Ltd, 2 Clementi Loop #02-01,
Jin Xing Distripark, Singapore 0512

British Library Cataloguing in Publication Data

A catalogue record for this book is available from the British Library

ISBN 0 471 94006 2 (cloth); 0 471 95857 3 (pbk)

Produced from camera-ready copy supplied by the author.
Printed and bound in Great Britain by Bookcraft (Bath) Ltd
This book is printed on acid-free paper responsibly manufactured from sustainable forestation, for which at least two trees are planted for each one used for paper production.

Formal Methods Fact File

Straightforward words
seem paradoxical

LXXVIII

Lao Tzu by Tao Te Ching

Contents

Preface

Formal methods offer ways of specifying computer systems that have many advantages over current conventional specification techniques. Despite this they have not been universally embraced.

Part of the reason for this is that people are put off by the mathematics of formal methods; specifications seem abstruse and cryptic, full of strange symbols and words, in many ways resembling some magical text only understood by a chosen few. In fact, learning a formal method is not as difficult as it might seem; you are probably writing small formal specifications already. If you wanted to add two numbers together you might write:

$$A = 1 + 2$$

You would not write the natural language equivalent:

Put one with two and place in A.

The former mathematical text is as much a formal specification as any of the specifications given in the rest of this book. It displays many of the properties of formal specifications; being unambiguous, concise and complete.

Learning any language, whether a computer based or a social one takes time. It takes even longer to become proficient in their use. Formal methods are no exception.

They do not, as is a popular misconception, take the creativity out of programming. There are as many ways of writing a formal specification as there are of programming it. Needless to say, only a few of these ways are good. Like programming there are both good ways and bad ways of developing and writing specifications. A good formal specification will not constrain a programmer, it will guide them, helping to remove the necessity for clarification that so often comes with a natural language text. A formal specification is written by an individual for another individual to read; write your specifications accordingly.

This book serves as an introduction to formal methods. It is designed to show:

- Why we need formal methods,
- the mathematics behind formal notations,
- how the many different styles of formal method fit together,
- the constructs and notation of two specific formal notations,
- how semantics can be used to prove formal specifications,
- what tools are available.

A. HARRY
June 1996

Acknowledgements

Although this book has one author, in truth it is only through the help and advice of numerous friends and colleagues that I have managed to write it.

In particular I would like to thank the following. Nick North and Graeme Parkin for providing help, and patiently explaining much of the work that has gone into this book. Richard Lampard for supplying the Estelle example given in Chapter 3 and Harold Munster for providing the LOTOS example in the same chapter. Mr Tim Denvir for reviewing and providing many helpful comments on the book. Andy Lovering for giving encouragement and support.

I would also like to thank the DTI and in particular Eric Roche for allowing me to use extracts from reports produced for them, and my editor Rosemary Altoft for her patience and assistance. There are many other people, far too numerous to mention.

1

Why do we need formal methods?

With the increasing complexity of software, and a greater requirement for reliability, it has become clear that the old *ad hoc* informal methods of programming are no longer stringent enough. Even with the use of software engineering and structured design methods the quality of software is often still poor. In cases where computer failure could cause life endangering situations this is plainly inadequate and a rigorous methodology for specifying and designing software is required.

Formal methods are based on the idea that computer programming is built upon a relatively small number of fundamental concepts, most of which are present in mathematics in some form or another (for example; equality, arithmetic operation etc.). It is therefore possible that specifications for programs can be given in a *formal mathematical notation* which unambiguously defines the requirements.

Formal methods do not provide a universal panacea to software problems. We cannot expect them to solve everything. Most of us rely in some way or other on computerised systems, but this does not mean that we can reasonably expect them to take care of everything. You may rely on the braking system on your car, but this does not mean it will never fail. The world is far too complex for us to foresee and predict every possible eventuality.

However, whilst we cannot prevent disasters we can certainly reduce the chances of them occurring, through rigorous quality assurance in design and testing. Most of us would expect that the items we use in everyday life have been quality tested for safety and reliability. Formal methods offer a way of increasing that assurance in the design and operation of software. Using them can help reduce the possibility of errors that creep in during the creation of software due to impreciseness and misinterpretation.

There is no way they will give total immunity. There is no way to guarantee that the formal specification matches the original requirements and that all possible situations have been taken into account. It is still quite possible to make errors in specification and proof. This said, however, their use can greatly increase confidence in the correctness of software produced with them.

A formal notation, correctly used, facilitates exact description, and provides a basis for the verification of the properties of the application it describes, and the development of conformance tests. Like any tool it can be used wisely or badly.

1.1. WHY FORMAL METHODS WERE DEVELOPED

Formal methods came about for two main reasons.

- **The interpretation of natural languages**. Just as there was a need for a specific legal language to deal with issues of law because normal everyday wording could be misconstrued and loopholes discovered, there has been found to be a need for specific languages for developing computer systems. By developing notations that have precise, unambiguous meanings that are not open to multiple interpretations there is reduction in the freedom of interpretation which reduces the chance of misunderstandings arising and the introduction of errors.

- **The manipulation of specifications**. Natural language is large and complex and cannot easily be manipulated. Attempts at creating systems capable of analysing and manipulating natural language in a meaningful way have met with limited success. If the work involved in the creation and testing of programs is to be helped by the use of tools it is necessary for specifications to be in a form which can be interpreted and manipulated by machines. Because of their precise meaning formal notations offer distinct advantages in this area. Being rigidly defined they allow new rules to be defined from specified ones in provable ways (such as by pattern matching) allowing such things as automatic algebraic simplification and proof analysis.

1.2. NATURAL LANGUAGE SPECIFICATIONS

The most obvious way of describing requirements is to use natural language; it is easily readable and widely understood. However, natural language descriptions tend to be verbose and can suffer from a variety of problems. In this section we look at some of the problems that can occur when describing computer systems in a natural language.

1.2.1 Ambiguity

Many words in natural language have multiple meanings and interpretations depending on their context. Sentences can therefore be interpreted in many different ways. Poetry and literature often rely on this ambiguity to produce powerful images. Humour too is often based around the double meaning of a word or situation. There is thus a fundamental need for ambiguity in natural languages. In software development, however, this ambiguity becomes a drawback rather than an asset.

Ambiguity in natural language means that many words and sentences are context-sensitive. Understanding and interpretation are inferred from the general surrounding text, often intuitively. It is unlikely that computers could carry out this type of interpretation with any degree of accuracy. Take for example the following requirement:

> The program will take a sequence of numbers and return a sorted list.

What is meant by sorted? This has not been defined clearly; Does it mean in ascending order, descending order, or within classes (for example, into whole numbers and fractions)? The specification does not clearly state what the sorted list consists of. We can infer from the surrounding text that it is the sequence of numbers, but this is not clearly stated. A program that took a sequence of numbers and then returned a completely different set of sorted values would still be fulfilling this specification.

1.2.2 Incompleteness and vagueness

Taking the previous example, how many numbers do we input? When is the sorted list output? Both of these questions are left unanswered. Natural language allows us to leave details unspecified and incomplete.

1.2.3 Contradiction

A set of requirements may contain statements at odds with each other. Typically these contradictions may be spread throughout the requirements so it will not be self-evident that they exist.

An example of a contradiction occurs in the following requirements:

> When the retrieve function is activated the beta file will be locked and no other access allowed. The retrieve function is activated by pressing the F1 button.
>
> Pressing the F7 function key will carry out all the functions of the F1 button. Concurrently with this, the date (held as the first field on the beta file) will be obtained using the getdate function and displayed on the screen.

It can be seen that when the retrieve function is activated no other access is allowed on the beta file. However, in the second statement the retrieve function is activated indirectly, and this prevents any other access of the beta file. The second part of this statement requires access of the beta file to obtain the date. This leads to a contradiction.

If these two statements were spread widely apart in a requirement their variance could easily be overlooked, resulting in an error at run time as the getdate function tried to access the file, but was prevented by the retrieve function.

1.3. FORMAL VS INFORMAL PROGRAMMING

One of the first criticisms that people bring up is that many of the problems mentioned previously could be solved by writing the requirements in a programming language. After all, they argue, are not most programming languages unambiguous, with tools capable of detecting static and dynamic inconsistencies (such as compilers and debuggers)? This argument leads to the suggestion that formal specification is unnecessary and that we can go straight to writing code. This overlooks a number of points.

Firstly, programming languages are implementation specific; the way they operate depends on the compiler used, the version of the language used and the machine on which they operate. Although the semantics of a language may be well defined (and this is often not the case) it is still hard to predict the behaviour of a program. They are therefore not as unambiguous as we may have originally envisaged.

Secondly, the syntax and operation of programming languages varies; it is often hard, if not impossible, to convert a specification from one programming language to another. Symbols often vary, or mean entirely different things. Unless you are completely conversant with the language it is hard to understand what is going on.

What is required is a language that is not dependent on the environment in which it is placed and uses a set of symbols universally understood. Formal methods work in an abstract environment, they are not dependent on any particular machine. They are based on a mathematical notation which is universal to all languages.

Like computer programs a formal specification is made up of two things; data, which consists of the objects we wish to manipulate, and statements, explaining what we want to do with the data[1].

Most programming languages require the latter to be explained in terms of a series of steps (algorithms) explaining the explicit steps involved in obtaining the results we want. We can compare this with a cookery book. In a recipe we are given the ingredients required and a step by step account of how to mix and cook them to obtain the final result (in computer science our ingredients are data, the instructions algorithms).

Formal methods allow us to go to a higher level of abstraction than this. We start by saying what we want, not how to obtain it. In this way we define what our expectations are before we become bogged down in the detail of how to obtain them. This allows us to set our requirements out clearly and unambiguously before we have to get down to the nitty-gritty of actually defining how we go about obtaining them.

Whereas programming starts at the recipes, formal methods start at the point at which we decide what the meal will be. When we are making a meal we first of all decide what we want to eat; only after we have done this do we look at the recipe and find out how to cook it.

By having a clear idea of what we want, we get a clearer idea of what our goal is. This helps us navigate our way through the problem. If we wish to get from A to B we can normally go about it in two ways; either we can plan the route by first looking at a map and by determining our destination choose the most appropriate route to get to it, or we can just leave it to chance and head in the general direction, asking directions on the way. Both methods will eventually get us to our destination, but the former is likely to be a lot quicker and less frustrating.

With formal methods we have a clear idea of where we are going. We can progressively break the problem into a series of steps, or stages necessary to accomplish it.

With informal programming this is often not the case. We start off knowing the general direction and head for it. Often the requirements will change as we go along, so we have to go back and alter the code. The resultant program, even if it accomplishes the task we want it to do, is likely to do it in a tortuous and error-prone way. It will also be hard to read and understand making it more difficult to revise on a later date.

---

[1] This is not strictly true in the case of process-based and algebraic specifications as we shall see later.

1.4. THE ADVANTAGES OF FORMAL METHODS

Formal methods offer distinct advantages over the normal process of program development:

- Formal specifications allow precise interpretation; there is therefore no possibility of argument about what has been specified.

- Formal methods allow systems to be defined in abstract terms; in particular developers can look at what a system is to do before becoming bogged down in detail as to how it is to be accomplished.

- A formal methodology demands attention to issues of completeness[2] and consistency[3], therefore reducing the chances of overlooking certain areas or situations which could cause errors or bugs.

- The use of a formal methodology (based on mathematical principles), allows the progressive refinement of an abstract specification into a concrete specification using well-defined rules. This leads to the possibility of generating programs from formal specifications automatically.

- Using formal descriptions it is possible to detect deviations (intentional or otherwise) of a program from its original specification. It may be possible to create tools to carry out much of this detection work.

Used early in system development they help reveal design flaws, used later they can help determine the correctness of a system and whether it has been implemented properly.

An additional benefit of formal description methods occurs in international projects. Because of the problems already mentioned in interpreting natural language it is often very hard to translate a natural language specification written in one language into another foreign language. Automatic translators have met with very limited success in this area. Formal methods can help in this area. Being based on mathematics, which is universally understood, the only language-dependent parts of a formal specification are variable and function names, which usually consist of simple words or phrases that can be easily converted using a lookup table consisting of equivalent words. This is in comparison to a natural language specification which will probably contain complex sentences and paragraphs. A formal specification is therefore more likely to be translated correctly, and can therefore be used to augment understanding of the

---

[2] A specification is complete if it covers all possible situations that can occur.

[3] A specification shows consistency if it contains no contradictions.

natural language part of the standard. With the ever increasing demand for the use of international standards and research this may play a greater role in the application of formal descriptions.

1.5. REQUIREMENTS OF A FORMAL SYSTEM

For a formal methodology to be complete it must be able to fulfil the following requirements:

1) **Specification**. It must be possible to state what a program is meant to do in a formal precise way.

2) **Verification**. Given the specification and a program obtained, it should be possible to prove using formal mathematical methods that the program does what the specification states.

Contemporary formal methods incorporate a *formal description technique* (FDT) for the production of the *specifications*.

A *formal development method* (FDM) is also incorporated in some formal systems to provide the mathematical apparatus whereby design steps may be checked against the specification and shown to satisfy it (*verification*).

Formal methods can therefore be seen as covering two areas: specification and development. In order to carry out verification it is necessary to be able to formally represent the program itself; that is, an exact specification of the semantics or meaning of each programming language construct is required.

2

Background material

To understand the theory behind formal methods notation a background in discrete mathematics is required. This chapter gives a brief introduction to this, as well as giving details of some of the basic operators common to many of the formal notations found in this book. Later chapters are devoted to specific languages and examine operators and constructs particular to each of them.

The symbols given for operators in this section are commonly used ones and are likely to be the same for most notations. There is a great deal of variance, however, in the notations.

At the end of this chapter the reader should be familiar with the basic operators underlying most formal methods. In later chapters these operators are used in working examples. This will clarify how the operators are used in practice.

2.1. ELEMENTARY SET THEORY

Sets form the backbone of mathematics. Nearly everything in mathematics and computer theory can be represented in terms of sets. It is therefore important to understand the theory behind these basic objects and their operators.

2.1.1 Sets

A set is an unordered collection of associated objects, each entity of which is distinct from the other members of the set. There are no duplicate elements in a set. Take any fixed collection of objects, for example, a, b, c, d. We can form sets of objects taken from this collection. Thus A = {a, b, d} means that set A contains the elements a, b and d. Sets can also contain other sets as members, so we can say, for example, A = {{a, b, c}, { a}} which means set A contains the sets {a} and {a, b, c}. A set can also be empty in which case we represent it by {} (or alternately by the null symbol ∅).

Sets are simple unstructured collections. Order and repetition do not apply to them, thus A = {b, a, d} and A = {d, a, b} are equivalent definitions of the same set. If we make a set B of the elements a, b, b, d, d then the set will consist of B = {a, b, d}. Set A is the same as set B since they both contain exactly the same elements.

$b \in A$ means element b is a member of set A and $c \notin A$ means that c is *not* a member of set A.

If every element of set A is a member of set B we can say set A is a subset of set B, thus if A = {1, 3} and B = {1, 2, 3, 4} then A is a subset of B represented by $A \subset B$. Often a subset is represented by the more general notation $A \subseteq B$ which also allows A to be equal to B, a property which the proper subset operator '⊂' specifically excludes. Thus both {1, 2} and {1, 2, 3, 4} would be valid subsets of B when using $A \subseteq B$. It follows that A = B iff[1] $A \subseteq B$ and $B \subseteq A$.

The *powerset* of a set is the set of *all* possible subsets of it and is represented by '$\mathbb{P}$'. For example, if

$$A = \{a, b, c\}$$

then:

$$\mathbb{P}(A) = \{\{\}, \{a\}, \{b\}, \{c\}, \{a, b\}, \{a, c\}, \{b, c\}, \{a, b, c\}\}$$

Note that the powerset includes the empty set and the set itself.

In the previous examples we have defined sets by stating the contents, or members of the set explicitly; this is referred to as *set enumeration*. Often sets are too large to be specified in this way, and are therefore specified by some property all the members of the set possess. We say that such a set is described *implicitly*. We represent the set S of all objects that have the property P in common in the form:

$$S = \{x \mid P(x)\}$$

---

[1] iff means if and only if.

which can be read as 'S is the set of all elements x with the property P'. This type of notation (defining a set by properties of the elements) is known as *set comprehension*.

For example, we could define natural numbers (the set of all non-negative whole numbers) as:

$$\mathbb{N} = \{ x \mid x \text{ modulus } 1 = 0 \text{ and } x \geq 0 \}$$

The *union* $A \cup B$ of two sets A and B is the set which has as its members exactly those objects which belong either to A or to B (or to both), as shown by the shaded area in Fig. 2.1.

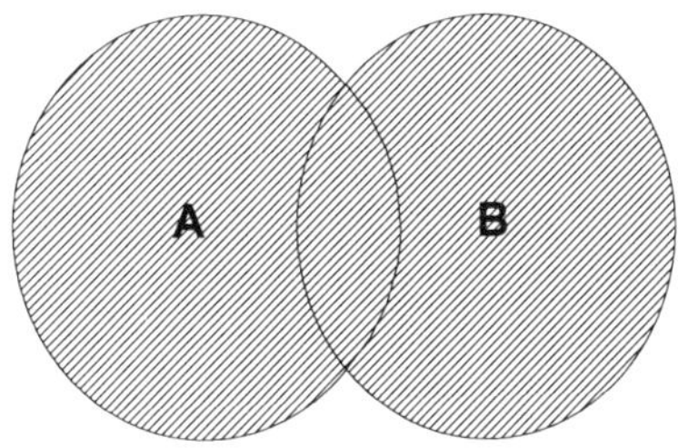

Figure 2.1: $A \cup B = \{x \mid x \in A \text{ or } x \in B\}$

For example:

$$\{a, b, c\} \cup \{c, d, e, f\} = \{a, b, c, d, e, f\}$$

The *intersection* $A \cap B$ of two sets A and B is the set that has as its members exactly those objects which belong to both A and B (Fig. 2.2). For example:

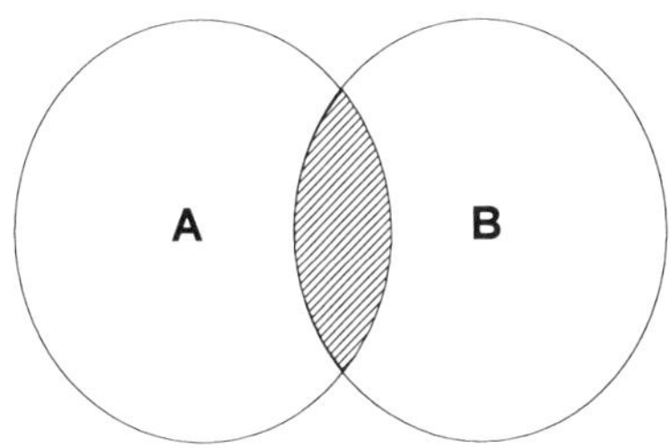

Figure 2.2: $A \cap B = \{x \mid x \in A \text{ and } x \in B\}$

$$\{a, b, c, d\} \cap \{c, d, e, f\} = \{c, d\}$$

It is also possible to have distributed or generalised union and intersection. In these cases the operator applies to a set of sets. Distributed or generalised union $\bigcup SS$ of a set of sets (SS) results in a set containing those elements that occur in at least one of the component sets. For example:

$$\bigcup\{\{a, b, c\}, \{c, d, e\}, \{d, e, f\}\} = \{a, b, c, d, e, f\}$$

Distributed or generalised intersection $\bigcap SS$ of a set of sets results in a set containing only those elements which occur in all of the component sets. For example:

$$\bigcap\{\{a, b, c, d,\}, \{c, d, e\}, \{c, d, e, f\}\} = \{c, d\}$$

The *relative complement* (or *difference*) A - B of two sets A and B is the set which has as its members exactly those objects in A that are not in B (Fig. 2.3).

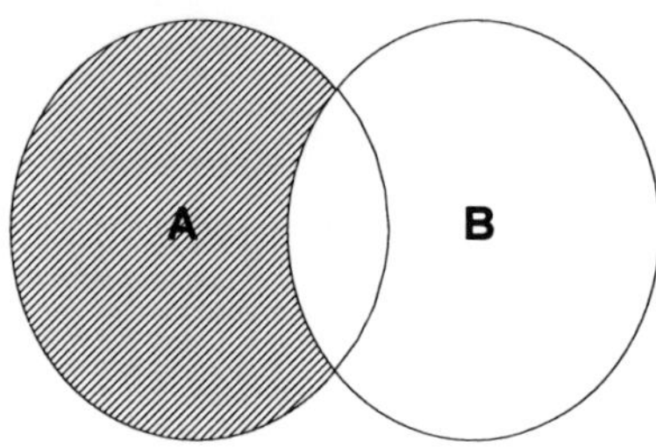

Figure 2.3: $A - B = \{x \mid x \in A \text{ and } x \notin B\}$

For example:

$$\{a, b, c, d, e\} - \{d, e, f, g\} = \{a, b, c\}$$

The *absolute complement* (or *symmetric difference*) A + B of two sets A and B is the set which has as its members exactly those members of each set that are not members of the other set (Fig. 2.4). For example:

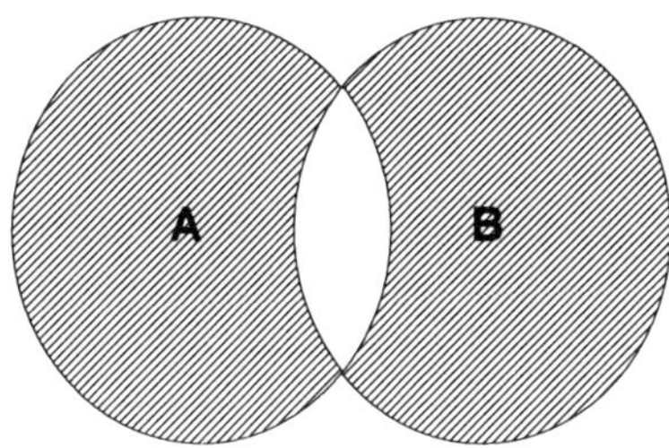

Figure 2.4: A + B = (A - B) ∪ (B - A)

{a, b, c, d, e} + {d, e, f, g} = {a, b, c, f, g}

If two sets have no elements in common, their intersection is the empty set {} and they are said to be *disjoint.*

The *cardinality* of a set is a count of the number of *members* in a set. It is symbolised by **card**(A). For example:

A = {2, 3, 4}	**card**(A) = 3
B = {{a, b, c}, {b}}	**card**(B) = 2

Cardinality only applies to sets of a finite size. Sometimes it is known by the alternate title of 'size' in which case it is usually represented by the hash symbol '#'.

In this book the symbols $\mathbb{B}$, $\mathbb{Z}$, $\mathbb{N}$, $\mathbb{Q}$ and $\mathbb{R}$ are used to represent the sets Boolean, Integer, Natural, Rational and Real numbers respectively.

Boolean consists only of the two truth values true and false (sometimes represented by the values 0 and 1 or *tt* and *ff*)

The set of Integers consists of all *whole* numbers, both negative and non-negative. e.g. ..., -3, -2, -1, 0, 1, 2, 3, ...

The set of Natural numbers is a subset of the integers which consists of only *non-negative* integers 0, 1, 2, ... There is some contention whether zero is a natural number, though this is generally accepted as being true. If we wish to define the set of natural numbers without zero we use the notation $\mathbb{N}^+$ to represent the values from one onwards 1, 2, 3, ...

The set of rational numbers consists of expressions $^a/_b$ where a and b are integers and b is not equal to zero[2], and two expressions $^a/_b$ and $^c/_d$ are said to be equal if a * d = b * c.

---

[2] 'a' is known as the numerator and 'b' the denominator.

The set of Real numbers we can regard as all numbers that can be represented by a terminating or non-terminating decimal value. All the number sets mentioned previously are subsets of the type Real.

Generally these sets can have an infinite number of elements, though some formal notations restrict their sets to finite ones. In languages where sets are normally defined as being infinite there is often a symbol which can be used to make such sets finite (such as the finite set symbol '$\mathbb{F}$' in the **Z** notation).

Sets used in formal specifications are always made up of elements having the same *type* or *class*, where the elements of the sets share some associated property or restriction such as, for example, all belonging to the set of natural numbers. Types and their properties are explained later on in this chapter.

2.1.2 Cartesian products

Sets are lacking in structure; in set notation {x, y} is the same set as {y, x}. If we want order we use round (or sometimes angular brackets) to say that this is important For example, (x, y) is an *ordered pair*. Thus:

{1, 2} is equal to {2, 1}

But (1, 2) is *not* equal to (2, 1)

The *Cartesian product* $A \times B$ of two sets A and B is the set of all *ordered pairs* (a, b) such that $a \in A$ and $b \in B$. For example, if:

$$A = \{a, b, c\}$$
$$B = \{1, 2\}$$

then the Cartesian product is:

$$A \times B = \{(a, 1), (a, 2), (b, 1), (b, 2), (c, 1), (c, 2)\}$$

consisting of all possible combinations of the elements of set A with the elements of set B.

Cartesian products can be made up of any number of sets. Their elements are referred to as *tuples*, though where such a tuple consists only of two members we usually call this an *ordered pair* (as above). Where it consists of three members we call it a *triple* and where it consists of n members we refer to it as an *n-tuple*.

2.2. TYPES

The definition of what constitutes a type is very much dependent upon the formal notation used; there is no single comprehensive definition that could encompass them all. We can broadly view a type as being a special kind of set, constraining the values that an object or expression of the type can take. They help to prevent meaningless expressions and ensure that a specification is well formed. Types can be looked on as consisting of a logically related set of values, or literals and a set of predefined operators for generating, manipulating and collating these values. In most formal notations there exist three distinct types:

i) **Predefined basic types**, corresponding to Boolean, Integer, Real and Natural numbers. These types inherit all the properties of their respective sets, for example types consisting of integers can be multiplied, added and subtracted. Boolean types can be compared for equality.

   Some languages also have subsets of the Real numbers defined as basic types, and others the types character (**char**) and text (**text**). The latter types being used to hold individual and strings of characters respectively; they have the equality operators defined for them.

ii) **User defined types** consist of sets defined by the specifier, for example

$$\text{DEFINEDTYPE} = \{2, 4, 8\}$$

   These types can be defined explicitly as above, or by some property, or invariant, that applies to all the members of the set as we saw with set comprehension.

iii) **Compound types** are types that are constructed of other types by application of a type operator to one or more types: for example, the powerset of a type, or the Cartesian product type.

By defining an object to be of a certain type we constrain it to only being capable of holding values of that type; for example, an object defined to be of type integer can only take on integer values. Objects of a certain type also inherit the operations associated with the type. Thus an object of type integer can, for example, be added, subtracted and multiplied with another number of the same type because the type integer has these operations associated with it.

2.2.1 Products and tuples

A product is a collection of values. A product type consists of a set of tuples (each consisting of an ordered collection of two or more values). For example, each element of the following product type:

$$\text{NAME} \times \text{ADDRESS} \times \text{TELEPHONENO}$$

consists of a tuple containing a name, address and telephone number. A product type consists of the set of tuples corresponding to its component types. If, for example, we take the following product type expression:

$$\mathbb{B} \times \mathbb{B}$$

we could list the entire set of tuples of this product type as:

$$\langle \text{true, true} \rangle$$
$$\langle \text{true, false} \rangle$$
$$\langle \text{false, true} \rangle$$
$$\langle \text{false, false} \rangle$$

In many formal languages the type operator $\times$ is not associative. For example, given three types T_1, T_2 and T_3 then $(T_1 \times T_2) \times T_3$ is not the same as $T_1 \times (T_2 \times T_3)$ or $T_1 \times T_2 \times T_3$.

Product types are usually not used for named types[3], which are better represented with more strongly typed composite types. Their main application is in function and operation *signatures* where they can show that more than one parameter is being passed. For example:

$$\text{func} : \mathbb{R} \times \mathbb{N} \rightarrow \mathbb{N}$$

would declare a function receiving a real and natural number as its parameters and returning a natural number as its result.

Another compound type, similar to the Cartesian product type, is the record type. A record type consists of a collection of component values or fields. Each of these fields may have an identifier associated with it by which it can be referenced. For example:

```
Person_details ::  name : NAME
                   address: ADDRESS
                   telno: TELEPHONE_NO
```

---

[3] A named type has an identifier or tag attached to it.

which consists of a record type Person_details containing field types NAME, ADDRESS and TELEPHONENO associated with the identifiers name, address and telno. The record type Person_details therefore contains three component fields. Records differ from product types in that they represent unique types.

Two product types with the same components would represent the same product type, thus:

$$PT_1 = NAME \times ADDRESS \times TELEPHONENO$$

and

$$PT_2 = NAME \times ADDRESS \times TELEPHONENO$$

would both represent the same type, whereas two record types:

```
Person_details ::   name : NAME
                    address: ADDRESS
                    telno: TELEPHONE_NO

Mail_details ::     name : NAME
                    address: ADDRESS
                    telno: TELEPHONE_NO
```

although having the same components would represent distinct types due to their name tags being different. Even if the components of the record type are the same if their name tags differ they are distinct.

Record types are generally used to represent data structures containing various items of data that are mutually connected. They are therefore composite types.

The syntax and construction of product types and records vary; this will be detailed in later chapters when we look at specific languages.

2.2.2 Enumerated types

Another complex type is the enumerated type. An enumerated type consists of the union of a number of named literals. In many languages the value and the type of each literal is represented by a single name consisting of a sequence of distinguished letters (CAPITAL LETTERS). For example:

RED

Enumerated types are formed by the type unions of a number of these literals, representing a small set of distinct values in which the order is not important. For example:

signal = RED | AMBER | GREEN

which states that signal consists of the union of the three literals RED, AMBER and GREEN, where each of the literals represents one particular value.

These literals only have the equality operators defined for them, enabling comparison between the values of the types, For example:

RED = RED is true
RED = GREEN is false

A literal will always represent the same value throughout a specification.

2.2.3 Mathematical operators

Types inherit the mathematical operators of their respective sets. As we have previously stated, all sets of numbers are restricted subsets of the real numbers[4]. Many of the more common operators are therefore ubiquitous to all these types such as addition, subtraction, multiplication and division.

Given a value X, the absolute operator **abs** X returns the absolute value of X, that is, a non-negative value of the same magnitude as X. For example:

abs -20 = 20
abs 2.3 = 2.3

Given a value X, the floor, or integer part operator floor X will return the greatest (most positive) integer value not greater than X. For example:

floor -1.5 = -2
floor 5.5 = 5
floor 20 = 20

Given two values X and Y, the integer division operator X **div** Y returns the integer quotient. For example:

5 **div** 2 = 2

---

[4] Ignoring complex numbers which can be regarded as a Cartesian product with operators.

The integer remainder operator returns the remainder from the division:

5 **rem** 2 = 1

and the modulus operator X mod Y returns the modulus:

5 **mod** 2 = 1

The remainder and modulus operators are essentially the same, but differ in some notations when the arguments are of different signs, with the remainder operator taking the sign of the first argument and the modulus taking the sign of the second argument. Thus:

-11 **rem** 3 = -2
-11 **mod** 3 = 2

and:

11 **rem** -3 = 2
11 **mod** -3 = -2

There are six comparison operators; equality =, inequality ≠, less than <, less than or equal to ≤, greater than >, and greater or equal to ≥. These all return Boolean values, for example:

$2 \neq 2$ returns false,
$2 < 3$ returns true,
$2 \leq 3$ returns true,
$3 \leq 3$ returns true,
$2 > 3$ returns false,
$3 \geq 2$ returns true,
$3 \geq 3$ returns true.

2.2.4 Bags

Whilst sets are unordered structures in which every element is unique, in bags, or multisets, duplicates are allowed. However, as with sets there is still no ordering to the elements, thus ⟦a, b, b, c, c⟧ is the same as ⟦c, b, a, b, c⟧ Bags are written with outlined curly or square brackets.

The count operator tells how many times a particular element occurs in the list.

count ⟦a, b, b, c, c, c⟧ b = 2

Most of the bag operators, such as cardinality, are the same as for sets. However, there are important differences when it comes to the union, intersection and difference operations.

There is some contention over what constitutes *bag union* and there are currently two distinct definitions. In the first, the resultant bag is formed by including the maximum number of times an element occurs in either of the two bags, thus:

$$[\![a, b, b, c, d, d, d]\!] \cup [\![b, c, c, d, d]\!] = [\![a, b, b, c, c, d, d, d]\!]$$

In the second definition the resultant bag contains the sum of the elements of the two bags, thus:

$$[\![a, b, b, c, d, d, d]\!] \cup [\![b, c, c, d, d]\!] = [\![a, b, b, b, c, c, c, d, d, d, d, d]\!]$$

Which definition applies depends on the notation being used. In most cases the latter definition is the more commonly used. It is sometimes referred to as *bag sum* to avoid confusion.

Bag intersection is defined as having the resultant bag formed by including for each element that occurs in both bags the minimum number of times it occurs in either bag, thus:

$$[\![a, b, b, c, c, c]\!] \cap [\![b, c, c]\!] = [\![b, c, c]\!]$$

There is doubt, however, as to whether intersection is a legitimate operation on bags, and some formal specification languages such as **Z** eschew it.

In *bag difference* we subtract the number of elements in the second bag from the first bag, thus:

$$[\![a, b, b, c, c, c]\!] - [\![a, b, c]\!] = [\![b, c, c]\!]$$

Bags are useful where we wish to count the number of occurrences of objects and can be thought of as sets with duplicates. Most formal methods do not, however, include bags as a standard data type. This is partly because they are not as clearly defined as other data types.

2.2.5 Sequences

A sequence, or list, is an *ordered* collection of objects or values of the same type, possibly containing repetitions. An object within a sequence is an *element* of that sequence. Sequences are usually represented with square brackets[5] [...].

The empty sequence is represented by []. A sequence containing the elements a, b, b, d *in that order* would be represented as [a, b, b, d]. Sequences are normally defined explicitly (as in the previous example), though in many formal languages they can also be defined implicitly (by defining some property of the elements). The implicit representation follows the same format as that for set comprehension except that sequence brackets are used instead of set ones. For example:

$$[n \mid 0 \leq n \leq 5]$$

which states a sequence [0, 1, 2, 3, 4, 5].

The head of a sequence (**hd**) is the first element of the sequence, and the tail (**tl**) is the sequence of remaining elements, thus if:

A = [a, b, c, d, d, e, f]

hd A = a
tl A = [b, c, d, d, e, f]

Note that **hd** A is *an element,* whilst **tl** A is another *sequence.*

The length of a sequence (**len**) is the number of elements in a sequence, including any repetitions, i.e. in the previous set:

len A = 7

Because a sequence is ordered each element of the sequence can be indexed. We can select an element of a sequence by application. Thus, for example, we could select the third element of the sequence A:

A(3) = c

The number given in the brackets is the position of the element in the sequence.

The indices (**inds**) of a sequence is a set corresponding to the index of the values in the sequence, i.e. for the previous sequence:

inds A = {1, 2, 3, 4, 5, 6 , 7}

It is important to note that in formal notations the first element of a sequence is indexed by the value one, not as in many programming languages zero.

---

[5] Though some formal notations have used angular brackets '⟨...⟩' and refer to these as lists in their documentation.

Thus:

$$\textbf{hd}\ A = A(1)$$

When converting from a formal notation to a programming language this must be taken into account.

The elements (**elems**) of a sequence is a set of the values in the sequence. Simplistically, it can be thought of as converting a sequence into a set.

$$\textbf{elems}\ A = \{a, b, c, d, e, f\}$$

Notice 'd' is not repeated, as the result is a set and therefore contains no duplicates.

The *concatenation* of two sequences is a sequence consisting of all the elements in the first sequence followed by all the elements in the second sequence. For example, [a, b, b, c] concatenated with [c, d, d, e] is [a, b, b, c, c, d, d, e].

A distributed concatenation operator exists in some languages which allows a sequence of sequences to be concatenated together. The symbol used for the concatenation operator varies greatly from formal method to formal method and has therefore not been introduced at this stage.

2.3. FORMAL LOGIC

Logic is concerned with the study of valid reasoning or arguments. Arguments occur in everyday life and in mathematics (in the form of proofs and derivations). In such cases a conclusion is derived from some premises or assumptions. *Assumptions* have some truth value. For example:

$$3^2 = 9$$

All grass is green

Deductions or *conclusions* are *derived* from assumptions. For example:

> Either there is a largest prime,
> or there is an infinite number of primes.
> There is no largest prime.
> Therefore, there is an infinite number of primes.

The truth or otherwise of the conclusion depends on the truth values of the assumptions. Logic defines structures enabling us to represent knowledge, which we would normally express in words, in a formal way describing and prescribing the relationships that hold between facts and allowing new relationships to be inferred.

2.3.1 Propositional logic

Propositional logic is the simplest level of classical logic. It is related to Boolean algebra in that propositions have the values true (*tt*) or false (*ff*).

Propositions can be made up of other propositions connected by one of the logical connectors:

$\wedge$	AND (also represented by & or .).
$\vee$	OR (also represented by | or +).
$\neg$	NOT (also represented by ~).
$\rightarrow$	IMPLIES (also represented by $\Rightarrow$ or $\supset$).
$\leftrightarrow$	EQUIVALENCE (also represented by $\Leftrightarrow$ or $\equiv$).

in which case their values depend on the values of their constituent propositions. Propositions are usually represented as alphabetic characters. For example:

IF it rains THEN I will get wet

The statements 'it rains' and 'I will get wet' are atomic propositions, each with a value true *tt* or false *ff*. They can be represented, for example, by the alphabetic characters, a and b:

IF a THEN b

We use these in Propositional logic in the same way:

$$a \rightarrow b$$

The implies symbol ($\rightarrow$) describes a relationship between the truth values of the two statements a and b. We call the first of these statements the *premise* and the second the *conclusion*. For the proposition to be valid the truth values of the statements must follow certain constraints. For example, if it is raining and I am wet is a valid condition, it does not refute the proposition. The situation where both the premise and conclusion are true therefore does not invalidate the proposition.

Although rain can be the cause of getting wet, you can get wet in other ways apart from being rained upon, so it is also possible that it is not raining and yet you still get wet. In this case the premise is false and the conclusion true. The proposition *permits* the conclusion to be true even when the premise is false without affecting the validity of the proposition.

If it is not raining and I am not wet also does not refute the proposition, since the proposition only states your condition when it is raining. The proposition is therefore still valid.

What the proposition does *not* allow, however, is the situation where it is raining and you do not get wet. If it is raining and you do not get wet then the proposition is clearly not a valid one since there are situations in which the rule does not apply.

It is important to realise that such a statement does not imply any causal connection between the premise and the conclusion; the proposition merely designates the situations to make the implication either true (valid) or false (invalid).

These situations can be summed up in a truth table which shows all possible combinations of values for the propositions a and b:

a	b	$a \rightarrow b$
ff	*ff*	*tt*
ff	*tt*	*tt*
tt	*ff*	*ff*
tt	*tt*	*tt*

IMPLIES truth table

It can be seen from this that the only time $a \rightarrow b$ is false is when a is true and b is false. We can make truth tables for the other connectors too:

a	b	$a \wedge b$
ff	*ff*	*ff*
ff	*tt*	*ff*
tt	*ff*	*ff*
tt	*tt*	*tt*

AND truth table

In this case the only time $a \wedge b$ is true is when both its constituent propositions are true.

a	b	$a \vee b$
ff	*ff*	*ff*
ff	*tt*	*tt*
tt	*ff*	*tt*
tt	*tt*	*tt*

OR truth table

a ∨ b is only false when both constituent propositions are false. Notice in Boolean logic that both propositions can be true and it is still correct; a ∨ b is true when one *or both* of the constituent propositions are true.

a	b	a ↔ b
ff	*ff*	*tt*
ff	*tt*	*ff*
tt	*ff*	*ff*
tt	*tt*	*tt*

EQUIVALENCE truth table

As you would expect in equivalence the proposition is true only if the two constituent propositions are equivalent.

The NOT operator is slightly different in that it is a unary operator applying to only one variable.

a	¬a
ff	*tt*
tt	*ff*

NOT truth Table

The connectors have a precedence order of ¬, ∧, ∨, →, ↔. In a proposition containing a number of operators you would evaluate the NOT first and the EQUIVALENCE last, though brackets can be used to override this order.

Let us now look at another proposition (¬a ∨ b) ↔ (a → b). In finding the values of this proposition the propositions in brackets would be evaluated first, the equivalence last.

a	b	¬a ∨ b	↔	a → b
ff	*ff*	*tt*	*tt*	*tt*
ff	*tt*	*tt*	*tt*	*tt*
tt	*ff*	*ff*	*tt*	*ff*
tt	*tt*	*tt*	*tt*	*tt*

Truth table for proposition

It can be seen from column three (under the equivalence sign) that this proposition is ALWAYS true.

A *Tautology* is a proposition that is always true (for example, a ∨ ¬ a must always be true). For a formula to be *valid* (or *analytic*) it must be true for all possible valuations (truth values) as in the previous truth table, and therefore a tautology. In all other cases it is *invalid*.

A *Contradiction* (or *inconsistency*) is a formula that is ALWAYS false (for example, $a \wedge \neg a$).

A *Contingent* (or *synthetic*) formula is one that is sometimes but not always true.

A formula is *satisfiable* if and only if there is at least one situation in which it is true (thus tautologies and contingent arguments are satisfiable, but contradictions are not).

A formula is *unsatisfiable* if and only if there are no circumstances in which it is true (thus a contradiction is unsatisfiable, but a contingent is not).

Proof by truth table is not very practical as each identifier doubles the size of the table. In the proposition above we saw that $(\neg a \vee b)$ is equivalent to $(a \rightarrow b)$; we could therefore replace the first law with the second and still have the same proposition and vice versa. This proposition forms one of the rules known as the laws of equivalence.

Laws of Equivalence

Where E1, E2 and E3 represent expressions or propositions:

1.	$(E1 \wedge E2) \equiv (E2 \wedge E1)$ $(E1 \vee E2) \equiv (E2 \vee E1)$ $(E1 \leftrightarrow E2) \equiv (E2 \leftrightarrow E1)$	Commutation
2.	$E1 \wedge (E2 \wedge E3) \equiv (E1 \wedge E2) \wedge E3$ $E1 \vee (E2 \vee E3) \equiv (E1 \vee E2) \vee E3$	Association
3.	$E1 \vee (E2 \wedge E3) \equiv (E1 \vee E2) \wedge (E1 \vee E3)$ $E1 \wedge (E2 \vee E3) \equiv (E1 \wedge E2) \vee (E1 \wedge E3)$	Distribution
4.	$\neg(E1 \wedge E2) \equiv \neg E1 \vee \neg E2$ $\neg(E1 \vee E2) \equiv \neg E1 \wedge \neg E2$	De Morgan's
5.	$\neg\neg E1 \equiv E1$	Double Negation
6.	$E1 \vee \neg E1 \equiv tt$	Excluded Middle
7.	$E1 \wedge \neg E1 \equiv ff$	Contradiction
8.	$E1 \rightarrow E2 \equiv \neg E1 \vee E2$	Material Implication

9. $(E1 \leftrightarrow E2) \equiv (E1 \rightarrow E2) \wedge (E2 \rightarrow E1)$ Material Equivalence
$(E1 \leftrightarrow E2) \equiv (E1 \wedge E2) \vee (\neg E1 \wedge \neg E2)$

10. $(E1 \wedge E2) \rightarrow E3 \equiv E1 \rightarrow (E2 \rightarrow E3)$ Exportation

11. $(E1 \vee E1) \equiv E1$ Or-Simplification
$E1 \vee tt \equiv tt$
$E1 \vee ff \equiv E1$

12. $(E1 \wedge E1) \equiv E1$ And-Simplification
$E1 \wedge tt \equiv E1$
$E1 \wedge ff \equiv ff$

Any of the propositions on the left of the equivalence '≡' sign can be exchanged for the proposition on their right-hand side and vice versa. These rules are all *tautologies*.

Using these rules and substitution it is possible to reduce a valid proposition to the single value *true* (*tt*). For example, take the proposition below:

$$x \vee (y \vee x) \vee \neg y$$

We can prove this proposition is a tautology by a series of *rewrites*:

$x \vee (y \vee x) \vee \neg y,$	
$\equiv x \vee \neg y \vee (y \vee x),$	Rule 1 Commutation
$\equiv x \vee (\neg y \vee y) \vee x,$	Rule 2 Association
$\equiv x \vee tt \vee x$	Rule 6 Excluded Middle
$\equiv x \vee x \vee tt$	Rule 1 Commutation
$\equiv x \vee tt$	Rule 11 Or-Simplification
$\equiv tt$	

There are seven additional laws that can be used to help prove propositions. The first of these is called Moden Ponens:

1. $E1 \rightarrow E2$ Modus Ponens
$E1$
$\therefore E2$

It expresses the fact that if we know E1 implies E2 and we can state E1, we can therefore also state E2. The '∴' symbol denotes 'therefore' in the rule. For example, taking our previous argument 'If it rains then I will get wet', if we know it is raining then we can state that we have got wet. The complete set of laws are:

1.	$E1 \rightarrow E2$ $E1$ $\therefore E2$	Modus Ponens
2.	$E1 \rightarrow E2$ $\neg E2$ $\therefore \neg E1$	Modus Tollens
3.	$E1 \rightarrow E2$ $E2 \rightarrow E3$ $\therefore E1 \rightarrow E3$	Hypothetical Syllogism
4.	$E1 \vee E2$ $\neg E1$ $\therefore E2$	Disjunctive Syllogism
5.	$E1 \rightarrow E2 \wedge E3 \rightarrow E4$ $E1 \vee E3$ $\therefore E2 \vee E4$	Constructive Dilemma
6.	$E1 \rightarrow E2 \wedge E3 \rightarrow E4$ $\neg E2 \vee \neg E4$ $\therefore \neg E1 \vee \neg E3$	Destructive Dilemma
7.	$E1$ $E2$ $\therefore E1 \wedge E2$	Conjunction
8.	$E1$ $\therefore E1 \vee E2$	Addition

These rules are constructed from the laws of equivalence and can be proved using them. For example, rules 7 and 8 are merely the reversing of the simplification laws.

2.3.2 Predicate logic

Although Propositional logic enables us to assess arguments whose validity depends only on the properties of the connectives it is not sufficiently powerful to deal with arguments (or syllogisms) such as:

1. All men are mortal
2. Socrates is a man

$\therefore$ Socrates is mortal

These types of arguments are *asyllogistic.* The above is a valid argument, but when it is interpreted in Propositional logic it would be represented as:

$$a \wedge b \rightarrow c.$$

This is inadequate to express the relationship between the propositions and the conclusion; we cannot prove whether the formula is valid or not by using this notation, and it is therefore necessary to reveal the internal structure of the proposition.

If we examine the arguments and what they say, we can interpret them according to set theory.

The first statement says there is a set called men and that this set is a subset of mortal things.

The second statement says there is an element called Socrates which is member of the set of men.

The conclusion says that since Socrates is a part of the set of men and that since all of the set of men are mortal then Socrates too must be mortal.

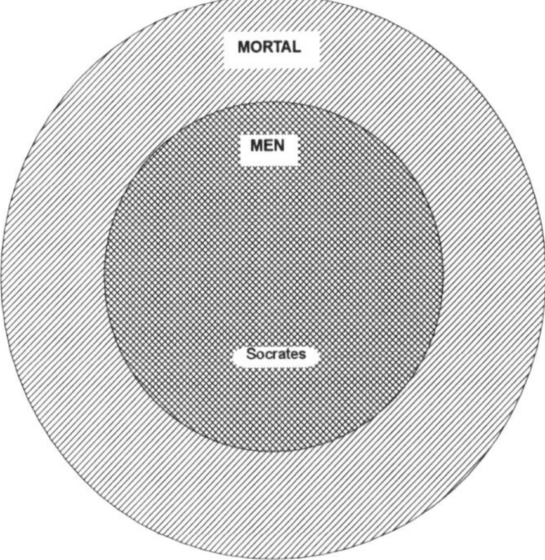

Figure 2.5: Socrates $\in$ Men $\subseteq$ Mortal

In the previous argument we stated 'ALL men are mortal'. This means that the entire set of men is contained within the set of mortal beings.

Predicate logic allows us to represent this by using quantifiers; in this case the *universal quantifier* ALL (represented by an ∀). To link the quantifier to a property we use variables or terms (in the example below x). We restate the proposition 'all men are mortal' by saying that all objects that have the property of being a man also have the property of being mortal. That is, being a man implies being mortal:

$$\forall_x \bullet \text{man}(x) \rightarrow \text{mortal}(x)$$

For all x that has the property of being a man it also has *by implication* of being a man the property of being mortal.

A property of a term is described by a *predicate*. Thus in the previous statement, the predicates of x are *being a man* (represented by the predicate *man*) and *being mortal* (represented by the predicate *mortal*). A separator symbol '•' is usually used to separate the predicates from the quantifiers (or to separate individual quantifiers).

The second proposition 'Socrates is a man' can be restated as saying there is *some individual* with the property of being called Socrates that also has the property of being a man. Unlike the first proposition it does not say ALL individuals called Socrates are men (for example, there might be a cat called Socrates), just that there exists at least one individual.

This is represented by an Existential Quantifier (∃) which stands for 'There exists at least one[6] ... that has the property of ...

$$\exists_x \bullet \text{Socrates}(x) \wedge \text{man}(x)$$

There exists at least one x that has the property of being called Socrates and the property of being a man.

Implies is not used in this case; having the property of being Socrates does not *always* imply being a man. All we can say is there exists at least one item that has the property of being called Socrates AND the property of being a man.

Since being a man implies being mortal and there exists an individual called Socrates that is a man we can conclude that there exists an individual called Socrates who is mortal.

$$\exists_x \bullet \text{Socrates}(x) \wedge \text{mortal}(x)$$

In Propositional logic propositions only range over the Boolean values {*tt*, *ff*}. Predicate logic extends this to allow variables to range over other

---

[6] There is a variation of the existential quantifier called the *singular existential quantifier* represented by ∃! which represents unique existence - there is one *and only one* such that ...

types e.g. ℕ (natural numbers), ℤ (integers), ℝ (reals) etc. Predicate logic allows us to write precise specifications, for example:

$\exists_x \in \mathbb{Z} \bullet x < 100$	There exists some integer less than 100.
$\forall_x \in \mathbb{R} \bullet x^2 \in \mathbb{R}$	Every number has a real square.
$\forall_x \in \mathbb{Z} \bullet \exists_y \in \mathbb{Z} \bullet x - y = 0$	For every integer x there is an integer y such that x - y = 0.

In some formal notations, instead of saying that a variable is a member of the *set* of a certain type, such as Boolean, Integer etc. An alternative notation is available to say that a variable is of a certain type.

$$\text{Quantifier}_{\text{variable}} : \text{Type}$$

So the last example given above could be restated as:

$$\forall_x : \mathbb{Z} \bullet \exists_y : \mathbb{Z} \bullet x - y = 0$$

2.3.2.1 *Scope of quantifiers*

We have stated that we use variables or terms to link the quantifiers to properties. If a variable is linked to a quantifier we say it is *bound* to that quantifier. If a variable is not linked to a particular quantifier we state that it is *free* with respect to that quantifier. Thus in predicate logic there are two types of variable, *free* and *bound.*

The scope[7] of a quantifier is only to the immediately following predicate. e.g.

$$\forall_x \bullet \underbrace{(E_1(x) \wedge E_2(y))}_{\text{Scope of } \forall}$$

In this expression x is bound and y is free with respect to the quantifier. All bound variables must be bound to *only* one quantifier each and no more.

---

[7] The scope of an object is the area in which an object is visible and can be referred to. It consists of a definition of the object and rules defining where the value of the object is applicable.

2.3.2.2 *Rules of quantification*

We have learnt how to specify in Predicate logic, now we need to define the rules for proving these specifications. There are four additional laws in Predicate logic corresponding to the universal and existential quantifiers. These are:

- Universal Instantiation
- Universal Generalisation
- Existential Instantiation
- Existential Generalisation

2.3.2.2.1 *Universal Instantiation*

Suppose we take the following statement:

1.	All plants are organic things
2.	All organic things contain carbon
∴	All plants contain carbon

It can be seen that the conclusion necessarily follows from the statements, but how do we derive this? If we turn these statements into formal logic we get:

1	$\forall_x \bullet \text{plant}(x) \rightarrow \text{organic\_thing}(x)$
2	$\forall_x \bullet \text{organic\_thing}(x) \rightarrow \text{contains\_carbon}(x)$
∴	$\forall_x \bullet \text{plant}(x) \rightarrow \text{contains\_carbon}(x)$

We cannot, however, prove these laws because they are not truth functionally related, we must first eliminate the quantifiers. We do this by a process known as Universal Instantiation.

What we can say is if a property is true for all items of a certain class[8] then it is true for each member of that class. For example, if all plants are organic_things then any member of the class plants will also be organic. We can therefore select this member of the class (which we shall call y) and so eliminate the quantifier:

1 $\text{plant}(y) \rightarrow \text{organic\_thing}(y)$

If this general premise is true of y (as an individual of the class), then the second premise must also be true of y, since we are entitled to pick the

[8] Class being a category or set to which an object belongs to, or is a member of.

same individual as we did in the first premise and we know that this individual is encompassed by the second class (being an organic thing).

2 organic_thing(y) → contains_carbon(y)

We can now use the Hypothetical syllogism rule to prove the rule.

1 plant(y) → organic_thing(y)
2 organic_thing(y) → contains_carbon(y)
∴ plant(y) → contains_carbon(y) *Hypothetical Syllogism 1 & 2*

However, we have only proved the case for an individual of the class we selected. In order to complete the proof we have to prove it for all members of the class. This requires the use of universal generalisation.

2.3.2.2.2 *Universal Generalisation*

This rule enables us to move from an assertion about a particular case to a general assertion. That is, if something is true of a member of a class it is true of all members of the class.

The rule has to be used with care. For example, just because my cat has no tail I could not conclude that all cats have no tails. The generalisation rule can *only* be applied when we have already *arbitrarily* chosen an individual of whom the premises were true. Since the individual was *arbitrarily* chosen, then whatever was true of it should also be true of any other individual in the class.

In the previous argument we have done this, choosing an arbitrary individual from the class 'plant', we can therefore use the universal generalisation rule to convert the conclusion:

plant(y) → contains_carbon(y) *Hypothetical syllogism*

into a universally quantified expression:

$\forall_x \bullet$ plant(x) → contains_carbon(x) *Universal generalisation*

2.3.2.2.3 *Existential Instantiation*

The existential quantifier restricts us to looking at part of a class and not the whole; there is therefore a crucial difference in the selection of an individual in these circumstances to that given previously for Universal instantiation.

Existential instantiation is similar to Universal instantiation in that we eliminate the quantifier by instantiating to an individual, but, there are two important conditions that must be adhered to when using this rule:

1. If you apply existential instantiation in a proof you must do it before universally instantiating with respect to any given individual.
2. You must never existentially instantiate twice with respect to the same individual.

The reason for the second condition can be displayed by the following fallacious argument:

1	Some cats have tails
2	Some dogs have tails
$\therefore$	Some dogs are cats

This is clearly wrong, but unless we heed the second condition about not existentially instantiating twice to the same individual the following proof can be given:

1	$\exists_x \bullet \text{cats}(x) \wedge \text{tails}(x)$	
2	$\exists_x \bullet \text{dogs}(x) \wedge \text{tails}(x)$	
3	$\text{cats}(y) \wedge \text{tails}(y)$	*Existential Instantiation*
4	$\text{dogs}(y) \wedge \text{tails}(y)$	*Existential Instantiation*
5	$\text{cats}(y)$	*Simplification* 3
6	$\text{dogs}(y)$	*Simplification* 4
7	$\text{cats}(y) \wedge \text{dogs}(y)$	*Conjunction 5 & 6*
$\therefore$	$\exists_x \bullet \text{cats}(x) \wedge \text{dogs}(x)$	*Existential Generalisation (see below)*

This is because the proof assumes that the individual y which occurred in the subclass of having tails in the first premise also occurred in the subclass of having tails in the second one. This assumption cannot be made and highlights the fact that existential instantiation should be used with care.

This rule can be used to prove that the conclusion about Socrates in Section 2.3.2 is valid:

1	$\forall_x \bullet \text{man}(x) \rightarrow \text{mortal}(x)$	
2	$\exists_x \bullet \text{Socrates}(x) \wedge \text{man}(x)$	
3	$\text{Socrates}(y) \wedge \text{man}(y)$	*Existential Instantiation*
4	$\text{man}(y)$	*Simplification* 3
5	$\text{man}(y) \rightarrow \text{mortal}(y)$	*Universal Instantiation*
6	$\text{mortal}(y)$	*Modus Ponens* 5 & 4
7	$\text{Socrates}(y)$	*Simplification* 3
8	$\text{Socrates}(y) \wedge \text{mortal}(y)$	*Conjunction* 6 & 7

However, the proof is not yet complete. In order to able to complete the proof we introduce a new rule.

2.3.2.2.4 Existential Generalisation

If we have defined that an individual has a property then we know that there is at least one member of the class to which it belongs which has this property. We are therefore entitled to add the existential quantifier to express this, making:

$$\text{Socrates}(y) \wedge \text{mortal}(y)$$

into the form:

$$\exists_x \bullet \text{Socrates}(x) \wedge \text{mortal}(x)$$

This completes the proof about the conclusion we drew about Socrates.

2.3.2.2.5 Conversion between quantifiers

It is sometimes useful to be able to interchange between existential and universal quantification. By rephrasing the formula this is sometimes possible. For example, if we state that all x has the property P, then we can also say that there is not a single x not having the property P. The following transformations provide such equivalences:

1. $\forall_x \bullet P_x \equiv \neg\exists_x \bullet \neg P_x$
2. $\neg\forall_x \bullet P_x \equiv \exists_x \bullet \neg P_x$
3. $\neg\forall_x \bullet \neg P_x \equiv \exists_x \bullet P_x$
4. $\forall_x \bullet \neg P_x \equiv \neg\exists_x \bullet P_x$

2.4. RELATIONSHIPS AND FUNCTIONS

In the previous section we used one place predicates (that is, each predicate described a property of a single entity). It is, however, possible to have two or more place predicates; these describe a *relationship,* or property between two or more terms. Take, for example, the statement:

x is less than y

This can be described with the predicate **less than**:

less_than(x, y)

For example, if we say x = 2 and y = 3 then we can state:

less_than(2, 3)

In normal mathematical notation we usually represent the predicate **less_than** with the symbol '<' and place it between the two terms (infix notation):

$$x < y$$

A *function* can been seen as a special kind of relation which given a value (x) will yield a value (y). Whereas, strictly speaking, relations 'relate' pairs, in functions there is a 'mapping' between values.

For two sets X and Y, where $x \in X$ and $y \in Y$, a *total function* (see later) is a relationship f such that for each value of the set X (i.e. each x) there is an element y such that there is a mapping from X to Y. A function can be seen as consisting of two sets and a rule associating an element of the first set with an element of the second set. This mapping is usually represented by the notation:

$$f : X \rightarrow Y$$

which represents the *signature* of the function.

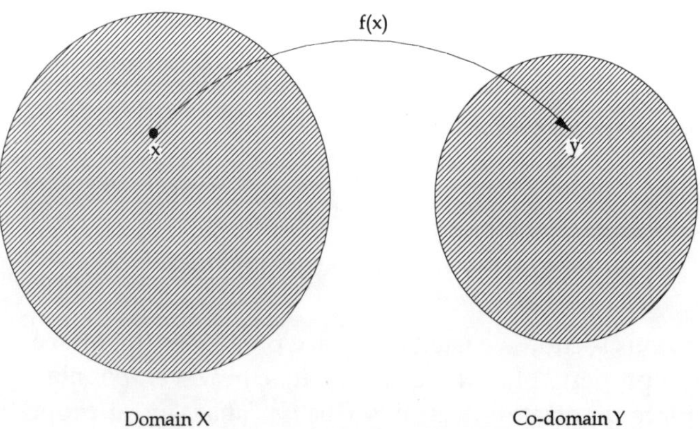

Figure 2.6: Schematic representation of a function

We therefore think of a function as consisting of a mapping of two sets:

- Set X consisting of the initial states or inputs; the data supplied to the function (the set of allowable states or inputs usually being described in a specification by a *precondition*).
- Set Y describing the corresponding final states; the required output or data produced by the function (usually described in a specification in the *postcondition*).

Suppose we create a function **square**, which returns the square of any number between 1 and 5:

$$\textbf{square}(x) = x^2 \text{ where } 1 \leq x \leq 5$$

where, for example, if 2 is the value passed to the function then 4 is the value yielded by the function (the result of squaring the parameter):

$$\textbf{square}(2) = 4$$

We can represent the input values allowed by the function as a set X:

$$X = \{1, 2, 3, 4, 5\}$$

This set is known as the *domain* of the function.

We can also make a set of values that can be returned by the function since we know $1^2 = 1$, $2^2 = 4$, $3^2 = 9$, $4^2 = 16$ and $5^2 = 25$.

$$Y = \{1, 4, 9, 16, 25\}$$

This set is known as the *co-domain* of the function. The set of possible results of the function.

It can be seen that for each value of x (where $x \in X$) there is a unique value y (where $y \in Y$). Each x has a mapping to a value y.

$$x \mapsto y$$

We can represent each of these mappings as an ordered pair with the left value x and the right value y,

$$(x, y)$$

and represent the **square** function as a set of these ordered pairs,

$$\textbf{square} = \{(1, 1), (2, 4), (3, 9), (4, 16), (5, 25)\}$$

with the left value of each ordered pair being the argument and the right value the result of applying that argument to the function.

The set of all the left co-ordinates of the ordered pairs are the *domain* of the function (Set X). The set of the right co-ordinates of the ordered pairs are the *range* of the function, a subset of the co-domain. In this example the co-domain and the range are equivalent. However, there are cases where the co-domain and range may differ.

To show the difference between the range and the co-domain it is best to use another example; a function which given a number returns a letter. If we define the set X (the domain) and Y (the co-domain) as:

$$X = \{1, 2, 3, 4\}$$
$$Y = \{a, b, c, d, e\}$$

we can define the function **num_to_letter** as:

num_to_letter = {(1, a), (2, b), (3, c), (4, d)}

If we take the values of the right co-ordinates we obtain the range:

range(**num_to_letter**) = {a, b, c, d}

The range consists only of those values that can be obtained by applying the arguments of X to the function. The letter e, although part of the co-domain, is therefore not part of the range. This difference may be important if say we define the domain and co-domain as the set of natural numbers, but only allow certain values as arguments to be returned. For example, we could define an electronic telephone directory which given a person's name (a sequence of characters) would return their telephone number (a sequence of natural numbers) as[9]:

Look-up : Name ⇸ Telephone-Number

It would also have the facility for adding to and deleting from the directory.

The domain would be sequences of characters (names), and the co-domain sequences of natural numbers (Telephone Numbers). The range, however, would only be those sequences of numbers which map from names present in the directory.

If a new name was added to the directory, the new telephone number would be added to the range. If a name was deleted from the directory the

[9] The arrow is crossed to show that it is a partial function. This will become clearer in the next section.

range would be reduced. The co-domain, however, would remain constant as all possible sequences of the natural numbers.

2.4.1 Total and partial functions

A *total function* is one which has as its domain the whole of the set of the type for which it is defined. For example, the standard arithmetic functions add and multiply are said to be total functions of the set of natural numbers.

The previous example of a lookup table introduces the concept of a *partial function*. Although we have defined Name and Telephone Number as types consisting of all possible names and telephone numbers, in any application we would be only likely to use a small subset of this type. The domain of the function would therefore not be the whole of the type Name (which would consist of every possible name in the universe!) but only the names currently held in the directory. The function is therefore a partial function of the set Name.

A solution to this partiality might seem to be to define Name as a set consisting only of those names held in the book, thus making the function total over its domain. However, we have already stated that we wish to add and delete entries from the book; this means the set of Names would be variable and could change so it cannot be initialised to a particular value.

Even where we appear to be using the whole of the domain, care must be taken. Take, for example, the function **predecessor**:

$$\textbf{predecessor}(x) = x - 1$$

where the domain and co-domain are the set of natural numbers. If the value of x is given as zero (which we allow as a natural number in this example) then there is no value in the co-domain for the result (which would be -1, a non-natural number). We would say the result is undefined. Thus the function **predecessor** is not defined for *all* values of $\mathbb{N}$ (the natural numbers) and is therefore a *partial* function.

A total function mapping (one which has as its domain the whole of the type) is usually represented by an arrow:

$$\mathbf{f} : \mathbb{N} \rightarrow \mathbb{N}$$

Partial function mapping, on the other hand, is usually represented by a crossed arrow symbol:

$$\mathbf{f} : \mathbb{N} \nrightarrow \mathbb{N}$$

Most useful functions, because of their dynamic behaviour, are partial functions of the standard types. This does not, however, mean that total functions are never used. Most of the mathematical and logical functions are total and by the use of mappings (to be discussed later) we can define functions which are total over their types.

2.4.2 Classification of functions

A function is a special form of relationship in which, at most, one element in the range can be mapped to from one element in the domain. You cannot therefore have a value in the domain mapped to a number of values in the range. Thus any application to an element of the domain will always yield an unambiguous result. Functions can be classified into three main groups according to how they map their values.

2.4.2.1 *Injective functions*

A function $f : X \rightarrow Y$ is injective if for every value in domain X there is a distinct value in Y. Every value of X therefore has a unique value in Y (though the reverse is not necessarily true) and the function can map at most one element in X to any element in Y. For example:

$$\text{charconvert} = \{\langle a, 1\rangle, \langle b, 2\rangle, \langle c, 3\rangle\} \text{ is injective}$$

but:

$$\text{charconvert} = \{\langle a, 1\rangle, \langle b, 2\rangle, \langle c, 2\rangle\} \text{ is not}$$

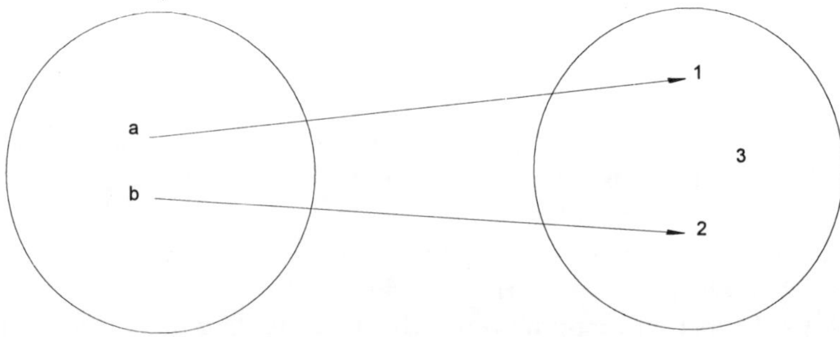

Figure 2.7: Injective mapping

An injective function can contain values in Y which are not mapped onto by any value in X. For example, the values of the injective char function given previously might be:

$$X = \{a\ b, c\}$$
$$Y = \{1, 2, 3, 4\}$$

with the value 4 not being associated with any X value.

This is the main difference between injective and bijective functions, which are examined shortly.

2.4.2.2 *Surjective*

A function $f: X \rightarrow Y$ is surjective if for every value in Y, there is at least one value in X that maps onto it. The upshot of this is that more than one value in X can map to the same value in Y, but that every Y has at least one X value associated with it. For example:

primes = {⟨1, true⟩, ⟨2, false⟩, ⟨3, true⟩} is surjective

A surjective function is sometimes represented by the $\twoheadrightarrow$ symbol. It should be noted that whilst the inverse of an injective function would also be a function (though its domain would not, in general, be the whole of Y) this does not follow with a surjective function, since any instances involving a many to one relationship could not give an unambiguous inverse relationship.

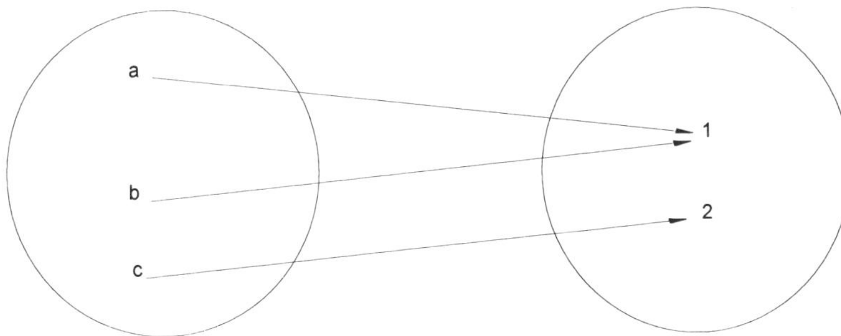

Figure 2.8: Surjective mapping

2.4.2.3 *Bijective*

A function $f: X \rightarrow Y$ is bijective if it is both injective and surjective. Every element in X produces a distinct value in Y, and every element in Y has an X value associated with it. This results in a function in which every value of X has a unique value in Y and vice versa. In other words, there is a one to one mapping between each value in X and Y.

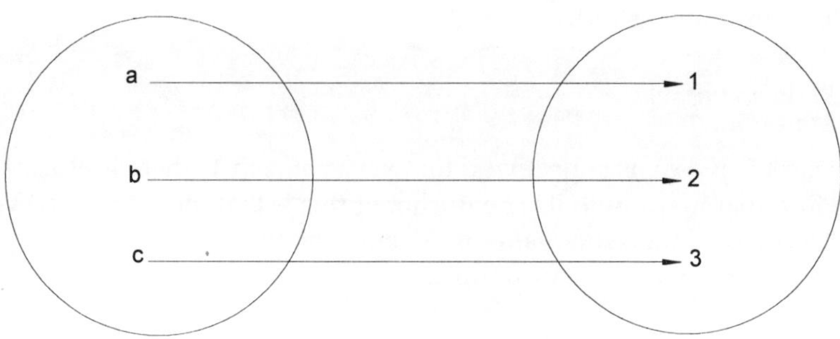

Figure 2.9: Bijective mapping

A bijective function cannot contain additional values in Y which are not mapped onto by elements in X, so:

$$X = \{a, b, c\}$$
$$Y = \{1, 2, 3\}$$

is bijective, but:

$$X = \{a, b, c\}$$
$$Y = \{1, 2, 3, 4\}$$

is not.

2.4.3 Function type

Consider the function **add**, which is a two-place function[10] taking two natural numbers and delivering a third, its sum. We could represent this as:

$$\text{add} = \{\langle\langle 0, 0\rangle, 0\rangle, \langle\langle 0, 1\rangle, 1\rangle, \ldots, \langle\langle 1, 0\rangle, 1\rangle, \langle\langle 1, 1\rangle, 2\rangle, \ldots\rangle \ldots$$

The argument or domain consists of two natural numbers and the co-domain of one natural number. We express this by writing:

$$\text{add} : \mathbb{N} \times \mathbb{N} \rightarrow \mathbb{N}$$

This characterises the *type* of the function and is sometimes referred to as its *signature*.

[10] Place refers to the number of values (or arguments) the function takes.

2.4.4 Lambda notation

Lambda notation provides a means of referring to a function without naming it. It is mainly used where we wish to define an expression whose scope is limited to a small part of the specification.

We define a lambda expression by prefixing it with an abstraction operator 'λ'. For example, we could define a lambda operation which returned the square of a value:

$$\lambda\, x \bullet x^2$$

This would be equivalent to the function

$$\text{square}(x) = x^2$$

The abstraction operator binds the variable x to the equation, in the same way as a quantifier in predicate logic binds the variables. The variable takes on the value of any argument passed to the equation, thus if we pass the lambda expression the value 3:

$$\lambda\, x \bullet x^2(3) = 9$$

the result is 3^2, which is 9.

Like Predicate logic we can also have free variables (variables not linked to an abstraction operator). For example:

$$\lambda\, x \bullet x + y$$

In this case the value y is free, since we have only bound x and the expression will still only accept one argument, that of x.

$$\lambda\, x \bullet x + y\ (2) = 2 + y$$

However, like Predicate logic we can bind more than one variable:

$$\lambda\, x\, y \bullet x + y$$

This expression now accepts two arguments:

$$\lambda\, x\, y \bullet x + y\ (5, 2) = 7$$

Lambda expressions are similar to functions and can contain conditional statements (which we will discuss later). There are problems when applying the lambda notation to recursive definitions, however, and it is best to avoid their use in such cases.

2.4.5 Currying

We can see that the previous expression

$$\lambda\, x\, y \bullet x + y$$

corresponds to the two-place function

$$f : (\mathbb{N} \times \mathbb{N}) \rightarrow \mathbb{N}$$

Using a process known as Currying[11], we can express this two argument function in terms of a one-place curried definition:

$$\begin{array}{l} \lambda x \bullet (\lambda y \bullet x + y) \\ \lambda x \bullet (\lambda y \bullet x + y\ (2))(5) \\ \lambda x \bullet x + 2\ (5) \\ = 7 \end{array}$$

Where the first definition essentially corresponded to a two-place function this definition corresponds to the one-place function:

$$f : \mathbb{N} \rightarrow (\mathbb{N} \rightarrow \mathbb{N})$$

whose returned value is itself a function.

Thus if we took the sets of the domains and ranges of the two definitions we would get:

$$\begin{array}{l} \lambda\, x\, y \bullet x + y = \{\langle\langle 0, 0\rangle, 0\rangle, \langle\, \langle 0, 1\rangle, 1\rangle, \ldots \langle\langle 1, 0\rangle, 1\rangle, \langle\langle 1, 1\rangle, 2\rangle, \ldots\} \\ \lambda\, x \bullet \lambda\, y \bullet x + y = \{\langle 0, \langle\langle 0, 0\rangle, \langle 1, 1\rangle, \ldots\rangle, \langle 1, \langle\langle 0, 1\rangle, \langle 1, 2\rangle \ldots\rangle, \ldots\rangle \ldots\} \end{array}$$

Currying allows an n-place function (of $n > 2$) to be turned into a one-place function whose co-domain is an n-1 place function.

2.4.6 Overloading and polymorphism

If we look at the basic mathematical operators such as add, subtract and multiply we can see that they can operate on many different types, including whole and floating point numbers. For example:

$$\begin{array}{l} 2 + 6 = 8 \\ 2.4 + 3.1 = 5.5 \end{array}$$

[11] Named after Haskell B. Curry, an American logician who discovered the property.

The operator is therefore not constrained to a particular type, but will work on a class of types (in this case numbers). We can therefore think of each operator as consisting of a series of signatures:

$$+ : \mathbb{Z} \times \mathbb{Z} \rightarrow \mathbb{Z}$$
$$+ : \mathbb{R} \times \mathbb{R} \rightarrow \mathbb{R}$$

We say that such an operator is *overloaded*. That is, there are several definitions of the operator, each consisting of different types.

A few formal methods allow user defined operators to be overloaded. In these cases it is important to ensure that the types used in the definitions are disjoint. For example, suppose we define an operator called div which divides two values and represent it with the types

$$\text{div} : \mathbb{R} \times \mathbb{R} \rightarrow \mathbb{R}$$
$$\text{div} : \mathbb{Z} \times \mathbb{Z} \rightarrow \mathbb{Z}$$
$$\text{div} : \mathbb{N} \times \mathbb{N} \rightarrow \mathbb{N}$$

Each of these would have associated with it a different operational definition. With real numbers the operator can return a floating point number. When used with integers it can return a whole number (which can be positive or negative), when using natural numbers it can only return a positive natural number. If we then use this operator:

$$3.3 \text{ div } 1.2 = 2.75$$
$$-4 \text{ div } 2 = -2$$
$$13 \text{ div } 2 = 6$$

With the first two of these equations there is no difficulty in determining the types used. The first equation obviously uses real numbers, the second (because of the negative value) uses integers. However, the third equation represents a dilemma; are we using integers or natural numbers in this case? Without being able to distinguish which type we are using we are unable to determine which of the operational definitions to use. The reason for this is that natural numbers are a subclass of integers. The two definitions therefore belong to the same class (that of integers).

Finding which is the right definition for an occurrence of an overloaded operator is called *overload resolution*. Resolution will fail if there is more than one definition which fulfils the properties.

In some languages we can define functions that operate on a number of different types; these are referred to as **polymorphic** functions. The same conditions apply as to overloading in that we must define a set of operations and signatures for each type allowed and the definitions must be disparate from each other.

2.4.7 Operations on functions

There are a number of operators on functions that appear in many formal notations. These include:

- domain restriction,
- domain subtraction,
- range restriction,
- range subtraction,
- override,
- composition.

2.4.7.1 The domain restriction operator

Given the function f the application of the domain restriction operator (◁) with a set s to this function will be to construct a partial function with a domain restricted to the elements of s.

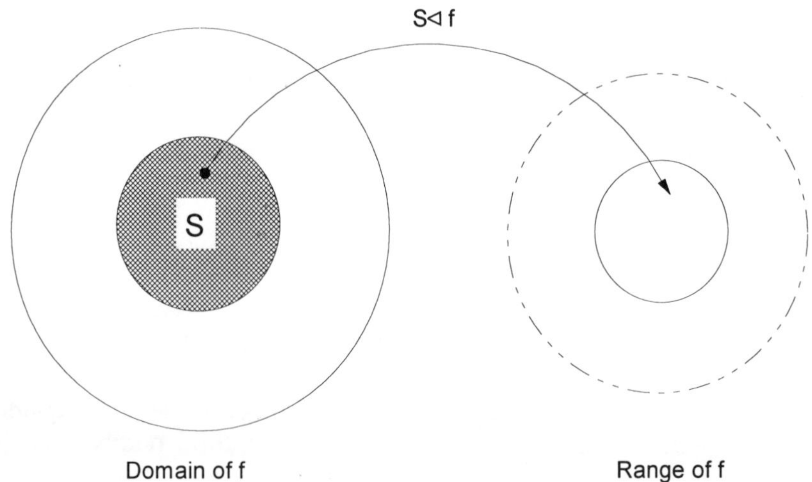

Figure 2.10: s ◁ f

For example, if:

$$f = \{a \mapsto 1, b \mapsto 2, c \mapsto 3, d \mapsto 4\}$$
$$s = \{c, d, e\}$$

then:

$$s \lhd f = \{c \mapsto 3, d \mapsto 4\}$$

It can be seen that the resultant operational domain is equivalent to the intersection of the domain of f and the set s.

2.4.7.2 The domain subtraction operator

Also known as the map deletion operator (⩤), given the function f the application of this operator with a set s to this function will be to construct a partial function with a domain restricted to elements that are not in s. For example, if:

$$f = \{a \mapsto 1, b \mapsto 2, c \mapsto 3, d \mapsto 4\}$$
$$s = \{c, d, e\}$$

then:

$$s \mathbin{⩤} f = \{a \mapsto 1, b \mapsto 2\}$$

It can be seen that the resultant operational domain is equivalent to the relative complement of the domain of f and set s. Note, that in both domain operators the domain operand is on the left-hand side.

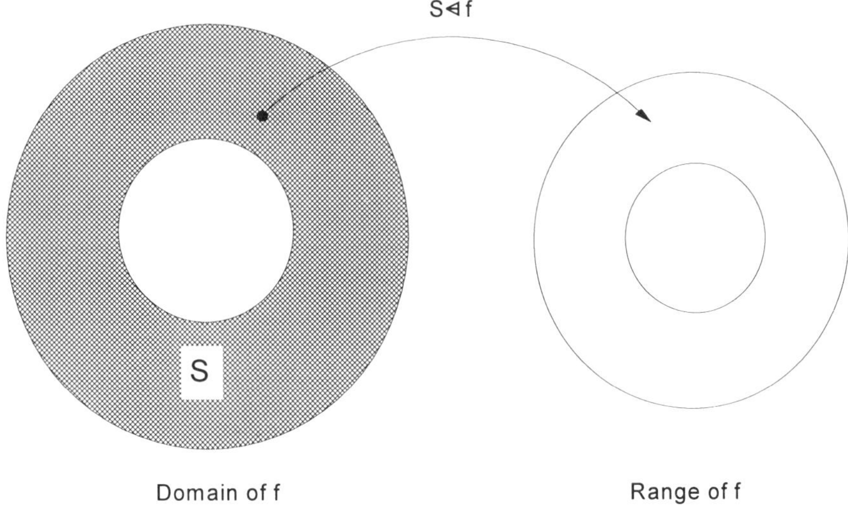

Figure 2.11: s ⩤ f

2.4.7.3 The range restriction operator

Given the function f the application of the range restriction operator (▷) with a set s to this function will be to construct a partial function with members restricted to those whose range values lie in s.

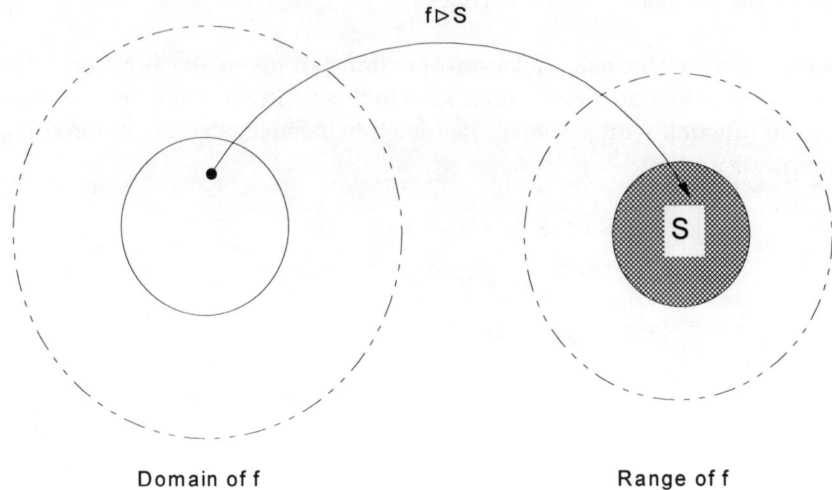

Figure 2.12: $f \rhd s$

For example, if:

$$f = \{a \mapsto 1, b \mapsto 2, c \mapsto 3, d \mapsto 4\}$$
$$s = \{1, 3, 5\}$$

then:

$$f \rhd s = \{a \mapsto 1, c \mapsto 3\}$$

2.4.7.4 *The range subtraction operator*

Given the function f the application of the range subtraction operator (⩥) with a set s to this function will be to construct a partial function with members restricted to those whose range values lie outside those of s. For example, if:

$$f = \{a \mapsto 1, b \mapsto 2, c \mapsto 3, d \mapsto 4\}$$
$$s = \{1, 3, 5\}$$

then:

$$f ⩥ s = \{b \mapsto 2, d \mapsto 4\}$$

Note that in both range operators the domain operand is on the right-hand side.

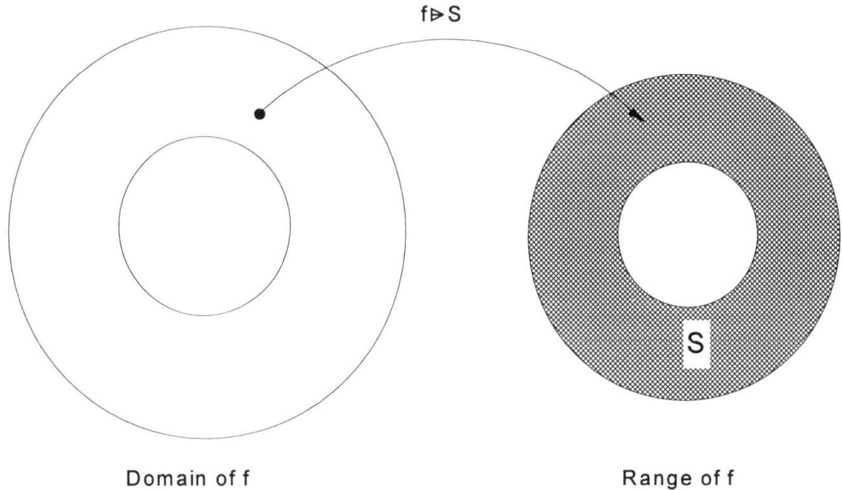

Figure 2.13: f ⊳ s

2.4.7.5 *The override operator*

The override operator is useful for modelling small changes in functions, relationships or maps (see next section). Application of the override operator (⊕) to two functions f_1 and f_2 (which must be of the same type) results in a new function that has the combined properties of both functions. The domain of the new function is equivalent to the union of the domains of both the functions. In this operation f_2 always overrides f_1, so if both functions have a common domain value it will always be replaced by f_2's. For example:

$$f_1 = \{a \mapsto 1, b \mapsto 2, c \mapsto 3\}$$
$$f_2 = \{b \mapsto 5, d \mapsto 4\}$$
$$f_1 \oplus f_2 = \{a \mapsto 1, b \mapsto 5, c \mapsto 3, d \mapsto 4\}$$

It can be seen in this example that b is common to both mappings, but f_2's value takes precedence. The override operator is sometimes represented by the dagger symbol (†).

2.4.7.6 *Composition operator*

Given two functions $f_1 \circ f_2$ the composition operator (°) yields a result equivalent to first applying f_2, and then applying f_1 to the result of this application. This is conditional on the range of f_2 being equivalent to the domain of f_1.

For example, given:

$$f_1 = \{1 \mapsto 2, 3 \mapsto 9, 2 \mapsto 4\}$$
$$f_2 = \{a \mapsto 1, b \mapsto 2, c \mapsto 3\}$$

then:

$$f_1 \circ f_2(a) \text{ is equivalent to } f_1(f_2(a)) = 2$$
$$f_1 \circ f_2(b) \text{ is equivalent to } f_1(f_2(b)) = 4$$
$$f_1 \circ f_2(c) \text{ is equivalent to } f_1(f_2(c)) = 9$$

and:

$$f_1 \circ f_2 = \{a \mapsto 2, b \mapsto 4, c \mapsto 9\}$$

2.4.8 Mappings

As we have seen, a function consists of a set of mappings. However, we can also define mappings explicitly.

A single mapping from one element to another (an ordered pair) can be represented using a maplet.

$$a \mapsto b$$

The maplet symbol ($\mapsto$) is used to map a single value. A set of these values can be placed together to represent a set of mappings.

$$\text{CHARCONVERT} = \{a \mapsto 1, b \mapsto 2, c \mapsto 3\}$$

The set of elements on the left-hand side of the arrows, which the map associates with those on the right, form the *domain* of the map. The set of elements on the right-hand side form the *range*.

The order of the pairs is not important since the map is just a set. Like sets, maps can be defined explicitly, as above, or implicitly in terms of properties. An empty map is represented in the same way as an empty set {}, though sometimes a maplet arrow is included to show it is a mapping, as in $\{\mapsto\}$.

In much the same way as functions, values can be applied to their domains to return associated range values. However, whilst functions are seen as having static domains or arguments on which they operate this is not necessarily true of mappings. Maps can be viewed as finite or infinite domain/range maps capable of being merged, reduced, restricted and operated on in many other ways. They are thus dynamic structures which are easily altered. The type of a mapping is usually represented by an arrow with a letter *m* either above or below it (depending on the notation).

$$\mathit{Directory} = \mathit{Name} \xrightarrow{m} \mathit{TelephoneNo}$$

A map can be applied to a value, if the value belongs to the domain of the map, by a process known as *map application*. Using map application applying a value corresponding to a value from the domain will return the corresponding value from the range associated with this value. For example, for the previously defined mapping CHARCONVERT:

CHARCONVERT(b) = 2

we can obtain the set of values present in the domain of a map by use of the *domain operator*. For example:

domain CHARCONVERT = {a, b, c}

and those of the range, with the *range operator*:

range CHARCONVERT = {1, 2, 3}

Most of the operators that apply to functions also apply to maps such as domain and range restriction, subtraction, override and composition.

Maps can be merged using the map merge operator ∪ which performs a function similar to union. The maps must be compatible, meaning that any elements common to the domains of the two maps must map to the same value. For example:

$$\{a \mapsto 1, b \mapsto 2, c \mapsto 3\} \cup \{c \mapsto 3, d \mapsto 4, e \mapsto 5\}$$

can be merged to give:

$$\{a \mapsto 1, b \mapsto 2, c \mapsto 3, d \mapsto 4, e \mapsto 5\}$$

because the common element (c) maps to the same value in both cases. However:

$$\{a \mapsto 1, b \mapsto 2, c \mapsto 3\} \cup \{c \mapsto 4, d \mapsto 5, e \mapsto 6\}$$

cannot be merged because the (c) element maps to a different value. To combine the latter requires the use of the map override operator:

$$\{a \mapsto 1, b \mapsto 2, c \mapsto 3\} \oplus \{c \mapsto 4, d \mapsto 5, e \mapsto 6\}$$

giving:

$$\{a \mapsto 1, b \mapsto 2, c \mapsto 4, d \mapsto 5, e \mapsto 6\}$$

In this case the second map always overrides any common maplets.

Like sets, maps can be represented explicitly (by map enumeration) or implicitly (by map comprehension) by some property common to all the elements.

2.5. OPERATIONS

Operations are like functions and can be defined implicitly or explicitly. They have one major difference over functions; they can refer to or change the value of external variables (values outside their own scope[12]). This affecting of what is essentially the state of the system is referred to as a side-effect.

Operations are influenced by the state of the system at the time they are called and may alter the state of the system through their invocation. Whereas a function will always return the same result for the same parameters, an operation will not necessarily do so and the value returned will be a consequence of the state of the system at the time the operation was called[13].

For example, we could define an operation to increment a counter held in the computer store and return the value. This would add one to the value currently held in the store. If the counter held the value six before the operation was called it would equal seven after the operation. However, if the counter was equal to nine before the operation was called then the new value would be ten. The effect of the operation is therefore dependent on the state of the entity it is accessing.

2.6. ABSTRACT DATA TYPES

A data type is a high-level object such as a queue, stack, tree etc. that is independent of the structure that implements it. For example, a queue may be implemented by either arrays or pointers. Provided the actual details of the implementation are hidden inside appropriately named procedures and functions, it does not matter which is chosen.

An abstract data type is specified by a class of states (or values) and a set of private operations to act upon the states. They are described by the behaviour of operations on them, providing functionality without the internal workings of the data type being accessible; the interface is described, but not the actual structure itself and as such it is implementation free.

---

[12] The local scope (or environment) of a function is the text contained within the definition of the function. A function cannot alter anything outside its environment (such as global variables) and can only interface with the outside world via parameters passed to and from it.

[13] Because of this operations cannot be curried.

A stack, for example, consists of a collection of elements all of the same type in which the last element put on the stack is the first element to be taken off. Such a structure uses two main operations; *push* which places an element on the top of the stack, and *pop* which takes the top element off the stack. Such a construct can be defined in terms of the results of these operations:

$$\begin{aligned}
&push : \mathbb{N} \times \mathbb{N}_s \rightarrow \mathbb{N}_s \\
&pop : \mathbb{N}_s \rightarrow \mathbb{N}_s \\
&top : \mathbb{N}_s \nrightarrow \mathbb{N} \\
&empty : \mathbb{N}_s \rightarrow \mathbb{B}
\end{aligned}$$

where $\mathbb{N}_s$ is the set of stacks of natural numbers, $\mathbb{N}$ the set of natural numbers and **B** the set of Booleans. These sets are often described as the *sorts*.

- *push* takes a number and the stack and places the number on the stack.
- *pop* takes a stack and results in a stack minus the top number.
- *top* takes a stack of numbers and returns the top number off the stack.
- *empty* takes a stack of numbers and returns the Boolean value true if empty.

The stack can be manipulated only by these specified operations.

An example in the **LOTOS** specification language of an abstract type using this principle could be a type called *extended natural numbers*:

```
type ext_nat_numbers is
      sorts   nat                    (* natural numbers *)
      (* operations *)
               (* 0 is a constant returning a natural number *)
      opns    0 -> nat
               (* successor takes and returns a natural number *)
                    succ:nat -> nat
               (* plus takes two natural numbers and returns one *)
               _+_:nat,nat -> nat
      (* equations *)
      eqns
               forall x,y:nat
               ofsort nat
               (* The result of adding 0 to x is the value x *)
               x + 0 = x;
               x + succ(y) = succ(x + y);
endtype
```

Here the data type is defined with two operations; successor (succ) which returns the next natural number, and plus (+) which adds two numbers together returning a natural number.

2.7. RECURSION

Recursion is the ability of code to call itself, and can be used in most specification languages to define data types, operations and functions. Recursive definitions are usually smaller and more elegant than their counterparts, but they must be treated with care.

Recursive functions are defined in terms of themselves; that is, they contain calls to themselves. The following is an example of a function which returns the sum of a list of numbers:

sequence → ℕ
sum(List) :-
    if List = [] **then** 0
    else hd List + sum(**tl** List)

If we called this with a sequence of [1, 32, 5] we could trace the operation as:

sum([1, 32, 5]) = 1 + sum([32, 5])
    sum([32, 5]) = 32 + sum([5])
        sum([5]) = 5 + sum([])
            sum([]) = 0

If we substitute in, we get:

sum([1, 32, 5]) = 1 + 32 + 5 + 0

which gives:

sum([1, 32, 5]) = 38

Recursive definitions appear circular and can indeed be infinite if care is not taken; generally we require finite functions. For a recursive function to be able to terminate it must contain a base case, or terminating condition which concludes the recursion. Each time the function is called in the application the new call must get nearer to this terminating condition. It is important that there is no situation in which this condition will never be applied. For example, in the above the terminating condition was:

if List = [] then 0

Each time a call was made the new sequence passed on was smaller. The function terminated on receiving an empty list.

Suppose instead, we decided to use a sentinel value placed at the end of a list to tell the function that it had come to the end.

if List = [-1] then 0

If we sent it a list with the sentinel value included[14], for example:

sum([1, 32, 5, -1])

then the function would terminate correctly. If, however, this value was not included:

sum([1, 32, 5])

then the function would fail to terminate correctly. This shows the importance of considering a correct terminating condition. Recursion can also be used to define data types elegantly.

[14]A sentinel is a marker that tells us we have reached the end of our data. This is useful if, for example, you have a fixed size array, but are only likely to use part of it at any particular time. If you have a sequence for thirty names, but only have three names in it, you can place the marker in the fourth element. Any operations can then terminate on the fourth element rather than searching through the rest of the list. Sentinels should be used with caution.

3

Formal specification styles

Formal methodologies can broadly be classified into two main categories:

- **Constructive**, where a mathematical model is constructed of the system.
- **Behavioural**, where a system is expressed in terms of properties of its inputs and outputs. The system being seen as a black box with the internal workings hidden.

These categories give rise to a large range of different specification styles and methodologies, though all are based on an underlying groundwork of discrete mathematics. There are both advantages and disadvantages to most of these styles; some are more suited to specifying particular types of computer systems (such as protocols), some are more amenable to mechanistic manipulation for proof analysis or animation. This diversity has a similarity in programming languages where a wide range of high and low level languages exist for different applications.

It is hard to separate the various styles into distinct classes, many overlap with each other and some form subclasses of others. Some formal methodologies allow a number of styles within their semantics allowing the user to choose the particular style depending on the application involved.

The tree in Fig. 3.1 represents a rough outline of some of the main styles available and their various subgroups. It should not be seen as definitive and there is some debate as to where the various systems fit together.

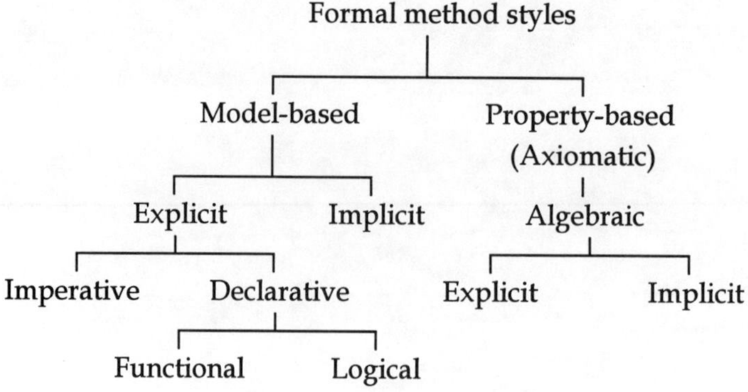

Figure 3.1: Specification styles

3.1. MODEL-ORIENTATED SPECIFICATIONS

In a model-orientated specification the system is represented as an abstract mathematical model. Operations and functions are expressed in terms of standard collections of basic data types and other type constructors. Specifications can be represented *implicitly* or *explicitly*, or in a mixture of these styles.

Model-based specification methods are sometimes criticised as being too operationally biased in the way they describe systems, with much of the design being visible within the abstract structure. They are, however, better suited to describing certain systems than other styles such as property-based.

3.1.1 Implicit specifications

Implicit specifications express operations in terms of *what* they are required to accomplish, without consideration as to *how* the task is to be carried out. This is usually done in the form of abstract pre- and post-conditions. Implicit specifications are normally more concise than explicit ones. They also enable the requirements to be written in a way that does not commit to a particular method of implementation; the developer is thus free to choose their own particular method of implementing it.

3.1.2 Explicit specifications

In explicit specifications definitions are given in terms of *how* the operation will be carried out. These are of a more concrete form than implicit statements. In *refinement*, implicit statements are normally refined to more explicit statements, converting the specification from *what* is required to *how* it will be carried out.

Explicit specifications can be expressed in a number of styles; *imperatively* (state-based), *declaratively* or in a mixture of both.

3.1.2.1 *Imperative (or state-based)*

When using an imperative style the specification is expressed in terms of actions upon variables. The basic concepts of state-based specifications are those of a variable and variable assignment. A variable is a container of a certain type, holding a value capable of being changed by operations upon it. Expressions which change the value of a variable are said to have *side-effects* on that variable.

The order of evaluation is important in state-based specifications and follows a sequential pattern. Changing the order of evaluation would produce different side-effects.

Programs written in traditional imperative languages such as Pascal and C are typically state-based. It is therefore easier to convert a state-based specification into one of these languages. State-based specifications reduce the number of parameters passed to them; this may be more concise than say functional-based specifications but can lead to problems in that it is often harder to see what variables are accessed by an operation. Never the less certain problems are best stated in this type of specification style.

3.1.2.2 *Declarative*

A declarative specification is one that declares data manipulations as a set of equations or relations. Declarative can be expressed as *applicative* (functional) or *logical*; the division between these two forms of specification style is difficult to differentiate and a wide spectrum exists between these two extremes.

3.1.2.2.1 *Applicative (or functional)*

Applicative or functional-based specifications are expressed in terms of functions (functions simply being mappings from one value of a type to another). In *purely functional specifications*, state and variables are not used; this means there are no side-effects. Parameters are passed to functions and the functions return a value; there is no notion of global or external variables. There is also no notion of a store (or state) containing values which are updated as the program executes.

Normally specifications are expressed in a *functional-style* rather than in a pure form; in these situations although variables are not used within the specification, a state is passed to functions (usually as a parameter to the program); the specification is then given in terms of functions upon this state.

Functional specifications correspond to programming languages such as ML, Miranda and Haskell. The lack of side-effects encourages modularity and structure and its inherent mathematical nature lends itself well to proof analysis.

3.1.2.2.2 Logical

In the logic-based style the specification is stated in terms of truth and falsehood. Usually, though not always, based on predicate logic, logical specifications represent systems in terms of a set of facts and inference rules (inter-relationships between the facts). A purely logical specification, like a functional one, does not allow *side-effects*.

There are no widespread logic-based specification languages, though there has been some attempt to use **Prolog**, a logic based programming language, for this purpose. The lack of strong typing in the language, though, generally makes it unsuitable, there being only one data type in the language; the *term*.

3.1.3 Property-based or axiomatic specifications

In property-based specifications the behaviour of a system is defined indirectly by stating a set of axioms defining properties that the system must satisfy. First-order predicates (based on Hoare logic) are used to specify pre- and post-conditions of operations in terms of axioms.

3.1.3.1 Algebraic specifications

If axioms are stated as equations the style is called algebraic. The algebraic style is a subset of the axiomatic style.

Operations are specified by their algebraic equivalences often in terms of other operations. As such, there is no model of the system, only the effect of operations upon it. Axioms are used to specify properties of systems, but are restricted to equations.

Using algebraic specifications enables *term rewriting*[1] to take place using symbolic manipulation of the specification.

Languages with the ability to define specifications algebraically include **Larch**, **LOTOS** and **OBJ3**. **RAISE** also has a limited ability to express in this form of notation.

---

[1] Term rewriting involves the replacement of one part of an equation by another. If, for example, we are given the rule ADD(0, X) = X then whenever we encounter the left-hand side of this equation 'ADD(0, X)' we can replace it with the right-hand side 'X'. Thus the equation ADD(0, ADD(0, X)) could be replaced in two rewrites by X.

3.2. CONCURRENCY-BASED SPECIFICATIONS

The basic concepts of concurrent specifications are those of inter-process communication and parallel composition. Concurrency can be applied in many of the styles given in Fig. 3.1.

In languages such as **RAISE** and **Estelle** channels are used to provide communication between processes. A channel is a medium along which values (of a particular type) can be sent or received. Value expressions executed in parallel may communicate with each other via these channels.

In specification languages like **LOTOS**, communication is given not by channels but by synchronised events and gates.

Most current concurrent specification languages are based on label transition diagrams and these can be in a number of different styles; constraint-orientated, extended automata and resource-orientated.

Concurrency is relevant only where the system to be modelled is inherently concurrent (conceptually concurrent) or where it is likely to become more efficient by the use of concurrency. Many problems cannot be converted to a concurrent form since they require a set order of evaluations and converting sequential programs to parallel for the latter reason is often difficult.

3.3. EXAMPLE SPECIFICATION LANGUAGES

The following sections give brief details of a number of formal languages, together with a small example of the notation in use. This attempts to give a broad view of the various styles of languages available. The examples are supposed to give only a flavour of the language and should not be seen as serious uses of the methods since they show only a small subset of the expressions available in any particular language. The same example, a telephone directory, has been used for all the languages in order to aid comparison. Where possible, structures particular to each language have been highlighted in the examples. Where two languages could have produced similar specifications (such as in **Z** and **RAISE**) an attempt has been made to show alternative ways of implementing the same specification which point out certain aspects of each language.

Some languages are better suited to describing this example than others. The examples are given in order to show how the various languages fit into the styles described previously, not to show each language to its best ability.

When choosing a formal notation you should be aware of its areas of application. Some formal methods are more suitable for describing sequential programs than parallel ones, some are good for describing transaction-based processes, but will fall down when used to describe protocol-based distributed systems. Without being aware of the domain to which the formal method can be applied, you may well try to apply a formal method to something it is totally unsuited to describing. Whilst in many cases you still might be able to describe the system using the wrong formal method it will result in overly complex code and a lot of headaches. The phrase 'using the right tools for the job' applies to formal methods as much as anything else.

Formal languages do not just vary in style; some languages contain a lot of syntactic sugar (in the form of more powerful constructs) to make specifications easier to read, others contain a minimal amount so that the specifications can more easily be manipulated. This is no different from programming languages where, for example, we have business languages such as COBOL which are highly readable but contain dozens of powerful constructs and programming languages such as C which contain a minimalistic set of primitive constructs that can be used to build more powerful ones. You should be aware of how you are going to use the specification and choose an appropriate one.

3.3.1 VDM

The Vienna Development Method (**VDM**) is a software specification and production method with three components: a notation for expressing software specification design and development; an inference system for constructing proofs of correctness; and a methodological framework for developing software from a specification in a formally verifiable manner.

Based on discrete mathematics, including the theory of sets and relations (with the underlying semantics of formal logic), a system is thought of as a composition of sets of objects.

VDM is a *formal development method* allowing not only specification, but the ability to move from the high-level abstract data types of the original specification to the data types of the target programming language. This can be done in a coherent and formally provable way by a process known as reification. **VDM** also embodies a principle known as operational decomposition which enables decomposition of specified functions and operations into more implementable versions for the target language.

VDM does not at present include the ability to specify concurrent processes and this does seem to be a disadvantage in the specification of communications protocol and other areas where such constructs would be useful.

3.3.1.1 Example - Electronic telephone directory

The requirements are for an electronic telephone directory which will store the names and telephone numbers of people indexed against the person's name.

Since the person's name is used to index the number we can say there is a mapping from the name to the number. We therefore define a data set called *Directory* which consists of mappings from names to telephone numbers.

$$Directory = Name \xrightarrow{m} TelephoneNo$$

In **VDM** this refers to a set of mappings. So the above consists of a *set of mappings* from name to telephone number. Objects in the domain Directory are of type Name, objects in the range are of type TelephoneNo. We can now define a state variable '*dir*' to represent our directory:

state *telbook* **of**
  dir : *Directory*
end

Here we declare the state of our telephone book as containing a single state variable called '*dir*' which is of the type '*Directory*'. This is similar in many respects to declaring a global variable in a programming language.

Initially, the directory should be empty. Our first operation is therefore to initialise the directory to the empty set:

INIT()
ext wr *dir* : *Directory*
post *dir* = {};

This operation alters the state of the external directory by setting it to empty. In the operation we need first to state that the directory is external to the operation. We do this by using the keyword **ext**.

ext wr *dir* : *Directory*

VDM has two words to specify how parameters are to be affected; **rd** meaning read-only access and **wr** meaning read and write access. The second line of the function uses **wr** to define that we wish to be able to write (or affect) the external Directory.

The final line of the operation gives the required effect, or goal, of the operation, referred to as the post-condition. In this case it is that the directory is set to empty.

post *dir* = {}

Now we want to be able to add a name and number to the directory. We therefore define a new operation called *ADD* which takes a name and corresponding number and adds them to the directory.

The operation requires two parameters of type Name and TelephoneNo.

$$ADD(name : Name, telno : TelephoneNo)$$

This states that two input parameters are expected: *name* and *telno* of type *Name* and *TelephoneNo* respectively. In the operation we will be altering the state of the external directory by adding a new name and number to it, so we use **wr**:

$$\textbf{ext wr } dir : Directory$$

Now we give the required effect of the operation; the post-condition.

$$\textbf{post } dir = \overleftharpoon{dir} \dagger \{name \mapsto telno\}$$

This says that the post-condition is that the new state of the directory *dir* is the old state of *dir* with the new name to number mapping added. It describes the addition of a maplet containing the new name and number to the directory. In **VDM** we describe the old state of a variable by placing a backward half arrow $\leftharpoonup$ (called a hook) above or beside it.

The dagger symbol '†' in **VDM** is the *map override* operator. In the statement it has the effect that if the name is not in the directory already then the new mapping {name $\mapsto$ telno} is added to the directory. However, if the name is already in the directory then the new mapping replaces the old mapping for that name. For example, if the directory contains the values:

$$dir = \{"John" \mapsto 031943, "Fred" \mapsto 421400\}$$

and we add the new mapping:

$$\{"Pat" \mapsto 071943\}$$

then:

$$\begin{aligned} dir &= \overleftharpoon{dir} \dagger \{name? \mapsto no?\} \\ &= \{"John" \mapsto 031943, "Fred" \mapsto 421400\} \dagger \{"Pat" \mapsto 071943\} \\ &= \{"John" \mapsto 031943, "Fred" \mapsto 421400, "Pat" \mapsto 071943\} \end{aligned}$$

The new mapping has been added. However, if the new mapping is:

$$\{"John" \mapsto \underline{077723}\}$$

and we add it to the directory, then:

$$
\begin{aligned}
dir &= \overleftarrow{dir} \dagger \{name? \mapsto no?\} \\
&= \{"John" \mapsto 031943, "Fred" \mapsto 421400\} \dagger \{"John" \mapsto \underline{077723}\} \\
&= \{"John" \mapsto \underline{077723}, "Fred" \mapsto 421400\}
\end{aligned}
$$

The new mapping replaces the previous mapping for the same name. It overrides the previous mapping. This is useful if a person we have in our telephone directory changes their telephone number. We can now state the complete operation:

$ADD(name : Name, telno : TelephoneNo)$
ext wr $dir : Directory$;
post $dir = \overleftarrow{dir} \dagger \{name \mapsto telno\}$;

We now wish to define the specification for the operation *LOOKUP* that given a name, will return the appropriate telephone number. Unlike the previous operation we wish to return a value (in this case a telephone number) so the first line is defined as:

$LOOKUP(name : Name)\ r : TelephoneNo$

We are not altering Directory in this case, only looking at it and so only read access is required.

ext rd $dir : Directory$

We need to define a precondition for the operation; the conditions necessary for the operation to work. The pre-condition in this case is that the name is in the directory.

pre $name \in$ **dom** dir

The operation will therefore only work if it is given a name that is currently in the directory. We would need to extend our specification if we wished to cover situations where the name given may not be in the directory.

We now define a post-condition describing the returning of the telephone number:

post $r = dir(name)$;

This uses *map application* to obtain the telephone number associated with the name.

This gives the final part of the operation:

LOOKUP(*name* : *Name*) *r* : *TelephoneNo*
ext rd *dir* : *Directory*
pre $name \in$ **dom** *dir*
post $r = dir(name)$;

We may also wish to delete a name and its associated telephone number from the directory. We do this with the operation *DELETE* which given a name removes it from the directory:

DELETE(*name* : *Name*)
ext wr *dir* : *Directory*
post $dir = \{name\} ⩤ \overleftharpoon{dir}$

This uses the domain subtraction operator '⩤' which excludes those elements in the domain of the directory which are named in the set {*name*}. The new directory therefore consists of all the elements of the old directory except those in {*name*}.

VDM contains some imperative programming constructs as well as higher level specification constructs. These can be used as a pseudo-code for defining algorithmic structures during refinement. This makes it very much easier to develop an implementation from a **VDM** specification than from languages such as **Z** and **LOTOS**.

3.3.2 Z

Z is a specification method that uses a combination of logic and elementary set theory. Texts, describing programs, are organised by means of structures called schemas.

3.3.2.1 Example - Electronic Telephone Directory

Like the **VDM** example the directory will map names (denoted by NAME) to telephone numbers (denoted by NUM). It is possible to define the directory as a partial function (not defined on every value of NAME) from NAME to NUM, so that it may be given a name that does not have a mapping to a telephone number.

$$\mathrm{DIR} \triangleq [dir : \mathrm{NAME} ⇸ \mathrm{NUM}]$$

The symbol '⇸' is used to show that this is a partial function. It is necessary to make the function partial because out of the universe of all possible names (the set of names) we are only likely to refer to a few in our telephone directory. Most functions in **Z** are described as partial.

The symbol '$\triangleq$' represents 'is defined as' and means that the object *dir* is defined within a schema DIR. This will become clearer later.

You will notice this specification is slightly different from the **VDM** specification where DIR was expressed as a mapping between two types, though we could equally well have described it in this way.

The subset of NAME for which *dir* is defined is the domain of the directory:

$$\text{dom}(dir)$$

E.g. if *dir* = {"*John Smith*" $\mapsto$ 031943, "*Fred Jones*" $\mapsto$ 421400} Then
dom(*dir*) = {"*John Smith*", "*Fred Jones*"},
dir("*John Smith*") = 031943,
dir("*Fred Jones*") = 421400.

Similarly the *range* of the directory is the telephone numbers:

$$\text{ran}(dir) = \{031943, 421400\}.$$

Initially the directory will be empty. We define this property in a schema:

```
__ Init ____________________________
| DIR
|___________________
| dir= {}
|____________________________________
```

A schema consists of two parts: the part above the central line declares the objects used in the schema (in this case DIR), the part below the central line is a predicate which specifies additional constraints (in this case that the dir is empty). A schema can thus be seen as being similar to a set or sequence comprehension declaration turned on its side. The above schema can also be declared in a vertical format in the form:

$$\text{Init} \triangleq [\text{DIR} \mid dir = \{\}]$$

Schema calculus provides a concise means of composing different pieces of a specification in an inherently modular style, allowing a specification to be broken down into component parts.

An operation to update the directory and add a new name and telephone number would be represented as:

```
Add
ΔDIR
name? : NAME
no? : NUM
------------------
dir' = dir ⊕ {name? ↦ no?}
```

By convention input variables end in '?' and output variables in '!'. The symbol '⊕' is *the function override* operator, which has the same effect as the map override operator in the **VDM** specification.

The Delta symbol 'Δ' prefixing DIR means that the directory's state can be changed by the operation. Because of this change we need to differentiate between the old state of the directory and its new state after the operation. We do this by adding a prime symbol ''' to the end of the directory name to represent the state of the directory after the operation. Thus *dir* represents the state of the directory before the operation and *dir'* represents the new state of the directory after the operation. The operation to lookup an entry in the table can be defined as:

```
Lookup
ΞDIR
name? : NAME
no! : NUM
------------------
name? ∈ dom(dir) ∧
 no! = dir(name?)
```

with *name?* being the name looked up, and *no!* the value returned. Prefixing DIR with the Xi symbol 'Ξ' says that the directory is not changed by the operation; there is therefore no need to differentiate between the before and after state of the directory in this operation.

The operation to delete a name from the directory is defined as:

```
Delete
ΔDIR
name? : NAME
------------------
name? ∈ dom(dir) ∧
dir' = {name?} ⩤ dir
```

Again *dir* and *dir* ' represent the before and after states of the directory.

The first line of predicate states the name must be in the table and provides a pre-condition on the operation. The second part states that the new state of the directory after the operation (*dir'*) is the old state of the directory (*dir*) with *name*? removed. The '⩤' symbol represents the domain subtraction operator.

In the schemas it has been assumed that no errors will occur; this was to keep the code brief. It is possible to modify these definitions to cope with problems such as looking up a name that is not in the directory.

There is a basic similarity between the **Z** and **VDM** specifications. However, the use of schemas in **Z** is seen as providing a distinct advantage since **VDM** does not contain such structures. **Z** is generally seen as being a more expressive language and allows structures such as relationships to be defined, though this extra power can make it more difficult to follow than **VDM**. It is also more difficult to refine into programming code, since it does not contain many of the imperative programming constructs found in **VDM**.

3.3.3 RAISE

RAISE is an acronym for *Rigorous Approach to Industrial Software Engineering*, a complete software development system offering a systematic method of software design[2]. The **RAISE** specification language (**RSL**) is a wide-spectrum language, capable of expressing both high-level abstract specifications and low-level explicit designs. **RSL** supports a number of different specification design methods including model-orientated (as in **Z** or **VDM**) and algebraic (as in **LOTOS**) allowing both explicit and axiomatic definitions. It also allows concurrency to be defined.

Unlike **VDM**, the **RAISE** language supports concurrency and non-determinism enabling stepwise development of concurrent as well as sequential software.

3.3.3.1 Example - Electronic Telephone Directory

Based on the same requirements as the previous examples, the telephone directory will store the names and telephone numbers of people indexed against the person's name. This example (in a functional style) gives one of the many possible ways of specifying the system in **RAISE**.

---

[2] The term rigorous concerns the fact that the refinement process in RAISE suggests rather than demands that formal proof analysis be carried out during refinement. This differs from a more formal approach where formal proof is a requisite of any stage of program development.

The directory maps names to telephone numbers:

$$\text{Dir} = \text{Name} \xrightarrow[m]{} \text{TelephoneNo}$$

A mapping operator (denoted by the *m* under the arrow) is used, rather than a function operator (denoted by a plain arrow) because the set of names will be *finite*: whereas functions relate to infinite sets. The directory will initially be empty. We define empty as being of type Dir:

$$\text{empty} : \text{Dir}$$

with the property of being empty:

$$\text{empty} \equiv []$$

We will want to be able to add a name and number to the directory. Firstly, we define a type expression for the function:

$$\text{add} : \text{Name} \times \text{TelephoneNo} \times \text{Dir} \rightarrow \text{Dir}$$

This shows that the function add is passed values of type Name, TelephoneNo and Dir and returns a value of type Dir. We now have to state the axioms (or properties) of the function; in this case that it will return a directory consisting of the old directory with the new name and number added:

$$\text{add}(\text{name}, \text{number}, \text{dir}) \equiv$$
$$\text{dir} \dagger [\text{name} \mapsto \text{number}]$$

The symbol '†' represents the *override operator* which overrides one map with another (see the **VDM** example for an description of this operator). Thus add corresponds to overriding the original directory with the new association.

We now wish to define the function Lookup, which given a name will return the corresponding number:

$$\text{lookup}: \text{Name} \times \text{Dir} \xrightarrow{\sim} \text{TelephoneNo}$$

where '$\xrightarrow{\sim}$' represents a partial mapping (Lookup being a partial function).

For the number to be returned we require that the name is in the directory. We define this with a pre-condition:

$$\textbf{pre}\ \text{name} \in \textbf{dom}\ \text{dir}$$

This precondition means that the function will only work in cases where the name is in the directory (it is for this reason that it has been defined as a partial function). This gives the complete axiom:

lookup(name, dir) ≡
    dir(name)
    pre name ∈ **dom** dir

The statement dir(name) applies the name to the directory returning the corresponding number, thus dir(name) = TelephoneNo. We may also wish to delete a name from the directory.

delete : Name × Dir → Dir

which given the name and the directory will return the directory with the name deleted.

delete(name, dir) ≡
    dir \ {name}

where '\' represents the *domain restriction operator* which restricts the directory to all mappings in the directory with a domain not in the set {name}, i.e.

dir \ {name} =
    [d ↦ dir(name) | d : Name • d ∈ dom dir ∧ d ∉ {name}]

A pre-condition that the name is in the directory is not required for delete. This is because the domain restriction operator is *restricting* the new state of the directory to all values not including the name, not simply *deleting* the name from the directory. This gives the complete specification:

scheme
    MAP_DIRECTORY =
        class
            type
                Dir = Name $\overrightarrow{m}$ TelephoneNo,
                Name, TelephoneNo

            value
                empty : Dir,
                add : Name × TelephoneNo × Dir → Dir,
                lookup : Name × Dir $\xrightarrow{\sim}$ TelephoneNo,
                delete : Name × Dir → Dir

```
axiom forall name:Name,number:TelephoneNo,dir:Dir •
        empty ≡ [],
        add(name,number,dir) ≡
            dir † [name ↦ number],
        lookup(name,dir) ≡
            dir(name)
            pre name ∈ dom dir,
        delete(name,dir) ≡
            dir \ {name}
end
```

RAISE specifications can be in a number of styles. We could, for example, specify the same system in a state-based specification as in the **VDM** example, or in an algebraic style such as:

```
scheme
    ALGEBRAIC_DIRECTORY =
      class
          type
              Name, TelephoneNo, Dir
          value
              empty:Dir,
              add:Name × TelephoneNo × Dir → Dir,
              lookup: Name × Dir ⥲ TelephoneNo,
              delete:Name × Dir → Dir

      axiom forall name, name1:Name, telno:TelephoneNo, dir:Dir •
              delete(name, empty) ≡ empty
              delete(name, add(name1, telno, dir)) ≡
                  if name = name1
                  then delete(name, dir)
                  else add(name1, telno, delete(name, dir))
                  end,
              lookup(name, add(name1, telno, dir)) ≡
                  if name = name1
                  then telno
                  else lookup(name, dir)
                  end
                  pre name = name1 ∨ name ∈ dir
      end
```

It can be seen in this specification that lookup is a partial mapping.

RAISE also has a number of operators to specify concurrency, including:

[]	External choice operator
⊓	Internal choice operator.
‖	Parallel operator
‖̶	Intersection operator
;	Sequential operator.

The parallel operator allows us to specify that two processes run simultaneously. The sequential operator specifies that one process runs after another, but that the two processes are 'combined'. Thus:

lookup_channel!name ; result_channel?

would put a value from lookup_channel into the variable name which would be input into the result channel.

The external choice operator allows a process to offer several different kinds of communication at the same time, the choice of which are selected depending on an external factor (and therefore being deterministic). The internal choice operator is used in non-deterministic situations.

In order for processes to communicate with each other, as in the example given previously, channels are provided. Channels are declared to be of a specific type:

channel_name : type

For a function to use channels it must be stated whether the channel is inputting information to or sending information from a function. Two keywords are given to define this:

in	Declares the channel(s) to be input channels
out	Declares the channel(s) to be output channels

For example:

function: **in** channel1 **out** channel2

declares function to have an input channel called channel1 and an output channel called channel2.

channel1 → function → channel2

RSL has two operators on channels allowing reading or writing to a channel.

channel?x Input a value x into the channel ($x \rightarrow$ channel)
channel!y Output a value from the channel into y (channel $\rightarrow$ y)

That is:

$$x \rightarrow \underline{\overline{\text{channel}}} \rightarrow y$$

As well as the normal types (**Bool**, **Int**, **Nat** and **Real**), **RAISE** has a number of other types:

Char Represents single characters such as 'A', 'B' etc.
Text Represents sequences of characters, such as 'text'.
Unit Represents the null value.

Unit is used to declare that a function does not return (or is not given) a value. For example, in a state-based specification a function often changes an external value (as a side-effect), but the function itself returns nothing (acting like a procedure in a programming language).

These types and operators allow us to specify a concurrent form of the telephone directory which allows multiple concurrent choices:

```
scheme
    CONCURRENT_DIRECTORY =
        class
            type
                Name, TelephoneNo,
                Dir = Name ⇸ TelephoneNo
            channel
                empty_chl:Unit,
                add_chl:Name × TelephoneNo,
                lookup_chl:Name,
                delete_chl:Name,
                lookup_result_chl:TelephoneNo

            value
                directory: Dir → in    empty_chl, add_chl, lookup_chl
                                   out  lookup_result_chl Unit,
                empty : Unit → out empty_chl Unit,
                Add: Name × TelephoneNo → out add_chl Unit,
                Lookup: Name → out lookup_chl →
                                        lookup_result_chl TelephoneNo,
                Delete: Name → out delete_chl Unit
```

```
axiom forall dir:Dir, name:Name, telno:TelephoneNo •
        directory(dir) ≡
           empty? ; directory([])
           []
           let (name,number) = add_chl? in
                directory(dir † [name ↦ number])
           end
           []
           let name = delete_chl? in
                directory(dir \ {name})
           end
           []
           let name = lookup_chl? in
              if name ∈ dom dir
              then lookup_result_chl!(dir(name)) ;
                   directory(dir)
           end
        end,

        /* define interactions with channels */
        Empty() ≡
           empty_chl!(),
        Add(name, telno) ≡
           add_chl!(name, telno),
        Lookup(name) ≡
           lookup_chl!name ; lookup_result_chl?,
        Delete(name) ≡
           delete_chl!name
end
```

RAISE seems to offer the advantages of both model-based and algebraic specification styles. It encourages modularity and because it contains both high-level and low-level constructs it is easy to develop implementations from specifications. Its major disadvantage is that it was developed fairly recently and so is not so well established as other formal methods. The language is, as yet, not one of those accepted by the International Standards Organisation, though the notation has proved suprisingly stable with little or no changes from the original being required.

3.3.4 LOTOS

LOTOS stands for *Language Of Temporal Ordering Specification*. It is a formal description technique designed to describe distributed concurrent information processing systems, in particular for service definition and protocol specification within the OSI (Open Systems) architecture and related standards. It is a well-defined mathematical notation providing a good basis for analysis and the development of support tools, including simulators, compilers and test sequence generators.

The basic constructs of **LOTOS** allow modelling of sequencing, choice, concurrency and non-determinism in an entirely unambiguous way. **LOTOS** also permits modelling of synchronous and asynchronous communication. **LOTOS** specifications consist of two parts; one concerned with the process behaviour, the other with the description of data structures (called ACT 1). The latter is based on the theory of abstract data types (ADTs).

Basic entities in **LOTOS** are processes, with an entire system being seen as a single process. Only the externally observable behaviour is described; this behaviour consisting of the interactions of the process with its environment. These interactions are assumed to be discrete atomic events and occur at specific interaction points called *gates*. Processes that communicate with each other share a *common gate*.

3.3.4.1 Example - Electronic telephone directory

Like the previous examples the electronic telephone directory will again store the names and telephone numbers of people indexed against the person's name in a directory.

LOTOS provides no way of saying that, for example, **Name** is simply a set (of names). One is forced to specify exactly what names it contains. The following example does not specify names and telephone numbers in this way, but contains comments where these details have been left out. These details would have to be added before the specification is valid. Two data types are taken from a standard library provided by LOTOS.

```
library
   Boolean, Set
endlib
```

The following data type defines three sets, consisting of names, telephone numbers and all possible entries in a directory, i.e. all possible combinations of a name and a number. The details defining names and numbers are left out, but those defining entries and their relationship to names and numbers are given. The various sets are called *sorts*, while mappings between them are called *operations*.

```
type Entry is
  Boolean
  sorts Name, Number, Entry
  opns
    (* To be inserted: operations to construct names and numbers *)
    _eq_ : Name, Name -> Bool
    _eq_ : Number, Number -> Bool

    BuildEntry: Name, Number -> Entry
    NameOf: Entry -> Name
    NumberOf: Entry -> Number
    _eq_, _ne_ : Entry, Entry -> Bool
  eqns
    forall a: Name, n : Number, x, y : Entry

    (* To be inserted: equations to define eq for names and numbers *)
    ofsort Name
      NameOf(BuildEntry(a, n)) = a;
    ofsort Number
      NumberOf(BuildEntry(a, n)) = n;
    ofsort Bool
      x eq y = (NameOf(x) eq NameOf(y)) and
               (NumberOf(x) eq NumberOf(y));
      x ne y = not(x eq y);
endtype
```

The definition:

```
BuildEntry : Name, Number -> Entry
```

means that for any **Name a** and any **Number n**, **BuildEntry(a, n)** is an **Entry**. This operation is said to 'construct' **Entries**. For other operations, *equations* are used to define their results. For example, **NameOf** does not 'construct' any **Names**, because there is an equation defining **NameOf**, for any given **Entry**, as the **Name** that was used in 'constructing' that **Entry**.

The library type **Set** is a *parameterised* type, using a parameter **Element**, which represents an unspecified set of elements. It defines **Set** as the set of all sets of **Elements**, **{}** as the empty set of **Elements**, **Insert(x, s)** as the set obtained by inserting the **Element x** into the **Set s**, **Remove(x, s)** as the set obtained by removing the **Element x** from the **Set s**, and **x IsIn s** as **true** or **false** according to whether the **Element x** is a member of the **Set s**.

Before this parameterised type can be used, it must be *actualised*, by specifying a particular set of elements.

```
type BasicDirectory is
  Set actualizedby Entry using
    sortnames
      Bool for FBool
      Entry for Element
      Directory for Set
    opnnames
      EmptyDir for {}
endtype
```

This also specifies some *renaming* of sorts and operations. **FBool** is a technical name used in the definition of **Set**. The **Elements** are renamed to be the set of **Entries** defined earlier. **Set**, the set of all sets of **Entries**, i.e. the set of all possible directories, is renamed **Directory**. **{}**, the directory containing no **Entries** is renamed **EmptyDir**.

The above definition of **BasicDirectory** is then *imported* into another type **RicherDirectory**, which defines an extra operation to specify whether a given **Name** is listed in a given **Directory**.

```
type RicherDirectory is
  BasicDirectory
  opns
    _ListedIn_ :  Name, Directory -> Bool
  eqns
    forall x, a: Name, n: Number, d: Directory
    ofsort Bool
      x ListedIn EmptyDir = false;
      x ListedIn Insert(BuildEntry(a, n), d) = (x eq a) or (x ListedIn d);
endtype
```

Note that **ListedIn** is defined recursively over **Directories**.

The next type defines a set of three 'access tags', **ADD**, **LOOKUP** and **DELETE**, used later to identify the nature of every access to a directory. Each tag is a *constant*, represented by an operation which has no input arguments and whose 'result' is therefore constant.

```
type DirectoryAccess is
  sorts AccessTag
  opns
    ADD, LOOKUP, DELETE: -> AccessTag
endtype
```

Now we define a *process* which manages a directory. This process interacts with its environment through a *gate*, called **access**. The process definition specifies behaviour in terms of the interactions that occur. It uses a parameter, which gives the initial contents of the directory.

```
process directory[access](current_dir: Directory): noexit :=
  access ! ADD ? x : Entry [not(NameOf(x) ListedIn current_dir)];
  directory[access](Insert(x, current_dir))
   []
  access ! LOOKUP ? a : Name ?
             n : Number [BuildEntry(a, n) IsIn current_dir];
   directory[access](current_dir)
   []
  (
   choice n: Number []
     access ! DELETE ? a: Name [BuildEntry(a, n) IsIn current_dir];
     directory[access](Remove(BuildEntry(a, n), current_dir))
  )
endproc
```

There are three alternative courses of action, separated by the *choice operator* **[]**. The first alternative begins with the *event* (interaction).

```
access ! ADD ? x : Entry [not(NameOf(x) ListedIn current_dir)]
```

An event is specified by the gate involved, together with a string of zero or more data values. Here there are two data values. One is indicated by an exclamation mark with an expression, in this case a tag to indicate that a new entry is being added. The other is indicated by a question mark with a variable declaration; this value is called **x**, and can be any **Entry**. The square brackets contain a precondition for the event to be permitted.

If this event takes place, the process **directory** is invoked recursively. This means that subsequent events will proceed according to the behaviour specified by this process. The new invocation begins with updated directory contents, specified by the new parameter value.

The second alternative begins with a 'look-up' event. There are two variable data values, giving the **Name** to be looked up and the associated **Number**. The 'pre-condition' forces both the **Name** to be one that is listed in the directory and the **Number** to be that entered along with that **Name** in the directory. The subsequent reinvocation of process **directory** begins with unaltered directory contents.

The third alternative allows a *choice* of any **Number n**, subject to its involvement in the subsequent event. That event is tagged as deleting an entry, with a single variable data value giving the **Name** to be deleted. The pre-condition forces the **Name** to be one that is listed in the directory, and also constrains **n** to be the **Number** associated with that **Name**. Process **directory** is reinvoked, beginning with updated directory contents.

This process may then be specified to 'run' in parallel with other processes, with *synchronisation* at the gate **access**. This means that other processes can specify **access** events, which must be simultaneously executed by **directory**, with identical data values. So if a process contains a variable **customer** whose value is a **Name**, it can execute the event

access ! LOOKUP ! customer ? cust_number: Number

The constraints imposed by process **directory** then ensure that **cust_number** is the **Number** associated with **customer** in the directory.

LOTOS is well established, particularly in the protocols area. Its notation is also well defined, being described in an international standard. The language is well suited to describing systems in terms of their behaviour and it has advantages in that it can describe concurrency and non-determinism.

3.3.5 Estelle

Estelle, *Extended State Transition Language*, is a partly formalised formal description technique for the specification of distributed or concurrent processing systems, in particular those which implement OSI services and protocols.

The language is based on accepted concepts of communicating non-deterministic finite state machines. An **Estelle** specification defines a system of hierarchically structured state machines. The machines communicate by exchanging messages through bi-directional channels connecting their communications ports.

A distributed system specified in **Estelle** would be viewed as a collection of communicating components called *module instances*, each module having a number of access points called *interaction points*. Each module has a visible external interface; it receives and sends messages (interactions) through the interaction points. Modules communicate either by exchanging interactions or by sharing variables. Modules can interact when they are linked by either the *connect* or *attach* primitive. Channel definitions provide a way of specifying the external behaviour of modules at their interaction points.

Modules are declared either as *processes* or *activities*. You can use process modules to enforce tight, synchronous parallelism; you can use activities to represent loose parallelism, where concurrency is expressed by the *interleaving* of parallel actions.

A module is defined by a *header* and a *body*. The header defines the module's external visibility, including which information will be received and sent. The body defines the module's internal composition, which could include its behaviour and/or its structure, and contains definitions for data types, variables, auxiliary procedures and transition rules.

Each of the transition rules held in a module state what events trigger the transition, what actions are performed when it is triggered and the state resulting from the transition. Each transition rule is triggered by a specific state. Specification of a transition rule in Estelle is of the form:

```
trans
from state1                {current state}
to state2                  {resultant state}
when event                 {when some event occurs}
provided predicates        {provided Boolean condition holds}
priority expression        {priority of the transition}
begin
   {actions to take}
end
```

States can be given symbolic names in Estelle and these appear in the **from** and **to** clauses. Only when the process is in *state1* is the transition allowed to occur. The **when** clause tells what event will trigger it and the **provided** clause allows a Boolean condition of the process states variables to be stated which must hold for it to take place. The priority clause allows priorities to be assigned to transitions.

Estelle permits the clear separation of the description of the communication interface between components of a specified system from the description of their internal workings.

Estelle is a modification and extension to Pascal; program-level constructs have been replaced by constructs to define finite-state modules exchanging queued messages. As in Pascal there is strong typing; this assists in the static detection of specification inconsistencies. Familiarity with Pascal makes the reading of **Estelle** specifications easier.

3.3.5.1 Example - Electronic telephone directory

Again like the previous examples this electronic telephone directory will store the names and telephone numbers of people indexed against the person's name in a directory. In this case, however, there is a user module (which provides the interactions with the user) and a directory module (which manipulates the directory) linked by a channel.

The user can send a name (via the channel) to the directory, in which case the directory will provide (return) the appropriate telephone number, or they can send a new name and telephone number to the directory.

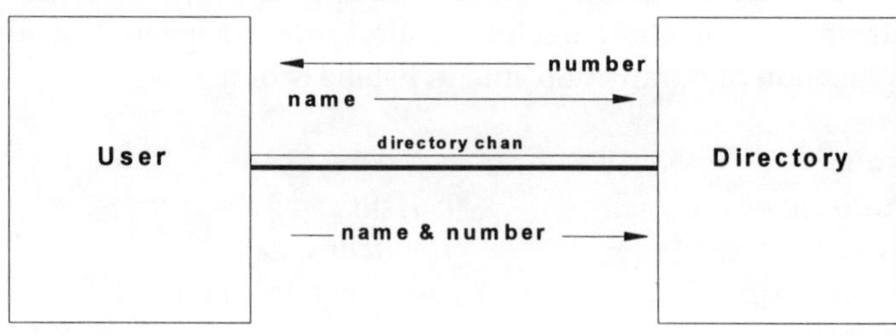

Figure 3.2: Graphical representation of electronic telephone directory

Since **Estelle** specifications are explicit they tend to be rather verbose. Comments (given in curly brackets) have therefore been added where appropriate to explain particular details rather than going through a step-by-step account of how the specification was derived.

```
specification telephone_directory;

const   length = ...;          { ellipsis indicates value is  }
                               { implementation dependent. }
        max_num = ...;         { ellipsis indicates structure of type is}
                               { implementation dependent. }
type    seq_of_char = ...;
        tel_no_range = 1..maxnum;
        directory_entry = record
            Name : seq_of_char;
            TelephoneNo : tel_no_range
          end;

{ Two possible types of users for this channel, a user and a provider. }
channel directory_chan(user, provider);
        { define what sort of message each user can send along the
          channel. }
        by user : send_name(nm:seq_of_char);
            send_name_&_number(nm:seq_of_char;
            telno:tel_no_range);
        by provider : send_number(telno: tel_no_range);
```

```
{ Modules may be activities or processes. Activities cannot run in parallel
   with other activities. Processes can run in parallel. }
module user_mod systemactivity;
        ip to_directory_mod : directory_chan(user);
end;

{ Body declaration for user_mod - 'external' indicates that contents of
   module are implementation dependent. }
body user_mod_body for user_mod; external;
{ Module header declaration. Indicates that user_mod has interaction point
  (ip) converted to a channel of type directory_chan. the role of this module
  or the channel is that of 'user'. }
module directory_mod systemactivity; { directory_mod has the role of}
                                     { 'provider' for this channel }
        ip to_user_mod : directory_chan(provider);
end;

body directory_mod_body for directory_mod;
        state initial;
        var dir: directory;

procedure add(nm:seq_of_char; telno:tel_no_range);
        begin
            if dir.pointer < length + 1 then
             begin
               dir.entries[dir.pointer].Name := nm;
               dir.entries[dir.pointer]. TelephoneNo := telno;
               dir.pointer := dir.pointer + 1
             end
         end
end;

function lookup(nm:seq_of_char):tel_no_range;
        var     count : 1..length;
                result : tel_no_range;
         begin
            result := 0;
            for count := 1 to length do
               if dir.entries[count].Name = nm
               then result:= dir.entries[count]. TelephoneNo;
            lookup := result
         end;
```

```
initialise to initial { Sets module to first state. }
      begin
          dir.pointer :=1 { Sets up module variables when }
                         { module 'initialised'. }
      end;

trans { Set of state transitions. }
      from initial to same { Indicates state transition to take place. }
          {When message received at interaction point. }
          when to_user_mod.Send_name_&_number
              begin
                  add(nm, telno)
              end
          when to_user_mod.send_name
              begin { Send this message back along channel in reply. }
                  output_to_user_mod.send_number(lookup(nm))
              end;
end; {Directory_mod_body}

modvar { Variable of type module. }
      Directory : directory_mod;
      User : user_mod;

initialize { Initialise specification. }
      begin
          init Directory with directory_mod_body;
          init User with user_mod_body;
          connect User.to_directory_mod to
          Directory.to_user_mod
      end
end. { End specification. }
```

3.3.6 Larch

Larch is a property-orientated specification language combining both axiomatic and algebraic specifications in a two-tier specification.

Firstly, an *auxiliary specification* consists of *traits* which each define a *sort* (analogous to a programming language type) and the operations that may be performed on a sort. The operations are specified using an algebraic style. Auxiliary specifications are independent of any particular implementation and are written in the *Larch Shared Language* (LSL).

The second part is the *interface specification*. This is intimately tied to a particular programming language, and thus forms the bridge between the abstract auxiliary specification and the implementation. A new interface specification can be produced for any number of programming languages, with each interface specification based on the same auxiliary specification.

Larch is especially convenient when one wishes to verify an implementation.

3.3.6.1 Example - Electronic telephone directory

The telephone directory used in the previous examples is again stated.

The following *trait* defines the *sort* DIR, which denotes a telephone directory, and contains a set of function declarations and equations:

```
DIR_SPEC : trait
        includes
                NAME_SPEC, TELNO_SPEC
        introduces
                EMPTY : → DIR
                ADD : NAME, TELNO, DIR → DIR
                LOOKUP : NAME, DIR → TELNO
                DELETE : NAME, DIR → DIR
       asserts DIR generated by EMPTY, ADD
                DIR partitioned by LOOKUP
                ∀n, m : NAME, t : TELNO, d : DIR
                    DELETE(n, EMPTY) == EMPTY;
                    LOOKUP(n, ADD(m, t, d)) ==
                        if n = m
                        then t
                        else LOOKUP(n, d);
                    DELETE(n, ADD(m, t, d)) ==
                        if n = m
                        then d
                        else ADD(m, t, DELETE(n, d))
```

Note that the trait imports two other traits, NAME_SPEC and TELNO_SPEC, which define names and telephone numbers respectively. The '*generated by*' clause indicates that all possible directories can be generated by the operations EMPTY and ADD. The '*partitioned by*' clause ensures that structurally different but equivalent DIRs are considered equal by the LOOKUP operation. It should be noted that the axioms are incomplete, in that no axiom is given for the case where a LOOKUP operation is attempted on an empty directory; the result in this case is undefined.

We now define the corresponding interface specification, written in **Larch**/Modula-2.

```
dir mutable type exports [empty, add, lookup, delete]
based on sort DIR
        from DIR_SPEC
        with [name for NAME, telno for TELNO]

PROCEDURE empty():(d:dir);
modifies nothing
effects d_post = ADD(n, t, d)

PROCEDURE add(n:name; t:telno; d:dir);
modifies at most (d)
effects d_post = ADD(n, t, d)

PROCEDURE lookup(n:name; d:dir):(t:telno);
requires d ≠ EMPTY
modifies nothing
effects t = LOOKUP(n, d)

PROCEDURE delete(n:name; d:dir);
modifies at most (d)
effects d_post = DELETE(n, d)
```

The first line of this interface specification indicates that dir is a mutable type, that is, certain operations modify objects of the type dir. Contrast this with the auxiliary specification, where all sorts are immutable.

The *exports* list indicates which procedures are exported. Thus, dir is an abstract data type that can only be accessed via the exported operations. Procedures can be defined within the interface that are used by other procedures but which are not exported, and thus remain hidden from the user of the type.

Each procedure definition consists of two or three clauses. A *requires* clause is the pre-condition and indicates what conditions must be met for the procedure to be defined. The *modifies* clause indicates which variables are modified; in this case the directory is modified by both add and delete. The *effects* clause[3] gives the post-condition, d_{post} being the new value of variable d if it has been modified.

Since the interface specification is tailored to a particular programming language, the construction and verification of implementations in that language is made easier. The tailoring of part of the specification to a

[3] More modern languages have replaced the term 'effects' by the more applicable term 'ensures'.

particular programming language was defined in Larch because it was felt that the environment in which the program would be embedded, and hence its observable behaviour, would be likely to depend in fundamental ways on the semantics of the programming language it was implemented in. Hence any attempt to disguise this dependency, by making the structure's language independent, would make specifications more obscure to both users and the implementors. It was seen as being easier to be precise, for example, about communication when the specification language reflected the programming language, as communications mechanisms differ from programming language to programming language and subtle differences could arise from the differing types of parameter passing and storage allocation mechanisms used in particular programming languages.

Although not shown in the example, if the target programming language supports *exception handling* the interfaces can specify under what conditions an operation signals an exception.

3.4. FINAL COMMENTS

Having looked at a number of formal notations and styles it can be seen that it is important to consider when choosing a notation what style is best suited for the type of system you wish to specify.

The mathematical basis of the notation of a language is important. Some languages are suited to the specification of protocols and communications, whereas others are better suited to other areas.

Which style you choose will depend on how the system is described. If the requirements are given in terms of behaviour then a property-based style is likely to be used. You will also need to determine if state is necessary or whether a functional style is better suited, and whether concurrency is required.

The rest of this book concentrates on the style known as model-orientated, or model-based specification, where we shall be looking at the two formal specification languages **VDM** and **Z** in closer detail.

4

Introduction to model-based languages

In model-based specification systems we build an abstract theoretical model of the system we wish to develop. This model formulates the more fundamental aspects of the system, initially ignoring irrelevant algorithmic details; describing what we want, not how we go about obtaining it. The model consists only of an axiomatic description describing behaviour and properties.

We can use this model to make inferences and draw conclusions about the system. It enables us to reason about a system, and determine inconsistencies and design decisions before actually building it.

In the next two chapters we examine two model-based languages and their constructs, **VDM** and **Z**. Both of these languages are in the process of being standardised and are the most commonly used in the commercial world.

Z was created with the view of describing abstract systems in terms of mathematics, whereas **VDM** could better be described as an attempt to abstract programming. In **VDM** this has resulted in a language in which many low-level as well as high-level constructs exist in the language. **Z** has kept low-level constructs to a minimum, with the result that only constructs that describe the properties of a system, rather than algorithms, can be specified.

Low-level constructs were specifically eliminated from **Z** because it was felt that only the properties of a system should be given in a specification, the algorithms used to achieve these properties being better left to the implementors. **VDM**, on the other hand, purports to incorporate a methodology for deriving programs from specifications; rules are given to allow verification of the steps in development whilst moving from an abstract specification to a concrete realisation. As such, low-level constructs need to be introduced during the process of refinement in order to aid the eventual translation into a programming language. Because of this, **VDM** specifications are usually easier to implement than **Z** specifications. However, the inclusion of lower-level constructs has resulted in many systems being initially described in **VDM** explicitly, when they may best have been written implicitly. This can result in operational bias where the specification is too prescriptive and restricts the freedom of the implementor to a particular way of carrying out the process. **VDM** is more open to abuse in this area than **Z**. There may, though, be times when an explicit style is the only way of describing a process, for example in describing an encryption system[1]. In these cases it is difficult to see how even **Z** could adequately describe such a process implicitly.

Z is more commonly used in academic circles than **VDM** and is a more powerful language. At the time of writing both **VDM** and **Z** were used an equal amount in the commercial world, but this seems to be changing with **Z** gaining dominance.

Model-based languages are best suited to stand-alone processes, rather than protocol and distributed systems. **VDM** and **Z** both suffer from having no explicit support for concurrency and time, and indeed such languages are not really suited to describing these sorts of processes, though some work has been carried out on extending them to support these areas.

RAISE, a language built on the general constructs in **VDM** and **Z**, has had concurrency explicitly built into it. It has done this, however, through allowing an axiomatic style of specification in a way similar to languages such as **LOTOS**.

Both **Z** and **VDM** have two syntactic representations; one mathematical (containing graphical symbols), and one text-based. The graphical notation makes specifications easier to read and most specifications are presented in this format. The text based notation is necessary to allow specifications to be typed in on a normal keyboard and to allow machine-based tools to analyse and manipulate the specification.

In this book the **Z** textual notation is based on an interchange language currently being defined as part of the work into the standardisation of **Z**. **VDM's** textual notation is based on ISO 646, and also forms part of the work of standardising the language. Where the mathematical and the text-based notation differ tables have been included giving both formats,

---

[1] With systems such as encryption and hashing functions there is often no meaningful way of implicitly describing the effect of the system on its input in a way that could easily be understood by an implementor. Often the only way of describing (and differentiating) between two different encryption or hashing methods is by describing the steps involved.

otherwise the format can be assumed to be the same. After introducing a construct it is referred to in later parts by its mathematical graphical notation only.

Although the two chapters can be read independently it is recommended that you cover both **VDM** and **Z**. **VDM** serves as a good introduction to model-based specification, and having been learnt it is a lot easier to go onto the more sophisticated constructs of **Z**. Indeed many of the constructs shared by **VDM** and **Z** are remarkably similar, with only a few subtle differences. A series of exercises are also given in each chapter by which the reader may become familiar with the languages. Sample solutions to these are given at the back of this book. However, it should be remembered that there are often many ways of writing the same specification and if your solutions do not agree with these then your answers may not necessarily be incorrect.

5

VDM

The Vienna Development Method encompasses both a formal description language **VDM-SL** and a methodology for program derivation. **VDM** can be seen as an abstraction of programming, its main difference from a programming language being the ability to specify a model without constraining it to a particular algorithm. Take, for example, the implicit add operation we looked at in Chapter 3:

$$\begin{aligned}&ADD(name : Name, telno : TelephoneNo)\\&\textbf{ext wr } dir : Directory;\\&\textbf{post } dir = \overleftarrow{dir} \dagger \{name \mapsto telno\}\end{aligned}$$

Any implementation that fulfils the post-condition of this operation is a correct implementation of it. Thus the operation represents a class (or set) of operations that would fulfil the post-condition, rather than a specific one. This allows implementors freedom to create efficient implementations, whilst still maintaining correctness.

Such aspects of **VDM** apply to all types of declaration of functions and operations, even explicit ones. An explicit function in **VDM** represents an example of a way of carrying out the function. It does not constrain the implementor to follow the steps described in the function exactly. The condition on an implementation of the function is that it must produce results consistent with those that would be obtained if the steps described explicitly in the function were carried out exactly. The specification thus serves as a control rather than an exact model.

It has been said that:

Algorithms + Data Structures = Programs[1]

Like programs, **VDM** specifications also consist of analogous structures incorporating function and operation definitions, as well as data structures in the form of type and value definitions.

VDM specifications separate these structures into distinct blocks consisting of types, values, functions, operations and state definitions. There is no particular order to these blocks and it is not necessary to include all of them in a specification, but each section included must start with the appropriate keyword[2] **types, values, functions** or **operations** defining the particular section:

types
    ... types definitions ...
values
    ... value definitions ...
functions
    ... function definitions ...
operations
    ... operation definitions ...

    ... state definition ..

The first two sections define the variables and constants used in the specification. The second two sections specify the algorithms used to manipulate this data, in the form of functions and operations. The definition of data structures and the operations on them are therefore separated within the specification. The operations section also defines any state variables required by the operations, such as used in our telephone book example:

state *telbook* **of**
    dir : *Directory*
end

which defined a state variable *dir* of type *Directory*.

---

[1] In a book of the same name by Niklaus Wirth, Prentice Hall 1976.

[2] Keywords are generally given in bold text in **VDM** to differentiate them from user-defined words.

5.1. USER-DEFINED IDENTIFIERS

User-defined words in **VDM**, such as value, type, function and operation names, must follow certain conventions. They must always start with, and consist of at least one letter (upper or lower case). This may be followed by any sequence of characters including letters, digits and Greek letters. The underscore character can be used to separate compound words. For example:

This_is_a_user_defined_word

The hyphen should not be used in this regard, as this can be confused with the subtraction operator. Spaces and **VDM** symbols also cannot be used in a user-defined word. Use of keywords, except as part of a compound word, should also be avoided in identifiers. Letter case in **VDM-SL** is significant, so:

User_defined_word
user_defined_word
User_Defined_Word

are all different identifiers and not related.

In **VDM** there is a convention that operation names are written entirely in upper case, whereas function names are written in lower case or a mixture. This is used to differentiate the two types of procedures.

Where Greek letters are used in the plaintext notation for user-defined identifiers and names, the letters are replaced by the corresponding alphabetic letter given below prefixed by a hash sign.

Greek letters with plaintext equivalencies											
α	a	ι	i	ρ	r	Α	A	Ι	I	Ρ	R
β	b	κ	k	σ	s	Β	B	Κ	K	Σ	S
γ	g	λ	l	τ	t	Γ	G	Λ	L	Τ	T
δ	d	μ	m	υ	u	Δ	D	Μ	M	Υ	U
ε	e	ν	n	φ	f	Ε	E	Ν	N	Φ	F
ζ	z	ξ	x	χ	c	Ζ	Z	Ξ	X	Χ	C
η	h	ο	o	ψ	y	Η	H	Ο	O	Ψ	Y
θ	q	π	p	ω	w	Θ	Q	Π	P	Ω	W

For example, capital Delta ('Δ') would be represented in plaintext as:

#D

5.2. COMMENTS

Comments can be included within a **VDM** specification, but, there are rules on how they are attached.

In the first form, recommended for short notes, the comment is prefaced with a double dash. Anything after this dash on the rest of the line is considered to be part of the comment. The end of the line terminates the comment. For example:

```
-- This function takes a name and corresponding
--  address and adds it to the directory
ADD(name : Name, telno : TelephoneNo)
ext wr dir : Directory;
post dir = dir↼ † {name ↦ telno}
```

For longer sections of text we use the keywords 'annotations' and 'end annotations'. Anything between these two keywords is considered to be comments. For example: we could place a comment at the beginning of the specification giving details about it.

```
annotations
        Specification: Example1
        Specification Language: VDM-SL
        Date Last altered: ...
        Specification writer: ...
        Short overview of what specification is about ...
end annotations
```

The rules about how comments are written are necessary in order for it to be clear which parts form the specification and which parts are simply notes clarifying the specification. This is similar to the situation in programming languages.

5.3. SEPARATORS

In a complete **VDM** specification all type, value, function and operation definitions are terminated with a semicolon placed at the end of their definition to separate them from the next definition. Where a new section heading (such as **types, values, functions, operations** etc.) occurs after the definition, however, the semicolon is omitted. This is because, like the semicolons in statements and expressions, the semicolon represents a separator, not a terminator, and is to separate one definition from the next. In the case of a section heading, the heading itself acts as the separator and so the semicolon is not required.

5.4. PATTERNS AND BINDINGS

Patterns are used in many of the constructs in **VDM-SL.** Their use involves the matching of the pattern to a value. If the value fits the template defined by the pattern, any identifiers are bound to their matched components. For example, in:

$$mk\_(x, y) = (1, 2)$$

the pattern on the left-hand side $mk\_(x, y)$ is matched with the value on the right-hand side (1, 2) binding the value 1 to x and 2 to y.

In most cases the pattern matches to at least some of the values, though in some circumstances, for example in conditional expressions, there may be situations where it does not. Patterns are used in various ways depending on the context, but are mainly seen in *set* and *type binds* where patterns are associated with sets:

$$\text{Pattern} \in \text{Set}$$

or types:

$$\text{Pattern} : \text{Type}$$

Such bindings either define or limit the choice of values the pattern can represent. For example, we can define a tuple bind:

$$\{mk\_(x, y) \mid x \in \mathbb{N}, y \in \mathbb{N} \bullet y = x * x\}$$

which implies all combinations of x and y are restricted to the set of natural numbers.

The pattern in many cases is simply an identifier, but it can also be defined in terms of an expression, a set or sequence enumeration, set union, sequence concatenation, a record pattern or a tuple pattern. It can also include do not care symbols '-' which match to any value or type but do not bind. These are useful where we do not need to know a value, for example:

$$\{a, -, c\} == \{X, Y, Z\}$$

where we do not require the value of the second element.

At this stage we do not need to know how patterns are defined in any great depth, though it is worth examining the grammar for patterns in the **VDM-SL** syntax given in the Appendix B, in order to gain a clearer understanding of their format. They will become clearer as we look at their use within the various constructs covered in this book.

5.5. VALUE DEFINITION

Values in a **VDM** specification define fixed values and are similar to constants in programming languages. A value definition in **VDM** has the form:

Pattern = Expression

For example:

$$PI = 3.142$$

Here, as in most cases, the pattern is simply an identifier.

A value definition can also have the type of the value defined, restricting the value of the expression to members of this type, in other words type binding the pattern. This has the form:

Pattern : Type = Expression

The expression in a value definition can be an unevaluated expression (which could, for example, include other values). The value will take on the *evaluated* value of the expression.

$$Max\_size : \mathbb{N} = 8,$$
$$Largest\_input = 4 \times Max\_size$$

So, in the above, Largest_input will take on the value 32.

The expression may also include functions, though not operations. For example:

$$Ten = Double(1 + 4)$$

Double would be a function, defined in the specification, which takes a value and returns the value doubled.

Exercise 5.1: Given the value Yen, how would you go about defining that the value of a Dollar is 100 Yen and a UK pound is 2.4 dollars?

5.6. TYPE DEFINITION

Data types in **VDM** are strongly typed and therefore, unlike operations, cannot be loosely defined. **VDM-SL** has a rich set of built-in standard data types and allows the construction of complex user-defined types such as sets, maps, records and products. Each type has associated with it a set of operators specific to the type. These have a variety of applications, from defining *type invariants* to manipulating data in functions and operations.

The simplest form of type definition in **VDM** has the form:

$$\text{Id} = \text{T}$$

where Id is an identifier and T its type. For example:

$$number = \mathbb{N}$$

which defines number to be of type natural. Composite types have slightly different definitions, which will be defined later.

In addition to defining an identifier to be of a specific type, **VDM** also allows us to constrain the values of the type to a specified subset of the type by the use of a *type invariant.*

5.6.1 Invariants on types

An invariant is a property that does not change, remaining constant throughout the life of the specification. We can constrain types by the use of an optional type invariant. This, like the Boolean expression in a set or sequence comprehension, constrains the type to those values for which the Boolean condition is true. An invariant condition in a type definition takes the form:

$$\begin{array}{l} \text{Id} = \text{T} \\ \textbf{inv} \text{ Pattern} \triangleq \text{Boolean condition} \end{array}$$

where it is appended to the end of the type definition. The word **inv** is a keyword and is short for invariant. The Definition symbol:

Symbol	Text	Mathematical
Definition	==	≜

can be considered to represent the statement 'is defined as'. We can therefore see the line states that the **invariant** on the type 'is defined' as the Boolean condition. For example:

$$\begin{array}{l} Bit = \mathbb{N} \\ \textbf{inv } Bit \triangleq Bit \in \{0, 1\} \end{array}$$

defines a type called Bit which consists of a single natural number, the invariant on which constrains the value of an element of the type to a member of the set {0, 1}. This is equivalent to a set comprehension of:

$$\{Bit \mid Bit \in \mathbb{N} \wedge Bit \in \{0, 1\}\}$$

A variable of type *Bit* in this case would thus only be allowed to take on a value of either 0 or 1 (where 0 and 1 are natural numbers).

In the example the name *Bit* used in the predicate part of the invariant is a variable or term used to represent a single value of Bit. Like a variable in predicate logic its name is unimportant and any name can be used, for example we could replace it with the letter *b*:

$$\begin{array}{l} Bit = \mathbb{N} \\ \textbf{inv } Bit \triangleq b \in \{0, 1\} \end{array}$$

However, this is not the case with the type-name 'Bit' following the invariant keyword, which must correspond with the earlier type-name.

Invariants can be expressed in terms of type operators and can contain user-defined values which have been previously expressed in the values section of the specification. For example:

$$\begin{array}{l} Byte = Bit^{+} \\ \textbf{inv } Byte \triangleq \textbf{len } b = Byte\_length \end{array}$$

where **len** is a keyword meaning length and Byte_length is a user-defined value set to 8.

Invariants are commonly used in defining types in **VDM** and can be used on all types including composite ones. They are always placed on the end of the type definition.

Exercise 5.2: Define a type *T_type* which cannot be greater than 200, and will always consist of a whole number.

5.7. BASIC TYPES

VDM has a number of predefined basic types including Boolean, natural numbers, natural numbers excluding zero (called the positive integers), integers, reals and rational numbers.

Type	Text	Mathematical
Boolean	bool	$\mathbb{B}$
Natural	nat	$\mathbb{N}$
Positive integers	nat1	$\mathbb{N}_1$
Integers	int	$\mathbb{Z}$
Real numbers	real	$\mathbb{R}$
Rationals	rat	$\mathbb{Q}$
Character	char	**char**
Token	token	**token**

There are also two additional predefined data types; **char**, which consists of the **VDM-SL** character set, and **token**, which consists of a set of distinct values. The character type **char** represents single alphanumeric characters. The **token** type is used to define a type with minimally specified properties which will be expanded in later refinement. For example:

$$Ingredients = \textbf{token}$$

We declare an identifier to be a basic type by saying that it equals that type. Thus we have defined the variable ingredients to be of type **token**.

5.7.1 Basic type values

VDM has built-in values for the Boolean types; **true** and **false**. We can thus set a Boolean type to one of these values:

$$on : \mathbb{B} = \textbf{true}$$
$$off : \mathbb{B} = \textbf{false}$$

When defining numerical values it is important to distinguish whole numbers from floating point numbers, and we do this by including or excluding the decimal point in the value. So, for example, if we wished to use the integer value for one we would type:

$$number : \mathbb{N} = 1$$

But if we wished to show it is a real value we should type:

$$number : \mathbb{R} = 1.0$$

If we wish to place a value in a char type we use single quotes to denote the literal. Thus:

$$one = \text{'1'}$$

would denote one to represent the character 1, rather than the value 1.

5.7.2 Basic type operators

VDM-SL contains all the normal Boolean operators:

Operator	Text	Mathematical
Not	not	$\neg$
And	and	$\wedge$
Or	or	$\vee$
Implies	=>	$\Rightarrow$
Equivalent	<=>	$\Leftrightarrow$

including those for Predicate logic:

Operator	Text	Mathematical
Universal quantifier	all	$\forall$
Existential quantifier	exists	$\exists$
Unique identifier	exists1	$\exists!$
Separator	&	$\bullet$

Layout of predicate expressions follows the standard format and brackets can also be used to change precedence.

As well as the standard numeric operators such as plus '+', minus '-' and divide '/' a number of other operators are also provided in **VDM-SL**.

Operator	Text	Mathematical
Multiply	*	$\times$
Power	**	$\uparrow$
Plus	+	+
Minus	-	-
Exponent	E	$\times 10\uparrow$
Integer division	div	**div**
Integer remainder	rem	**rem**
Integer modulus	mod	**mod**
Division	/	/

including the following comparison operators:

Operator	Text	Mathematical
Equals	=	=
Not equals	<>	$\neq$
Less than	<	$<$
Less than or equal to	<=	$\leq$
Greater than	>	$>$
Greater than or equal to	>=	$\geq$

All these are infix binary operators and correspond with their normal mathematical use.

The only two which might not be familiar are power, which is represented with an upward arrow, as in:

$$2\uparrow 3$$

instead of 2^3 and the exponent operator which can be represented either in the form x10↑n:

$$2.3 \times 10\uparrow -4$$

or the form $x10^n$:

$$2.3 \times 10^{-4}$$

in the mathematical notation, and as the more usual:

2.3E -4

in the textual notation.

VDM-SL also has two prefix operators **floor** and **abs** which correspond to the floor (or integer part) and the absolute value operators respectively.

floor X
abs X

Plus and minus can be prefix (unary) or infix (binary) operators. For example:

x = +2
2 + 2 = 4
y = -2
2 - 2 = 0

5.8. QUOTE TYPES

Quote types consist of a single identifier, written in capitals. For example:

QUOTE_TYPE

They are mainly used to represent the literals in enumerated types and their use will be seen later in this chapter when we look at union types. In the **VDM** plaintext format quote literals have to be enclosed in angular brackets '<>'. For example:

<QUOTE_TYPE>

Quote types consist of a single value, with both the value and the type being represented by the quote literal. They have no properties apart from equality, i.e.

$$\mathsf{RED} \neq \mathsf{BLUE}$$

Since such types are user defined they cannot be classified as basic types.

5.9. COMPOUND TYPES

In addition to the basic types **VDM** incorporates facilities for building compound types, including sets, maps, sequences and records.

5.9.1 Set types

A set type is defined in **VDM** by postfixing it with the set constructor:

Constructor	Text	Mathematical
Set	**set of** T	T-**set**

where T represents a type (though not a function type). T-**set** has values which are the finite sets of values of the type T. For example:

set of nat

or, alternatively:

$\mathbb{N}$-**set**

defines a set whose elements are themselves finite sets of values of the type nat. All sets in **VDM** are finite, so a set can only contain a finite number of elements.

5.9.1.1 Set values

Sets in **VDM** must be flat (i.e. containing no function types) and can be constructed either explicitly:

$$set1 = \{1, 3, 5, 4, 2\}$$

or by set comprehension:

$$set1 = \{\, n \mid n \in \mathbb{N}_1 \bullet n \leq 5\}$$

the above stating that *for all n belonging to the set of natural positive numbers n is less than or equal to 5* (thus this is the same set as in the previous explicit definition). Set comprehension in **VDM-SL** has the following form:

$$\{\, \mathrm{E} \mid \mathrm{B}_1, \mathrm{B}_2, \ldots, \mathrm{B}_n \bullet \text{Boolean condition} \,\}$$

where E consists of an expression representing one or more values. $B_1, B_2, \ldots, B_n$ represent set or type bindings on the values, and the Boolean condition constrains the values of the set to only those which fulfil the condition stated.

As we already know, set binds have the form Pattern ∈ Set and type binds the form Pattern : Type. These can be used to constrain the values of the pattern to a particular set or type. For example:

$$evens = \{ n \mid n : \mathbb{N}_1 \bullet (n \ \mathbf{mod}\ 2 = 0) \}$$

binds n to the type positive integers.

If more than one of the patterns is of the same set or type they may be bound in the shorter form $P_1, P_2, \ldots, P_n \in$ Set or $P_1, P_2, \ldots, P_n$: Type rather than individually being declared to be of the same binding. For example, $n_1 \in \mathbb{N}$, $n_2 \in \mathbb{N}$ can be represented alternatively as $n_1, n_2 \in \mathbb{N}$. Note that this is more complex than in sequences where set bindings are limited to one identifier. The Boolean expression is conditional and may be omitted:

$$\{ E \mid B_1, B_2, \ldots, B_n \}$$

For example:

$$\{ [x, y] \mid x \in X, y \in Y\}$$

which would be the set of sequences containing both a value from the set X and a value from the set Y.

A special form of set comprehension given in **VDM-SL** is the set range expression:

$$set1 = \{L, \ldots, U\}$$

where L represents the lower limit and U the upper limit of the range. For example:

$$set1 = \{1, \ldots, 5\}$$

represents the set containing the values 1, 2, 3, 4, 5.

5.9.1.2 *Set operators*

It is possible to determine whether a value is an element of a set in **VDM** by use of the membership operators:

Operator	Text	Mathematical
member	in set	∈
non-member	not in set	∉

For example:

$$a \in \{a, b, c\} = \mathbf{true}$$
$$d \notin \{a, b, c\} = \mathbf{true}$$

VDM also has the cardinality operator **card** giving the number of elements in a set. For example:

$$\mathbf{card}\ \{\} = 0$$
$$\mathbf{card}\ \{a, b, c\} = 3$$

Relationships between sets are defined by equality, inequality, proper subset and subset:

Operator	Text	Mathematical
Equality	=	$=$
Inequality	<>	$\neq$
Proper subset	psubset	$\subset$
Subset	subset	$\subseteq$

In **VDM** a proper subset cannot be equal to the set it is being compared with, thus:

$$\{a, b, c\} \subset \{a, b, c, d\} \ = \ \mathbf{true}$$
$$\{a, b, c\} \subset \{a, b, c\} \quad = \ \mathbf{false}$$

The proper subset **psubset** operator can be thought of as representing less than, whereas the normal subset operator represents less than *or equal to.* A normal subset may therefore be less than or equal to the set it is being compared with, whereas a proper subset must be less than the set it is compared with.

VDM has all of the standard set operators including **union**, relative complement (referred to as set difference in **VDM**) and intersection:

Operator	Text	Mathematical
Union	union	$\cup$
Difference	\	$\setminus$
Intersection	inter	$\cap$

Distributed union and intersection are also available and these are placed prefix:

Operator	Text	Mathematical
Distributed union	dunion	$\bigcup$
Distributed intersection	dinter	$\bigcap$

For example:

$$S = \{\{a, b, c\}, \{c, d, e\}, \{c, e, f\}\}$$
$$\bigcap S = \{c\}$$
$$\bigcup S = \{a, b, c, d, e, f\}$$

VDM does not have the standard powerset operator, but it does have something very similar called the finite subset operator. This behaves in exactly the same way as the powerset operator, but is limited, or constrained, to finite sets (all sets in **VDM** being finite). It will always produce a finite set.

Operator	Text	Mathematical
Finite subset	power	$\mathcal{F}$

For example:

$$\mathcal{F}\{a, b, c\} = \{\{\}, \{a\}, \{b\}, \{c\}, \{a, b\}, \{a, c\}, \{b, c\}, \{a, b, c\}\}$$

gives a set consisting of all combinations of the set $\{a, b, c\}$.

Exercise 5.3: A company has an assorted set of portable computers of varying power and facilities, each of which is uniquely identified by a serial number consisting of a whole number. An employee may obtain use of a particular computer, providing it is not already in use, by booking it. This operation requires its removal from the set of portables currently available. When the portable is returned it is placed back in the set available.

a) How might we represent the set of available computers?
b) What set operation could we use to model the operation *obtain* which represents the situation when an employee obtains a portable? What pre-condition would we require?
c) What set operation could we use to model the operation *release* which represents the situation where an employee returns the portable?
d) How could we tell how many portables are still available?

5.9.2 Maps

Map types can be defined in **VDM** as general or injective.

Constructor	Text	Mathematical
General map type	**map** T_1 **to** T_2	$T_1 \xrightarrow{m} T_2$
Injective map type	**inmap** T_1 **to** T_2	$T_1 \overset{m}{\leftrightarrow} T_2$
Maplet	E_1 |-> E_2	$E_1 \mapsto E_2$
Empty map type	{|->}	$\{\mapsto\}$

A map associates each element of the first type with an element of the second type. We have already seen this in our telephone book example:

$$Directory = Name \xrightarrow{m} TelephoneNo$$

where each element of type *Name* is associated with a telephone number of type *TelephoneNo*. The elements of each representing the domain and range of the map respectively. A map can thus be thought of as a collection of ordered pairs (x, y) where x is an element of the first type and y an element of the second type. It is important to note, however, that although a map represents a set of these ordered pairs it is not itself a set and as such the standard set operators cannot be applied to it.

In an injective map no element of the range is associated with more than one element of the domain. For example:

$$Char\_Ascii = Letter \overset{m}{\leftrightarrow} Number$$

where each character would have a corresponding numerical value and vice versa.

5.9.2.1 *Map values*

Maps can be stated directly by map enumeration in the form:

$$\{M_1, M_2, \ldots, M_n\}$$

where $M_1, \ldots, M_n$ represent a set of maplets, or by map comprehension in the form:

$$\{\, M \mid B_1, B_2, \ldots, B_n \bullet \text{Boolean condition} \,\}$$

where M is a mapping and $B_1, B_2, \ldots, B_n$ are set or type binds of the same form as used in set comprehension. As with set comprehension the Boolean condition constrains the values of the set and is optional. For example:

$$Square = \{\ t1 \mapsto t2 \mid t1 : \mathbb{N}, t2 : \mathbb{N} \bullet t1 \leq 4 \wedge t2 = (t1 \times t1)\ \}$$

represents a mapping of all natural numbers up to 4 to their squares such that $(x \mapsto x^2)$.

Note that the domain and range of all maps in **VDM-SL** must always be finite. If the constraint $t1 \leq 4$ had not been included in the above definition the mapping would have been infinite and although syntactically correct would have been semantically incorrect and therefore illegal.

5.9.2.2 *Map operators*

VDM has the basic map operators domain **dom**, range **rng**, and map application. Map application has the form:

map_name(Expression)

where the expression corresponds to an element of the maps domain, the result being the element of the maps range corresponding to the expression. For example, given:

$$Square = \{1 \mapsto 1, 2 \mapsto 4, 3 \mapsto 9, 4 \mapsto 16\}$$

then:

$$Square(2) = 4$$
$$Square(1 + 2) = 9$$

The domain and range operators follow their standard convention, so for the above example:

$$\mathbf{dom}\ Square = \{1, 2, 3, 4\}$$
$$\mathbf{rng}\ Square = \{1, 4, 9, 16\}$$

VDM-SL also has the common map operators:

Operator	Text	Mathematical
Map union	munion	$\uplus$ (m)
Distributed merge	merge _	$\bigcup\_$
Override	++	$\dagger$
Domain restriction	<:	$\lhd$
Domain subtraction	<-:	$\ntriangleleft$

and:

Operator	Text	Mathematical
Range restriction	:>	$\rhd$
Range subtraction	:->	$⩥$
Composition	compose	$\circ$
Iteration	**	$\uparrow$
Inverse	inverse _	$\_^{-1}$

Map union combines two maps so that the result maps the elements of the domains of the two maps. It is written:

$$M_1 \uplus M_2$$

where M_1 and M_2 are maps. Although similar to set union, a map union is more restrictive as it requires that the two maps are compatible with each other. Any element present in both the domain of M_1 and the domain of M_2 must be mapped to the same value. For example:

$$\{a \mapsto 1, b \mapsto \underline{2}, c \mapsto 3\} \uplus \{b \mapsto \underline{2}, d \mapsto 4\} = \{a \mapsto 1, b \mapsto \underline{2}, c \mapsto 3, d \mapsto 4\}$$

is a valid map union because the b is mapped to the value two in both cases, whereas:

$$\{a \mapsto 1, b \mapsto \underline{4}, c \mapsto 3\} \uplus \{b \mapsto \underline{2}, d \mapsto 4\}$$

would give an error since b maps to different elements in each case.

Where we wish to merge two maps which are incompatible (i.e. contain different mappings to values for elements common to both domains) we can use the map override operator:

$$M_1 \dagger M_2$$

This has the same effect as a merge except that any mappings with common elements in their domains are mapped to M_2's values. For example:

$$\{a \mapsto 1, b \mapsto 2, c \mapsto 3\} \dagger \{b \mapsto \underline{5}, d \mapsto 4\} = \{a \mapsto 1, b \mapsto \underline{5}, c \mapsto 3, d \mapsto 4\}$$

This conforms to the standard override operator as it is defined in Chapter 2.

The domain restriction, domain subtraction, range restriction and range subtraction operators conform to their standard use, having the form:

$$S \lhd M$$
$$S \mathbin{\blacktriangleleft} M$$
$$M \rhd S$$
$$M \mathbin{\blacktriangleright} S$$

where M is a map and S a set. For example:

$$\{Li, Na\} \lhd \{H \mapsto 1, Li \mapsto 3, Be \mapsto 4\} = \{ Li \mapsto 3\}$$
$$\{Li, Na\} \mathbin{\blacktriangleleft} \{H \mapsto 1, Li \mapsto 3, Be \mapsto 4\} = \{H \mapsto 1, Be \mapsto 4\}$$
$$\{Mg \mapsto 12, K \mapsto 19, Rb \mapsto 19\} \rhd \{ 19\} = \{ K \mapsto 19, Rb \mapsto 19\}$$
$$\{Mg \mapsto 12, K \mapsto 19, Rb \mapsto 19\} \mathbin{\blacktriangleright} \{19\} = \{Mg \mapsto 12\}$$

The map composition operator is also present, having the form:

$$M_1 \circ M_2$$

The result of this is a composite map obtained by first applying the map M_2 then applying the map M_1 to the result. For example:

$$\{ Li \mapsto 3, K \mapsto 19\} \circ \{ \text{"Lithium"} \mapsto Li, \text{"Sodium"} \mapsto Na\}$$

would give:

$$\{ \text{"Lithium"} \mapsto 3\}$$

Associations where no match exists are removed from the result.

Map composition is defined only if the map M_1 can be applied to M_2, so that the range of M_2 is a subset of the domain of M_1.

Provided the range of a mapping is a subset of its domain a map can be composed with itself using map iteration. This has the format:

$$M \uparrow N$$

where M is a map and N is the number of iterations. For example, given the map:

$$X = \{1 \mapsto 2, 2 \mapsto 1\}$$

then:

$$X \uparrow 2 = \{ 2 \mapsto 2, 1 \mapsto 1\}$$

since $1 \mapsto 2$ with $2 \mapsto 1$ results in $1 \mapsto 1$, and $2 \mapsto 1$ with $1 \mapsto 2$ gives $2 \mapsto 2$. This operation is only defined if the domain of the mapping is the same as the range.

The inverse operator is only valid with injective mappings and given a range value will return the domain value corresponding to it. Thus if the mapping Square given earlier had been defined as injective, then:

$$Square(9)^{-1} = 3$$
$$Square(16)^{-1} = 4$$

Exercise 5.4: In a company a number of employees pass messages to each other. In order to stop other people casually eavesdropping on their messages they decide to introduce a simple cipher system capable of converting their message into a jumble of letters, which can then be converted back by one of their group having the appropriate program. They decide to use a simple monoalphabetic substitution, since the threat is not that great. This involves simply replacing letters with other letters in a systematic fashion. Thus using an example cipher:

Plain: `ABCDEFGHIJKLMNOPQRSTUVWXYZ`

Cipher: `ZHXIGMALKVEJTSWRDPBCNUOYQF`

the message:

```
HI THERE
```

would become:

```
LK CLGPG
```

by transposing the letters. The program ignores white space, which we shall also do for the moment.

a) Using maps how could we describe the relationship between the plaintext and the cipher letters? Remember we will need to be able to both encode (scramble) and decode (unscramble) the messages.
b) What map operation would we use to convert a character to its equivalent ciphered form?
c) Given an enciphered character how would we convert it back to its original plain-text form?

5.9.3 Sequences

We can represent sequences of the basic types by post-fixing the type with a sequence constructor. **VDM** has two of these; the general sequence constructor and the non-empty sequence constructor.

Constructor	Text	Mathematical
General sequence	**seq of** T	T^*
Non-empty sequence	**seq1 of** T	T^+

Here T represents a basic type.

The general sequence type allows empty sequences, whereas a non-empty sequence must contain at least one element. We could, for example, represent the type Name as a sequence of char:

$$Name = \mathbf{char}^+$$

A sequence of **char** in **VDM** is referred to as a text string.

5.9.3.1 *Sequence values*

Like individual characters, text strings can be compared. Text string values are declared using double quotes, for example:

newname = "Fred Jones"

which denotes newname as having the value Fred Jones. This is shorthand for the more explicit definition:

newname = ['F', 'r', 'e', 'd', ' ', 'J', 'o', 'n', 'e', 's']

This shorthand only applies to text strings[3], if we want to represent a sequence of values we use the latter notation, i.e:

$$TelephoneNo = [4, 5, 0, 7, 6]$$

Sequence types in **VDM** can be constructed either directly:

$$sq1to5 = [1, 2, 3, 4, 5]$$

or by sequence comprehension:

$$sq1to5 = [n \mid n \in \mathbb{N}_1 \bullet n \leq 5]$$

Sequence comprehension in **VDM-SL** has the following form:

$$[\, \mathrm{E} \mid \mathrm{Id} \in \mathrm{S} \bullet \text{Boolean condition} \,]$$

where E consists of an expression, Id ∈ S is a *set bind* on a single identifier, and the Boolean condition constrains the values of the set to only those which fulfil the condition stated.

---

[3] If we wish to include the double-quote character within a string we must repeat it. Thus """"a""b" represents the sequence ['"','a','"','b'], that is, "a"b.

The set bind (Id ∈ Set) constrains the values of the identifier to a particular set and follows the same convention we have seen previously, except that the set in this bind *must* be an ℝ-**set** expression. A definition such as:

$$evens = [n \mid n \in \mathbb{N}_1 \bullet (n \textbf{ mod } 2 = 0)]$$

which binds n to the set of positive integers would therefore not be allowed. Sequence comprehensions in **VDM-SL** must also be finite (which this is not). The following is, however, an acceptable definition:

$$evens = [n \mid n \in \{1,\ldots,40\} \bullet (n \textbf{ mod } 2 = 0)]$$

The Boolean expression in sequence comprehension is conditional and may be omitted:

$$[\mathrm{E} \mid \mathrm{Id} \in \mathrm{S}]$$

For example:

$$[x \times 2 \mid x \in \{1,\ldots,n\} \bullet x \leq 5]$$
$$[x \times 2 \mid x \in \{1, 2, 3, 4, 5\}]$$

would both give the sequence:

$$[2, 4, 6, 8, 10]$$

provided *n* was equal, or greater than 5 in the first expression. Sequence types can have constraints, such as maximum length, placed upon them.

5.9.3.2 *Sequence operators*

All of the normal sequence operators are available in **VDM** including head **hd**, tail **tl**, length **len**, elements **elems**, indices **inds** and concatenation:

Constructor	Text	Mathematical
Head	hd	**hd**
Tail	tl	**tl**
Length	len	**len**
Indices	inds	**inds**
Elements	elems	**elems**
Concatenation	^	$\frown$

The head operator returns the first element of the list, and the tail operator the sequence with the first element removed. The length operator, as might be expected, returns the number of elements in the sequence. For example:

X = [*a*, *b*, *c*, *d*, *e*, *f*, *g*]
hd X = a
tl X = [*b*, *c*, *d*, *e*, *f*, *g*]
len X = 7

We can look upon a sequence as a set of mappings from natural numbers (the indices) to the elements of the sequence. The value '1' thus maps to the first element, the value '2' to the second element, and so on, up to the last element. A sequence can therefore be seen as having a domain, consisting of the numbers corresponding to the position of the elements in the sequence, and a range, consisting of the elements of the sequence. The indices and elements operators give the components of these two sets:

inds X = {1, 2, 3, 4, 5, 6, 7}
elems X = {a, b, c, d, e, f, g}

A component of a sequence can be accessed by sequence application which has the form:

X(N)

where X is the sequence name and N the position of the element to be extracted. Note that curved brackets are used in this case. A sub-sequence can also be accessed using the sub-sequence expression:

X(L,..., U)

where X is a sequence and L and U represent the upper and lower bounds of the sub-sequence. For example:

X = [*a*, *b*, *c*, *d*, *e*, *f*, *g*]
X(2) = *b*
X(2, ..., 6) = [*b*, *c*, *d*, *e*, *f*]

If the lower bound L is greater than the upper bound U then this will return the empty sequence [].

VDM-SL also has a sequence modification operator, similar to the override operator:

Constructor	Text	Mathematical
Sequence modification	Sq ++ St	Sq † St

where Sq is a sequence and St a set of mappings from numbers corresponding to the indices of the sequence to new values. For example:

$$Colours = [red, orange, yellow, cyan, blue, violet, black]$$
$$Colours \dagger \{4 \mapsto \underline{green}, 7 \mapsto \underline{indigo}\}$$

would give:

$$Colours = [red, orange, yellow, \underline{green}, blue, violet, \underline{indigo}]$$

Concatenation of two sequences uses the concatenation operator which is placed between the two sequences to be combined:

$$\mathrm{Sq1} \frown \mathrm{Sq2}$$

For example:

$$X = [a, b, c, d]$$
$$Y = [d, e, f]$$
$$X \frown Y = [a, b, c, d, d, e, f]$$

A distributed concatenation operator **conc** also exists in **VDM-SL** which can be prefixed to a sequence to allow distributed concatenation:

conc Sq

For example:

X = ["Con", "cat", "en", "ate"]
conc X = "Concatenate"

Exercise 5.5: A research establishment have developed a small robot capable of finding its way around mazes. The robot has four movements: "forward one unit", "backward one unit", "rotate left" and "rotate right". It also has one command "stop", which it issues on reaching its destination to switch itself off. Each movement or command is recorded, together with the order in which they where made. This allows the researchers to determine what path the robot took through the maze. How could we record this?

a) What would the initial state be?
b) How would we add a new move each time?
c) When the robot has reached its destination and stopped how would we determine the total number of movements made?
d) How could we determine if the robot had made any backward movements during its travels?
e) The record of the robot's travels always terminates with the "stop" command if the robot successfully reached the destination. The researchers decide that in future they will use the command "switch off" instead of “stop”. However, they have a number of old records of successful attempts which still have the "stop" command in them. How could they modify these records so that the "stop" command is replaced by the new command?

f) It is decided, in order to make the operation more efficient, to convert the records from sequence of strings to sequence of integers. A function called *translate* which converts a *movement* into a corresponding digit is written. A routine is then required to extract each element at a time in the order they are recorded and using the *translate* function convert each element to its corresponding digit. Think about how we could extract each element at a time in the order in which they exist in the record and what sequence operators we would need to do this. Give a rough outline of how we might go about this (we shall look at how to define this type of definition more formally later in this chapter). Hint: Consider recursion, discussed in the Chapter 2.

5.9.4 Records

A record in **VDM** consists of a collection of component fields:

$$
\begin{aligned}
\mathrm{Id} :: \; & \mathrm{Id}_1 : \mathrm{T}_1 \\
& \mathrm{Id}_2 : \mathrm{T}_2 \\
& \quad \ldots \\
& \mathrm{Id}_n : \mathrm{T}_n
\end{aligned}
$$

where Id is the name of the record type, $T_1, \ldots, T_n$ are the component types and $Id_1, \ldots, Id_n$ are identifiers associated with each of the fields. For example, we can declare the type Person_details consisting of a person's name, address and telephone number:

$$
\begin{aligned}
\mathit{Person\_details} :: \; & \mathit{name} && : \mathit{Nametype} \\
& \mathit{address} && : \mathit{Addresstype} \\
& \mathit{telephone} && : \mathit{Teltype}
\end{aligned}
$$

where Nametype, Addresstype and Teltype are previously defined types and name, address and telephone are the field names. Field identifiers are optional and a record type can simply be defined as:

$$
\begin{aligned}
\mathrm{Id} :: \; & \mathrm{T}_1 \\
& \mathrm{T}_2 \\
& \ldots \\
& \mathrm{T}_n
\end{aligned}
$$

in which case the individual fields cannot be referred to by field selection. Their use in this regard is explained later.

VDM-SL also has another form of record construction:

$$
\begin{array}{l}
\text{Id} = \textbf{compose}\ \text{ID}\ \textbf{of} \\
\quad \text{Id}_1\text{:T}_1 \\
\quad \text{Id}_2\text{:T}_2 \\
\quad \ldots \\
\quad \text{Id}_n\text{:T}_n \\
\textbf{end}
\end{array}
$$

This is equivalent to the first form of notation for records. Again the field identifiers are optional.
The identifier ID in this form of definition is a tag on the type and was originally designed to allow declaration of different composite types with the same fields. For example:

$$\text{Id}_a = \text{ID}$$

$$\text{Id}_b = \text{ID}$$

where Id (the name of the type) is the same as ID.

Record types can be nested and it is perfectly legitimate for one or more of the types in a record to also be record types. For example, we could have defined the type Addresstype in the record Person_details as another record:

$$
\begin{array}{l}
\mathit{Addresstype} :: \mathit{number} : \mathbb{N}^* \\
\qquad\qquad\qquad \mathit{street} : \textbf{char}^*
\end{array}
$$

5.9.4.1 Record values

Whenever a record type is declared, two functions *mk*_Id and *is*_Id are implicitly declared enabling type construction and type membership respectively. The record constructor allows values to be placed in a record and has the form:

$$mk\_\text{Id}(\text{E}_1, \text{E}_2, \ldots, \text{E}_n)$$

where Id is the tag of the composite type and $E_1, \ldots, E_n$ expressions of the field types of the record. There must be one expression for each field in the record. For example, suppose we use the type Person_details we declared earlier consisting of a person's name, address and telephone number:

$$
\begin{array}{l}
\mathit{Person\_details} :: \mathit{name} : \mathit{Nametype} \\
\qquad\qquad\qquad \mathit{address} : \mathit{Addresstype} \\
\qquad\qquad\qquad \mathit{telephoneNo} : \mathit{Teltype}
\end{array}
$$

where Nametype, Addresstype and Teltype are previously defined types. If we wished to place a value for a person in this type we would use:

*mk*_Person_details("Jones", "13 High St", 44076)

corresponding to the name, address and telephone number of the person. If we had declared Addresstype as:

$$\begin{aligned} \mathit{Addresstype} :: \mathit{number} &: \mathbb{N}^* \\ \mathit{street} &: \mathbf{char}^* \end{aligned}$$

as we did earlier, this would result in a slight alteration when creating values:

*mk*_Person_details("Jones", *mk*_Addresstype(13, "High St"), 44076)

We can see if the record is of the type Person details using the *is* of type operator. For example, given a record *PD1*:

*is*_Person_details(*PD1*)

will return either true or false dependent on whether the record is, or is not, of the type.

5.9.4.2 Record operators

Records can be compared using the equals and not equals operators. Individual fields can be selected using the field selection operator, which has the form:

R.Id

where R is the record value and Id is the identifier associated with the field we wish to select. For example, if we define a value of the type Person_details, given in the previous section:

PD1 = *mk*_Person_details("Jones","13 High St", 44076)

then:

PD1.name = "Jones"

This denotes the value held in the field corresponding to the field identifier (*name*) in the record value (*PD1*). When applying the field selector to nested records we use the selector to successively choose the field. For example: stating Addresstype as we defined in the previous section as a record type, and defining PD1 as:

PD1 =
*mk*_Person_details("Jones", *mk*_Addresstype(13, "High St"), 45076)

we can say:

$$PD1.address = \text{"13High Street"}$$
$$PD1.address.street = \text{"High St"}$$
$$PD1.address.number = 13$$

Record values can be modified using the record modification operator:

Operator	Text	Mathematical
Modification	mu	μ

This has the form:

$$\mu(R, Id_1 \mapsto E_1, Id_2 \mapsto E_2, \ldots, Id_n \mapsto E_n)$$

where R is a record expression, $Id_1, \ldots, Id_n$ are the name of the field identifiers of the record type and $E_1, \ldots, E_n$ are expressions or values of the corresponding field types.

The resultant value of this function will be the same as R except in the fields denoted by $Id_1, \ldots, Id_n$, which will consist of the new values $E_1, \ldots, E_n$. For example, if we had the value:

$$PD1 = mk\_\text{Person\_details}(\text{"Jones"}, \text{"13 High St"}, 45076)$$

then we could alter the telephone number and address by stating:

$$\mu(\text{PD1}, address \mapsto \text{"144 Church St"}, telephoneNo \mapsto 23451)$$

The new record would consist of the component values Jones, 144 Church St, and 23451, with only the field Name remaining unaltered. Here we have used values, though we could equally well use expressions. We can also refer to the previous value in the field. For example, suppose we had a value P consisting of the type Position (composed of x and y co-ordinates):

$$\begin{aligned} \text{Position} :: \ & x : \mathbb{Z} \\ & y : \mathbb{Z} \end{aligned}$$

$$P = mk\_\text{Position}(3, 5)$$

and we wished to double the value held in x, then we could say:

$$\mu(P, \text{x} \mapsto (2 * P.x))$$

in which case the new value in P.x would be 6. The new value is two times the old value. Note the use of the field select in the inner bracketed expression.

Exercise 5.6: A company wishes to set up a stock control system in which each product has the following information: product identifier, product name, supplier name, unit price, units in stock, units on order. The product identifier is a natural number, unique to each item, which can be used to look up the part. How could we represent the stock system?

a) How would we add a new item to the stock?
b) The unit price of an item might change from time to time. What operation would we need to do to replace a unit's price with the new price?
c) How could we find how many units we have in stock of a particular item?

5.9.5 Products

The product type operator is used to create tuples:

Constructor	Text	Mathematical
Product type	*	$\times$

in the form:

$$T_1 \times T_2 \times \ldots T_n$$

where $T_1,\ldots,T_n$ are Types.

Product types are used in function and operation signatures to allow more than one parameter to be passed. For example:

$$function : \mathbb{N} \times \mathbb{N} \rightarrow \mathbb{N}$$

which represents a function taking two natural numbers and returning a single number. Product types are rarely used in named types; composite types (such as records) are better suited in this area due to their stronger typing and the ability to select individual fields by name.

It is important to note that a product type is not the same as a record type in which the individual elements, or component fields, have not been named. A record type represents a unique type, whereas a tuple does not.

5.9.5.1 Tuples and product values

If we wish to place values in a product type we use the *mk_* function as we did in records. The only difference is that the type does not have a type name identifier:

$$mk\_(E_1, E_2,\ldots, E_n)$$

where $E_1,\ldots, E_n$ are expressions or values.

For example, given the product type:

$$NAME \times ADDRESS \times TELNO$$

We could place the following values in it:

*mk_*("Fred Jones", "13 High Street", 44076)

5.9.5.2 Product operators

Product types only have two operators: equality and inequality. For the two types to be equal each component of the types (T_1,...,T_n) must be equal. For example:

("Jones", 1, 4) = ("Jones", 1, 4)
("Smith", 1, 4) ≠ ("Jones", 1, 4)
("Smith", 1, 4) ≠ ("Smith", 4, 1)

These operators can only be used where both product types are flat.

5.9.6 Unions

A union type of $T_1 \mid T_2$ represents the union of the values of types T_1 and T_2 (where T_1 and T_2 are values of the same type). If T_1 and T_2 have any elements in common then those elements appear only once in the union. For example:

$$UT1 = \{1, 2, 3\}$$
$$UT2 = \{3, 4, 5\}$$
$$UT1 \mid UT2 = \{1, 2, 3, 4, 5\}$$

Any number of unions are allowed $T_1 \mid T_2, \ldots T_n$. The union operator '|' is associative and commutative so $(T_1 \mid T_2) \mid T_3$ is the same as $T_2 \mid (T_1 \mid T_3)$. The main use of union types is with quote types, to create what are effectively enumerated types. For example:

Signal = RED | AMBER | GREEN

Exercise 5.7: Using an enumerated type how could we define a type to represent a movements made by a robot able to go left, right, forward or backwards?

5.10. OPTIONAL TYPES

An optional type in **VDM-SL** can equal the **nil** value, **nil** being a predefined type/value in **VDM-SL** that represents the absence of a value.

An optional type therefore consists of the union of some type and the **nil** value; T | **nil**. Optional types in **VDM-SL** are represented by enclosing the type in square brackets [T], thus, for example, we might have a mapping:

$$\mathbb{N} \xrightarrow{m} [\mathbb{N}]$$

which delivers either a natural number or no value (**nil**). Since:

$$[\mathbb{N}] = \mathbb{N} \mid \mathbf{nil}$$

5.10.1 Optional type operators

Expressions of the type can be checked to see if they are nil values.

Expression = **nil**

Set membership, however, cannot be used with **nil**, even though it is a predefined type.

5.11. TYPE MEMBERSHIP

As we have seen previously, each of the types in **VDM** has a corresponding type membership identifier *is*_T implicitly defined to test whether a value is of the type T. For example:

$$is\_\mathbb{N}(a)$$

will test whether the value of a is a natural number. If a = 1 then this would be true, but if a = 1.2 then it would be false as the value is a real number.

5.12. FUNCTIONS AND OPERATIONS

We now examine the structure of functions and operations. Functions and operations in **VDM-SL** are procedures which enable us to break a specification down into component parts, encouraging modularisation of the specification. By reducing a specification to a series of sub-problems we make it very much easier to write, and to understand the complete specification. **VDM-SL** allows functions and operations to be defined implicitly or explicitly, and a mixture of both may be used within a single specification.

All parameters passed in both functions and operations are value parameters. They cannot be changed or altered by the procedure. Any parameters passed to procedures cannot be returned except as a value of the function itself. Functions and expressions may be passed as parameters, so, for example, it is perfectly possible to have a function call such as:

$$f(a + abs(-3) * 1)$$

where *abs* is a function. In these cases the value of the expression and/or function(s) are evaluated immediately before the call.

In **VDM** there is no need for a function or operation to been defined prior to it being referred to (though it must be defined somewhere within the specification). The scope of such a declaration is global to the specification this means it is possible to use both a top-down or bottom-up approach. It should be noted, however, that many tools used to assist in formal specification writing do not have this freedom, and therefore require definition before any references are made.

5.13. FUNCTIONS

Functions are basically rules for deriving values from other values passed to them in the form of parameters. They can be defined implicitly, in terms of a property which the result must hold, or explicitly, in terms of an expression. Unlike operations, which we shall discuss later, functions do not allow side-effects and so cannot refer to or alter the value of variables outside their scope. It is allowable for a function to have no parameters, in which case it is a constant, but it must always return a result. A function will always return the same result for the same values of parameters.

5.13.1 Implicit functions

Implicit functions have the form:

function_name ($Ids_1 : T_1$, $Ids_2 : T_2$, ..., $Ids_3 : T_3$) $Id_r : T$
pre B
post B'

where Ids_1,...,Ids_3 each represent one or more identifiers of the corresponding type T following them, Id_r represents a identifier (and its type T) corresponding to the returned result of the function. B represents the pre-condition which is optional and can be excluded if unnecessary. B' represents the post-condition, which defines the value of Id_r. For example:

-- returns maximum value of 3 natural numbers
max(*x*, *y*, *z* : ℕ) *max3* : ℕ
post $(x \le max3) \wedge (y \le max3) \wedge (z \le max3) \wedge (max3 \in \{x, y, z\})$

which states that x, y and z must be less than or equal to the returned value and the returned value must be one of the values. In this case a pre-condition has not been given because it is not necessary due to the function being total for its types.

Both implicit and explicit functions may recursively call themselves; the post-condition of the function may thus contain an application of the function itself. For example:

-- sum of a list of natural numbers

$sum(X : \mathbb{N}^+)\ res : \mathbb{N}$

$\textbf{post}\ (X = [] \wedge res = 0) \vee (res = \textbf{hd}\ X + sum(\textbf{tl}\ X))$

5.13.2 Explicit functions

Explicit functions have the form:

$\text{function\_name} : T_1 \times T_2 \times \ldots \times T_n \rightarrow T$

$\text{function\_name}\ (Id_1, Id_2, \ldots, Id_n) \triangleq$

E

pre B

where Id_1, $Id_2, \ldots,$ Id_n are the names of the parameters passed to the function and the signature of their T_1, $T_2, \ldots,$ T_n associated types. E represents an expression of the same type as T (the returned value type). B is an optional pre-condition and may be excluded if unnecessary. For example:

-- returns maximum value of 3 natural numbers.

$max : \mathbb{N} \times \mathbb{N} \times \mathbb{N} \xrightarrow{t} \mathbb{N}$

$max(x, y, z) \triangleq$

$\textbf{if}\ (y \leq x) \wedge (z < x)\ \textbf{then}\ x$

$\textbf{elseif}\ (x < y) \wedge (z < y)\ \textbf{then}\ y$

$\textbf{else}\ z$

5.13.2.1 *Function signatures*

Explicit functions require a signature expressing the types of the parameters being passed to and by it. This is usually placed just before the definition of the function body. Functions may be partial or total:

Signature	Text	Mathematical
Cartesian product	*	$\times$
Non-parameter	()	()
Partial function	->	$\rightarrow$
Total function	+>	$\xrightarrow{t}$

An explicit total function would thus have a signature of the form:

$$func\text{: } T_1 \xrightarrow{t} T_2$$

where *func* represents the name of the function, T_1 represents one of more types being passed to the function and T_2 represents the type of the value returned by the function. The arrow is superscripted with a '*t*' showing it is a total function[4]. For example:

-- Given a value, the function returns
-- the value incremented by one
$increment\_value: \mathbb{N} \xrightarrow{t} \mathbb{N}$
$increment\_value(n) \triangleq n + 1$

Functions allow a non-parameter definition '()' which states that no parameter is passed to the function. For example:

$$\text{func: } () \rightarrow T_2$$

The function always has a return type, since it must return a value. A function which returns a value without receiving one is a constant, since it will always return the same value[5].

The Cartesian product operator is used when a number of parameters are passed to a function or operation. For example:

-- function takes two numbers and returns their average
$average: \mathbb{R} \times \mathbb{R} \rightarrow \mathbb{R}$
$average(x, y) \triangleq x + y / 2$

Implicit function definitions do not require a signature as the types are expressed in their parameter lists. For example:

-- *function takes two numbers and returns their average*
$average(x, y : \mathbb{R})\ result : \mathbb{R}$
post $result = x + y / 2$

---

[4] Early versions of VDM-SL did not make a distinction between partial and total functions when defining explicit function signatures and used the plain arrow '$\rightarrow$' for both. At one stage of development partial functions were represented by the symbol '$\xrightarrow{\sim}$' but this was withdrawn due to compatability problems with earlier specifications and the reader is unlikely to come across any specifications using this particular symbol.

[5] This is true even when the function uses a non-deterministic statement in its definition to generate a value. Unlike operations, where a new value is generated every time, the function would only be evaluated once. The first time the function is called, a value would be non-deterministically determined. Every call after this would, however, produce the same result.

5.13.2.2 Polymorphic function definition

VDM-SL allows explicit functions to be defined as polymorphic functions. A polymorphic function definition is stated in the same way as a normal explicit function definition, the only difference being that one or more of the parameters and/or the result type are given as uninstantiated type expressions.

The type is left incompletely defined and can be instantiated when the function is called. We declare a type in this way by prefixing the identifier used to represent the arbitrary type with the type variable identifier '@'.

At the beginning of the function signature we place a list of the uninstantiated types we are using, in the form:

$$\text{function\_name } [@T_1, @T_2, \ldots, @T_n]$$

where $@T_1$, $@T_2, \ldots, @T_n$ are uninstantiated types used in the signature. If we took a *max* function, we could define this to be polymorphic:

-- returns maximum value of 3 natural numbers
max [*@num*] : *@num* × *@num* × *@num* → *@num*
max(*x*, *y*, *z*) $\triangleq$
if $(y \leq x) \wedge (z < x)$ **then** *x*
elseif $(x < y) \wedge (z < y)$ **then** *y*
else *z*

In this case we would only be using one abstracted type so the list would have only one element (*@num*). When we call the function we fill in this type, instantiating it to a specific type. For example:

$$result = max[\mathbb{N}](1, 3, 4)$$
$$result = max[\mathbb{R}](1.2, 3.7, 2.0)$$

In the first example the type *@num* is instantiated to the type natural numbers throughout the signature, in the second case *@num* is replaced by the type real numbers throughout the signature.

Exercise 5.8:

a) Look at your answer to the cipher Exercise 5.4. See if you can now write the complete functions for encoding and decoding.
b) Define an explicit function which returns the number of times a given number occurs in a sequence.
c) Using the previous function define an implicit function which returns the number that occurs most frequently in a list of natural numbers.

5.13.3 Operators on functions

VDM-SL has two operators on functions which provide function composition and function iteration:

Operator	Text	Mathematical
Composition	compose	$\circ$
Iteration	**	$\uparrow$

The function composition operator follows the same notation and operation as the map composition operator:

$$f_1 \circ f_2$$

This yields a function equivalent to applying first f_2 and then f_1. That is, it is equivalent to $f_1(f_2())$.

Function iteration allows a function to be applied a number of times, and has the form:

$$F \uparrow N$$

where F is the function name and N the number of iterations required. N must be a value greater than or equal to zero. For example, if we had a function *Inc* which increments a value by one, then:

$$Inc(2) \uparrow 3$$

would call the function three times finally returning the value 5 (two incremented three times). If N is set to zero then the function is not applied and the value of its parameter is returned:

$$f(x) \uparrow 0 = x$$

so:

$$Inc(2) \uparrow 0 = 2$$

5.14. OPERATIONS

Operations are used when we write in an imperative style; where we define the specification in terms of its effect on the state of the system. Operations can refer to or change the state variables. These variables, external to the operation, can be thought of as global values which retain a history of their state and thus affect the state of the system. We need therefore to first look at how we define such variables.

5.14.1 Defining state

Particularly when using an imperative style of specification we need to define the initial state of the system. We do this by including a *state* definition in the specification. This defines the initial values of the variables we wish to use.

A state definition is similar in form to a record declaration with state variables forming the fields of the record:

> **state** Id **of**
>   field_list
>   **inv** invariant definition
>   **init** initialisation definition
> **end**

The invariant and initialisation clauses are optional and can be omitted.

Both the state identifier Id and the state variables (which together with their types form the field list) have global scope. The state variables can only be referred to within operation bodies.

> **state** *maximum* **of**
> $max : \mathbb{N}$ -- declare variable in state
>   **init** $maximum(m) \triangleq m = 0$ -- initialise max to 0
> **end**

The initialise clause sets the initial value of the variable, that is, its value (or state) upon first entering the system.

The invariant defines a constraint on the types of the state variables. Their initial states must fulfil the invariant condition and any operations upon them must result in a state that fulfils the invariant.

> **state** *aircraft* **of**
> $speed : \mathbb{R}$
> $height : \mathbb{R}$
>   **init** $mk\_aircraft(s, h) \triangleq (s = 0.0) \wedge (h = 0.0)$
>   **inv** $mk\_aircraft(\text{-}, h) \triangleq (h \geq 0.0)$
> **end**

In the above, the state identifier is set in the invariant and initialisation definitions, with s and h corresponding to the fields *speed* and *height*. We have placed a constraint to ensure that the height cannot be negative and set the initial state of speed and height to zero. Since we are not concerned with the speed in the invariant clause, a dash is used in this field to show it is unimportant. The arguments in the brackets of the state identifier *mk_* clause correspond to the fields in the state definition in both number and order. Thus if you have, for example, five variables in the definition then the *mk_* clause must also have five elements within the brackets.

Using the state identifier in this way is optional; we can, if we want, just refer to the fields themselves (as we did in the maximum definition). The state identifier has no real purpose other than being used in this way, and though it provides a name for the specification it cannot be referred to in any other part of it. It must, however, always be stated.

5.14.2 Implicit operations

In an implicit operation we explain what we want in terms of some property that must be true after execution of the operation (the post-condition). They have the form:

> OPERATION_NAME ($Ids_1 : T_1$, $Ids_2 : T_2$, ..., $Ids_n : T_n$) $Id_r : T$
> **ext** Access Vrs
> **pre** B
> **post** B'

Id_r and its type T are not required if the operation does not return a result. The pre-condition is optional and may be left out if not required.

External variables (Vrs) can be accessed via the **ext** clause (which is optional). Access can be read only, in which case the variables are prefixed with the keyword **rd**.

rd $Vrs_1{:}T_1$, $Vrs_2{:}T_2$,..., $Vrs_n{:}T_n$

where Vrs_1,...,Vrs_n each consist of one or more variables and T_1,...,T_n are their respective types. Alternatively they can have read/write access in which case they are prefixed by the keyword **wr**:

wr Vrs_1:T1, Vrs_2:T2, ...,$Vrs_n{:}T_n$

In this case their state, or value, can be altered by the operation. For example:

> -- returns maximum value of 3 natural numbers
> *MAX3*()
> **ext rd** $x, y, z : \mathbb{N}$
>   **wr** $max : \mathbb{N}$
> **post** $(x \leq max) \wedge (y \leq max) \wedge (z \leq max) \wedge (max \in \{x, y, z\})$

In this example no parameters are being passed to the operation, though we could equally pass *x*, *y* and *z* as parameters. Notice we are writing to the external state variable *max* which we declared earlier on in our state definitions. Apart from accessing values external to the operation, this example is not substantially different from an implicit function of the type. Operations, however, can change the state of the system affecting external variables.

5.14.2.1 *Old state, new state*

We can see that using a read/write option on an external variable in an operation allows us to alter the state of the variable. We need some way of differentiating between the value of a variable before an operation and its value after the operation. We do this by the use of the hook symbol which we came across in the telephone book example:

Operator	Text	Mathematical
Hook (old state)	~	$\overleftarrow{\ }$

VDM-SL gives the option of placing this hook either directly over the identifier:

$$\overleftarrow{\text{variable}}$$

or immediately following it:

$$\text{variable}^{\overleftarrow{\ }}$$

The textual version of the hook '~' is always placed after the identifier.

Identifiers with a hook refer to the state of the variable at the time the operation was called. Identifiers without a hook (in this context) refer to the new state after the operation (in functions we cannot change state so there is no need for such differentiation). We could, for example, replace the previous operation we gave with the following:

-- if n > value currently stored in max then replace
-- value in max with new value.
$MAX\_NUM(n : \mathbb{N})$
ext wr $max : \mathbb{N}$
post $(n \leq max) \wedge (max = max^{\overleftarrow{\ }} \vee max = n)$

This operation upon being passed a number would compare it with the value currently stored in max. If the new value is greater than that in max then max will take on the value of the number[6]. We can thus simulate the

---

[6] Note in these cases we say that max equals the other value, rather than max is assigned the value. This is because the operation is implicit. It does not say how max gets the value, only that it requires that max is equal to this value after the operation.

previous operation max3 by calling this operation three times, passing it x, y and z consecutively. Unlike the previous operation, there is no limit in the number of values we can compare.

We must be careful, however, to ensure that max has been initialised to zero before we do this comparison, otherwise it may already contain a value greater than the numbers we compare it with, in which case this value and not one of the values we had passed to the operation, would be returned. This highlights one of the major concerns about using operations; the value returned by an operation will depend on the state of the system at the time and not necessarily on the values passed to it. It is thus harder to predict their behaviour than it is for functions which will always return the same result for the same inputs.

5.14.2.2 *Error definition in implicit operations*

In **VDM** we can extend an implicit operation to cover error conditions for which the pre-condition does not hold. Using an error definition block having the form:

$$
\begin{array}{l}
\textbf{errs}\ Id_1\text{: } EP_1 \rightarrow EP_1' \\
\qquad Id_2\text{: } EP_2 \rightarrow EP_2' \\
\qquad \ldots \\
\qquad Id_n\text{: } EP_n \rightarrow EP_n'
\end{array}
$$

where Id is an annotatory identifier identifying the error[7], $EP_1, \ldots, EP_n$ are the error pre-conditions and $EP_1', \ldots, EP_n'$ are the error post-conditions. For example:

-- puts value of current year into external location yr
-- year expected in format 19xx or 20xx where xx is
-- two digits e.g. 1994.

$$
\begin{array}{l}
\mathit{PUT\_CURRENT\_YEAR}(\mathit{year} : \mathbb{N}) \\
\textbf{ext wr}\ \mathit{yr} : \mathbb{N} \\
\textbf{pre}\ \mathit{year} \geq 1994 \\
\textbf{post}\ \mathit{yr} = \mathit{year} \\
\textbf{errs}\ \mathit{year\_format1}\text{: } 94 \leq \mathit{year} \wedge \mathit{year} \leq 99 \rightarrow \mathit{yr} = \mathit{year} + 1900 \\
\qquad \mathit{year\_format2}\text{: } \mathit{year} < 94 \rightarrow \mathit{yr} = \mathit{year} + 2000
\end{array}
$$

[7] Since the Ids are for annotation only it does really matter what they are called. But they must be different for each error.

This is equivalent to declaring the operation as:

$PUT\_CURRENT\_YEAR(year: \mathbb{N})$
ext wr $yr: \mathbb{N}$
pre $year \geq 1994 \vee 94 \leq year \wedge year \leq 99 \vee year < 94$
post $(year \geq 1994 \wedge yr = year) \vee$
$(94 \leq year \wedge year \leq 99 \wedge yr = year + 1900) \vee$
$(year < 94 \wedge yr = year + 2000)$

The effect of the error definition block is therefore to extend the pre-condition and post-condition of the operation so that if one of the error conditions holds then the effect of the operation is such that the corresponding post-condition holds.

5.14.3 Explicit operations

Explicit operations have the format:

$\text{OPERATION\_NAME}: T_1 \times T_2 \times \ldots \times T_n \xrightarrow{o} T$
$\text{OPERATION\_NAME}\ (\text{Id}_1, \text{Id}_2, \ldots, \text{Id}_n) \triangleq$
Expression
pre B

As with implicit operations external entities can be used, but unlike implicit operations, no **ext** clause is given in these cases[8]. The type and the read/write access of external entities are derived from the statements in the operation and the surrounding environment. The pre-condition is, again, optional. For example:

-- if n > value currently stored in max then replace
-- value in max with new value.
$MAX\_NUM : \mathbb{N} \xrightarrow{o} ()$
$MAX\_NUM\ (n) \triangleq$
if $max < n$ **then** $max := n$
else skip -- max remains unaltered

[8] This has not always been the case and early specifications may have the ext clause present in definitions of explicit operations.

5.14.3.1 *Operation signatures*

Explicit operations require a signature expressing the types of the parameters being passed to and by them. This is usually placed just before the definition of the operation:

Signature	Text	Mathematical
Cartesian product	*	$\times$
Non parameter	()	()
Operation	==>	$\xrightarrow{o}$

An explicit operation uses the signature:

$$\text{OPERATION: } T_1 \xrightarrow{o} T_2$$

where the arrow has a superscripted 'o' over the top of the arrow to represent the fact that it is an operation.

Operations allow the non-parameter definition '()' which states that no parameter is passed to and/or returned by the operation. For example:

$$\text{OPERATION: } () \xrightarrow{o} ()$$

would be the signature for an operation which neither receives or returns a value, and:

$$\text{OPERATION: } \mathbb{N} \xrightarrow{o} ()$$

is the signature for an operation that receives a natural number value as its parameter but does not return a value. Such signatures are useful where the operation reads or changes the state of an external entity, but does not itself return a value. For example:

-- Changes the state of counter by incrementing
-- the current value held by one.
$INCREMENT\_COUNTER : () \xrightarrow{o} ()$
$INCREMENT\_COUNTER() \triangleq$
$counter := counter + 1$

which changes the state of the system (the value of the external counter), but does not itself receive or return a value.

As with functions the Cartesian product operator is used when a number of parameters are passed to an operation. For example:

$$SETDATE : \text{Day} \times \text{Month} \times \text{Year} \xrightarrow{o} ()$$

Implicit operation definitions do not require a signature as the types are expressed in their parameter lists, as we have already seen in the telephone book example:

$$ADD(name : Name, telno : TelephoneNo)$$
$$\textbf{ext wr } dir : Directory;$$
$$\textbf{post } dir = \overleftarrow{dir} \dagger \{name \mapsto telno\}$$

Since the types are declared in the parameter list a signature is not necessary.

5.14.3.2 Assignment

Until now we have been using the equality operator '=' to state that an identifier is of a certain type or value. When carrying out explicit operations, however, we may be required to assign values dynamically to particular variables (within statements). We do this using the assign operator which has the form:

$$\text{Id} := \text{E}$$

where Id is an identifier and E an expression. For example:

$$x := 3$$

assigns the value 3 to x. This differs from, for example, value definitions where we are saying that the identifier is equal or equivalent to the value on the right-hand side.

With values, we are defining constants and so are stating the identifier is equal or equivalent to the expression. With an assignment operator we are saying that the identifier takes on the value given on the right-hand side, not that it is equal to it. The identifier on the left-hand side of an assignment statement must always be a variable of some form.

This distinction is important. When we compare two objects or define a constant value we use the equals operator:

$$a = b$$

but when we assign a value to a variable we use the assignment operator:

$$a := b$$

These are quite distinct. In assignment statements (denoted by ':=') we are stating something is *assigned* the value of something else. The assignment statement (as opposed to the equals sign) implicitly infers the state. We therefore do not need to use a hook (as we do in implicit operations) to differentiate between the old and new states.

For example, to increment a counter we could say:

$$counter := counter + 1$$

which means that *counter* is assigned the current value of the counter plus one.

In a post-condition, where we are using equality, not assignment, we would have to define the old state and new state explicitly:

$$\textbf{post}\ counter = \overleftarrow{counter} + 1$$

saying that the new state of counter is equal to the old state (denoted by the hook) plus one. Assignments are only allowed in statements, not expressions, and therefore can only occur within explicit operations.

5.14.3.3 *Statements*

Explicit operations use statements, rather than expressions to define the body of their definitions. Statements differ from expressions in that they are similar to commands in normal programming languages; allowing sequential ordering. They define events in operational terms allowing us to affect the value of state and local variables (by the use of the assignment operators).

Statements in **VDM-SL** may be atomic, consisting of a single indivisible statement, or may be compound, being made up of a sequence of other statements and commands. A sequence of statements will be executed in the order they are given. Statements within a compound statement are separated by semicolons and surrounded by parentheses. The following is a single block statement made up of other atomic statements:

```
(temp := x; x := y; y := temp) -- swap x and y
```

A semicolon is not needed before a closing parenthesis.

Compound statements may be nested within other compound statements. In these cases it is a good idea to indent the surrounding brackets to make it clear which closing bracket refers to which statement. For example:

```
( x:= a;
  y := b;
        ( temp := x;
          x := y;
          y:= temp
        )              -- inner nested statement
)                      -- outer compound statement
```

Whenever the term statement is used within this chapter this can be taken to mean either an atomic or a compound statement.

5.14.3.4 The null command

The null command is stated as:

skip

and can be used only within statements. It does nothing and therefore has no effect. This can be useful where you wish to define a situation in which no action is required. For example:

```
-- If x > y then swap values
if x > y
then swap(x, y) -- swap values
else skip -- else do nothing
```

Here if x is less than or equal to y no action is taken.

Exercise 5.9:

a) Look at your answer to the stock control system in Exercise 5.6. Define the state of the system and the actions as implicit operations.
b) A system holds the temperature of a probe in memory. How could we model this? Write an implicit operation which returns the temperature and an explicit operation which sets the temperature to a value given.

5.15. ADDITIONAL CONSTRUCTS

Having looked at how to define types and values, we need to look at how we manipulate these types within functions and operations. **VDM-SL** has two types of operators; those related to specific types (which we have already covered) and general operators which can be used on all types such as conditional, iteration and notational commands. These can be used in conjunction with the previously defined type operators within the body of functions and operations.

5.15.1 Conditional commands

In conditionals the action taken varies depending on whether a condition is true or false. **VDM-SL** has two types of conditionals; the **if** ... **else** and the **case**. These can be either expressions or statements.

An **if** ... **else** expression has the form:

if B_1 **then** E_1
elseif B_2 **then** E_2
...
elseif B_n **then** E_n
else E

where B_1,..., B_n are Boolean conditions and E_1,..., E_n and E are expressions giving a value of the same type as each other. An **if** ... **then** statement has a similar form except statements, rather than expressions, are used, i.e.

if B_1 **then** S_1
elseif B_2 **then** S_2
...
elseif B_n **then** S_n
else S

where S_1,..., S_n and S are statements

In both cases the **elseif** branches are optional, but the final **else** is obligatory and must be included. For example:

-- returns the maximum value of two numbers x and y.
if $y > x$ **then**
then y
else x

This is in order to ensure that all eventualities are covered.

Case statements and expressions are used in pattern matching. The **case** expression has the form:

cases E_s:
$Ps_1 \rightarrow E_1$,
$Ps_2 \rightarrow E_2$,
...
$Ps_n \rightarrow E_n$,
others $\rightarrow$ E
end

where Ps_1,..., Ps_n are lists of patterns, each consisting of one or more patterns, and E_s is an expression which the pattern is matched against.

The **case** statement differs only in that statements are used instead of expressions on the right-hand side of the arrows.

cases E_s:
    $Ps_1 \rightarrow S_1$,
    $Ps_2 \rightarrow S_2$,
    ...
    $Ps_n \rightarrow S_n$,
    others $\rightarrow$ S
end

We can use such structures to give a series of actions or values dependent upon the value of the pattern. For example:

```
-- Takes a string consisting of a country name
-- and returns postal classification
cases Address.country:
    "England", "Wales", "Scotland" → INLAND,
    "France", "Germany", "Greece" → EUROPE_EC,
    "Yugoslavia" → EUROPE_NON_EC,
    "Africa", "United States", "India" → OVERSEAS1,
    "Australia", "China", "Japan" → OVERSEAS2,
    others → UNKNOWN
end
```

The scope of the case statement in this case is the string Address.country (forming part of an Address record).

The **others** option performs a similar function to the final else statement in an **if**...**else** construct, in that if no pattern matches then the expression or statement stipulated by the **others** branch will be returned. The statement is, however, optional and may be excluded. If it is excluded you should ensure that the pattern statements cover all eventualities. In the above example we could not remove it since we have not specified all the countries possible. The case statement is similar to case constructs in programming languages.

In both types of conditional statement or expression, if more than one of the conditions matches, then only the statement or expression matching the first match will be carried out.

Exercise 5.10: The researchers using the maze travelling robot we defined in an earlier exercise decide to write a routine that will simplify the records produced by the robot. The routine will take a sequence of movements given by the robot and will produce a new sequence which records only changes in direction. Thus given a record:

```
[FORWARD, FORWARD, FORWARD, LEFT, LEFT, LEFT, RIGHT]
```

the routine would remove adjacent duplicate directions to give:

[FORWARD, LEFT, RIGHT]

a) Using **if** .. **then** how could we express a recursive routine to carry this out?
b) The robot occasionally fails, in which case it outputs a number between 1 and 4 relating to the reason for failure. The numbers relate to the following errors:

   1 - means there has been an internal arithmetic fault in the processor
   2 - means the battery power is low, or failing
   3 - means the motor is stuck
   4 - means the sensor has failed, or is damaged.

In order to make the error more understandable the researchers write a routine which given the error number returns a string stating the error message associated with the number. How could we use a case statement to carry this out?

5.15.2 Iteration

Iteration results in the repeated execution of some action whilst some condition holds. **VDM-SL** has two main forms of iterative loop structure, the **for** loop and the **while** loop. These structures are classified as statements and therefore can only be used within explicit operation definitions.

VDM-SL has three different for loops: indexed, sequence and set. The index loop will be familiar to most programmers and is useful for specifying loops where the increment is a regular step. It has the form:

for Id = E_1 **to** E_2 **by** Inc **do** St

where Id is an identifier, E_1 and E_2 the start and terminating expressions respectively, Inc is the increment expression and St the statement upon which the loop is operating. For example:

-- Sets every even element in an array A to 1
for *i* = 2 **to len** *A* **by** 2 **do** *A*[*i*] := 1

The increment need not be specified:

for Id = E_1 **to** E_2 **do** St

In this case the step is assumed to be one. For example:

```
-- Places fibonacci sequence in array A
A[1]:= 1; A[2] := 2;
for i = 3 to len A do
    A[i] := A[i - 1] + A[i - 2];
```

Sequence loops are useful where there is no regular increment and have the format:

for Id **in** Sq **do** St

where Id is an identifier (which can have an optional type or set bind), Sq a sequence and St the statement on which the loop is operating. The sequence may be given implicitly, by some property, or explicitly, by its elements. For example:

```
-- sum = A[1] + A[3] + A[7] + A[8] + A[11]
for i in [1, 3, 7, 8, 11] do sum := sum + A[i]
```

Sequence loops imply ordering. The first element of the sequence is used before the second and so on, until the last element is reached. The sequence loop can also be specified with a descending pattern:

for Id **in reverse** Sq **do** St

in which case the order of the contents is reversed. For example:

```
-- sum = A[25] + (A[25]²+ A[16]) etc.
for i : ℕ in reverse [1, 4, 9, 16, 25] do
    sum := A[i] + squared(sum)
```

Set loops are similar to sequence loops except that, because they use sets instead of sequences, there is no order in the way the elements are chosen (order is essentially non-deterministic[9]). They have the form:

for all Id ∈ E **do** St

The **for all** is usually written in text rather than mathematical notation.

Set loops reduce the constraints on the order that the loop is executed. For example, suppose we defined a loop to set the first six elements of an array A to zero using a sequence loop:

```
-- Set the values of all elements of the array
-- A[1,...6] to zero
for i = 1 : ℕ in [1, 2, 3, 4, 5, 6] do A[i] := 0
```

---

[9] That is, it is impossible to determine which element of the set will be chosen beforehand.

Here we are stating that the array is cleared from left to right. However, if we stated this with a set loop,

for all $i : \mathbb{N} \in \{1, 2, 3, 4, 5, 6\}$ **do** $A[i] := 0$

there is no order in the way the array is cleared. $A[5]$, for example, could be set to zero before $A[1]$. This distinction can be particularly important if the value of one element of the array is dependent on the value of another element in the array.

It should be noted that the index variable used in for loops (i in the example above) has a scope that is local to the loop. It does not need to be declared separately. This is not the case in while loops.

While loops are a familiar programming construct and repeatedly execute an operation or statement whilst some Boolean condition holds. A **while** loop in **VDM-SL** has the form:

while B **do** St

where B is a Boolean condition and St a statement. For example:

```
-- computes the factorial of n.
n := 10; -- initialise n to a value
factorial := 1;
 while n > 0 do
        (
          factorial := factorial * n;
           n:= n - 1
        )
```

If B is false on entering the loop then the loop is not activated and returns no value. If B is true on entering the loop then the statement St executed. The Boolean value is then re-evaluated and if still true the process is repeated. This continues until the Boolean condition becomes false at which time the process stops and a value is returned. For example:

```
-- Greatest common denominator
while x ≠ y do
       if x > y
       then x: := x - y
       else y: := y - x;
```

terminates when $x = y$.

Exercise 5.11: Given a file in memory consisting of a sequence of words, without using recursion, write an operation which will replace all occurrences of a given word in the file with a given new word.

5.15.3 Notational structuring

VDM has three constructs which allow values to be defined that are local to an expression or statement, the scope of the variables being a single statement or expression immediately following them. All three notations are essentially bindings introducing local declarations whose scope is the statement or expression immediately following them. The variables declared in these declarations can be seen as existing only during the execution of the statement or expression.

The first form of notational structure is the *declaration preamble* which, being a statement, can only be used in explicit operations and allows declaration of a single local identifier:

dcl Id: T := E;

where Id is an identifier, T a type expression and E an expression or operation call of type T. The expression is optional and can be omitted. For example:

dcl *num* : $\mathbb{R}$;

If the expression is included it is evaluated and assigned before evaluation of the statement following it. Declaration statements are used to declare variables local to statements or operations. For example:

```
-- make values in list = 1, 2, 4, 8, 16, 32 etc.
-- where list is an externally defined entity.
DOUBLE : () -o-> ()
DOUBLE () ≜
(dcl d : ℕ:= 1;
 for i = 1 to len list do
    (list(i):= d;  d := d + list(i)));
```

Note that the declaration preamble counts as a single statement, therefore the above operation requires brackets round it, and the statement following it (the for loop) to make a single 'block' statement.

The second form of binding is the *definition* construct which allows a number of definitions to be defined which are local to an expression or statement. **VDM-SL** has both **def** expressions and **def** statements, the construct can therefore be used in both functions and operations. The **def** construct has the form:

def $\text{Id}_1 = \text{E}_1$;
$\text{Id}_2 = \text{E}_2$;
...
$\text{Id}_n = \text{E}_n$ **in** E_s

where $Id_1,\ldots, Id_n$ are identifiers, $E_1,\ldots, E_n$ are expressions and E_s is an expression or statement that the definition construct applies to.

The identifiers $Id_1,\ldots, Id_n$ in a **def** expression can have a set or type binding placed on them, such as:

$$Id_1 : \mathbb{N} = E_1$$
$$Id_2 \in \mathbb{N} = E_2$$

The binding is optional and does not need to be expressed. For example, in the following def expression:

```
-- removes those elements from list that are already in memory
-- operation terminates when sentinel symbol is encountered
REMOVE: List -o-> List
REMOVE(list) ≜
if list(1) = sentinel then return list
else def top = hd list; rest = tl list in
     if top ∈ memory
     then return REMOVE(tl list)
     else return [hd list] ⌒ REMOVE(tl list)
pre sentinel ∈ list;
```

In **def** statements the expressions $E_1,\ldots, E_n$ can contain variables (such as state or local variables). For this reason **def** statements (as opposed to **def** expressions) can only be used in explicit operation definition. Because the statement is declaring definitions rather than declarations the expressions are mandatory in this case. An example of the use of the definition statement is:

```
-- returns true if first element of list is repeated in rest of list
-- and removes it from list if this is the case
DUPLICATE: () -o-> 𝔹
DUPLICATE() ≜
def top = hd list; rest = tl list in
if top ∈ elems rest
then (list:= tl list↼; return true)
else return false
```

A similar construct to the **def** construct is the **let** construct. Like **def** constructs, these can be expressions or statements. They have the form:

$$\textbf{let } Id_1 = E_1, Id_2 = E_2,\ldots, Id_n = E_n \textbf{ in } E_s$$

where $Id_1,\ldots,Id_n$ are identifiers, $E_1,\ldots,E_n$ are expressions and E_s an expression or statement on which the scope of the let construct operates. Like the **def** construct the identifiers can have set or type bindings. Unlike definition statements, however, local variables are not allowed in the expressions $E_1,...,E_n$. Replacement is purely textual (because the values to which the identifiers are bound are constant).

The **let** construct effectively states that all the identifiers $Id_1,...,Id_n$ textually replace the expressions on the right side of their equals signs within E_s. This is a form of macro substitution, where all occurrences of $E_1,..., E_n$ in E_s are replaced by their corresponding identifiers $Id_1,..., Id_n$. If we had the expression:

$$total\_price := amount + (amount \times rate / 100)$$

we could rephrase this as:

let *tax* = *amount* × *rate* / 100 **in**
total_price: = *amount* + *tax*;

Use of the let construct is particularly useful for improving readability, since they help reduce the size of expressions and allow meaningful names to replace equations. It should be noted that the replacement only applies to the expression or statement following the let expression. Lets can be nested. We might, for example, also require postage in the previous expression:

```
let tax = x × rate / 100 in
   let taxed_price = x + tax in
      if taxed_price < 200 then
         let postage = 20 in total_price := taxed_price + postage
      else
            total_price := taxed_price -- else postage is free
```

The scope of the identifier 'postage' in this example is only the first total_price statement (which follows the let statement in which it is defined). If postage had been mentioned in the second total_price expression another let statement would have been required after the else clause to define this too, even if it was of the same value. A let construct may also have the form:

let Bd **in** E_s

where Bd is a set or type binding, and E_s an expression or statement. For example:

let $x \in \{1, 2, 3, 4, 5, 6\}$ **in** *random* = x

In this case some element of the set expression is arbitrarily chosen then used in the expression. This type of expression should only be used in situations where it does not matter which member of the set is chosen. This is useful for abstracting away from an inessential choice of an element from a set where it is not important which element is chosen. There is a third form of let construct having the form:

let Bd **be st** Pd **in** E_s

where Bd is a binding, Pd is a predicate expression and E_s is an expression or statement. This is similar to the previous **let** construct and could be rephrased as:

let Id ∈ {Id | Pd} **in** E_s

where Id is an identifier and Pd a predicate. A value is chosen such that it satisfies the predicate. For example, in:

let *x* **be st** ($x \uparrow 2$) + *x* - 2 = 0 **in** *root* := x

The variable *x* could take on either the values 1 or -2.

Let ... **be** constructs are useful where the property of an element is known but an explicit definition is difficult to ascertain or express.

It should be noted that as in **for** loops the identifiers (Id) defined on the **let** construct's left-hand side (the assignment) may be considered local and therefore do not need to be declared separately. Also because the identifier is assigned a constant value the type of the identifier does not need to be declared as this can be ascertained from the expression on the right-hand side. Since the identifier is purely a textual substitution, in reality the variable has no independent existence.

Exercise 5.12: Expand the operation given in the previous exercise (5.11) so that it also returns the number of replacements made.

5.15.4 Exceptions and handlers

In explicit operation definitions the statement normally terminates with the value of the last command executed. In **VDM-SL**, however, it is possible to cause exiting from a statement before the last command. Two commands exist to allow this:

return

which terminates normally, and:

exit

which causes abnormal termination.

Both of these commands may prefix an expression representing the value to be returned in these cases:

return E   **exit** E

where E is an expression. If no expression is given no value is returned. An example of the use of these two operators is:

-- Operation to get number from memory and divide it by d
-- where 'mem' is a state variable.
$DIVIDE\_MEM: \mathbb{R} \xrightarrow{o} \mathbb{R}$
$DIVIDE\_MEM(y) \triangleq$
if $y = 0$ **then exit** -- Division by zero is an error
else return *mem* / *y*

where if the divisor is zero the operation terminates abnormally, otherwise it terminates normally returning the result.

In order to deal with termination under these situations **VDM-SL** incorporates handlers allowing exception conditions to be dealt with. **VDM-SL** has three types of handlers; always, nonrecursive and recursive which can be used to head a statement.

The **always** handler traps any terminating condition (normal or abnormal) and therefore applies to both return and exit conditions. It has the form:

always S_h **in** St

where S_h and St are statements. When St is terminated by either a return or exit command then the handler statement S_h is carried out. For example, if we had two routines, *close_system* which closes down a system and *run_system* which runs a system, we could state:

always (*close_system*; **exit**) **in** *run_system*

If the system terminated due to an exit or return, the handler statement would be called and would run *close_system* before exiting, thus carrying out a clean shutdown. This allows for all eventualities whether the system stops intentionally or through some exception.

The non-recursive handler (or trap) is slightly different in that it is activated only by abnormal terminations, such as that caused by the exit statement. It has the form:

trap P **with** S_h **in** St

where P is a pattern (which can include an optional set or type binding) and S_h and St statements. When St is terminated, if the value returned matches P then the handler statement S_h is activated. If the returned value does not match P then the statement terminates abnormally with the returned value unchanged. For example:

REMOVE: *List* $\xrightarrow{o}$ *List*
REMOVE(*list*) ≜
trap *error_message* **with** (*display*(*errror_message*); **return** []) **in**
if *list* = [] **then exit** EMPTYLIST
elseif len *list* = 1 ∧ *list* ≠ *sentinel* **then exit** NOSENTINEL
elseif *list*(1) = *sentinel* **then return** *list*
else def *top* = **hd** *list*; *rest* = **tl** *list* **in**
  (**if** *top* ∈ *memory*
  then return *REMOVE*(**tl** *list*)
  else return [**hd** *list*] ⌒ *REMOVE*(**tl** *list*))

If the list is empty then the operation is terminated abnormally by the **exit** command. The parameter EMPTYLIST is bound to the error_message binding in the **trap** statement and this is used in the statement following the **with** to display EMPTY_LIST (now bound to error_message), before returning the empty sequence. In the case of there being no sentinel the same thing happens except that NOSENTINEL is bound to the error_message.

The recursive handler, like the non-recursive handler, also traps only abnormal terminations and has the form:

$$\textbf{tixe}\ \{P_1 \rightarrow St_1, P_2 \rightarrow St_2, \ldots, P_n \rightarrow St_n\}\ \textbf{in}$$

In this case a whole list of patterns may exist, each associated with a different statement. For example:

-- ensures input value is in range min ≤ input ≤ max
-- by changing trapping and changing it to either min or max
-- if it is out of bounds.
-- min and max are global constants.
IN_RANGE : ℕ $\xrightarrow{o}$ ℕ
IN_RANGE(*input*) ≜
tixe { (CATCH1) ↦ **return** *min*,
    (CATCH2) ↦ **return** *max*} **in**
if *input* < *min* **then exit** CATCH1
elseif *max* < *input* **then exit** CATCH2
else return *input*

The recursive handler attempts to match the value returned by the abnormal termination against one of the patterns in its list. If it succeeds then it executes the statement associated with the pattern. If no pattern is found the statement terminates abnormally with the returned value unchanged. If more than one pattern matches then one of these is chosen at random, non-deterministically, and its associated statement executed.

The handler is recursive because it also applies to the handler statements it carries out. If the statement terminates abnormally then the process repeats itself and a new pattern is matched against the termination value of this statement. This will continue until one of the statements terminates successfully. It is therefore important to ensure that the recursive handler will always terminate at some point.

5.15.5 Non-deterministic commands

VDM has an operator which allows the execution of a series of statements in a non-deterministic fashion.

Operator	Text	Mathematical
Nondeterminism	||	||

It has the form:

$$|| (St_1, \dots , St_n)$$

where $St_1, \dots , St_n$ represent the component statements of the command.

The effect of this command is that the order of execution of the statements cannot be determined beforehand. In other words it is non-deterministic.

Such a command is useful where we wish to specify that the order of execution of a set of commands is of no consequence to the final result. For example, in a paint mixing machine:

|| (*add_red_paint*, *add_yellow_paint*) ;
mix

it would not matter if we added the red paint or the yellow paint first. In both cases after mixing we would end up with the same orange paint.

The operator is sometimes referred to as a parallel operator, since it represents the 'parallel' execution of the statements. This does not, however, mean that the commands are executed simultaneously. The statements are still executed one at a time. For example, given $x = 2$ and $y = 1$ the result of executing:

$$||(x{:=}y,\ y{:=}x)$$

would be that both x and y have exactly the same value, and not, as you might have expected, swapped values. One statement is always executed before the other. In this case there are only two possible orders in which the commands could be carried out, the first being:

$$(x{:=}y;\ y{:=}x)$$

which would result in $x = y = 1$, and the second being:

$$(y{:=}x;\ x{:=}y)$$

which would result in $x = y = 2$.

Because of the non-deterministic command, however, we would be unable to determine which of these orders would be chosen, and therefore could not determine the result of the operation.

The non-determinism operator is seldom used in **VDM** specifications and can only be applied to explicit definitions.

5.15.6 Lambda expressions

Lambda expressions can be used to defined abstract functions without naming them.

Operator	Text	Mathematical
Abstraction	lambda	λ
Separator	&	$\bullet$

In **VDM** the lambda expression has the form:

$$\lambda\ Bs_1{:}T_1,\ Bs_2{:}T_2,\ \ldots,\ Bs_n{:}T_n \bullet E$$

where $Bs_1,\ldots, Bs_n$ are each one or more bound variables, $T_1,\ldots,T_n$ their respective types and E an expression. For example:

$$\lambda\ x : \mathbb{N} \bullet x \times 2$$

Lambda expressions are particularly useful in **VDM** for defining abstract local function definitions. For example:

-- Gives x to the power of y, i.e. x^y

let $power = \lambda\ x, y : \mathbb{N} \bullet x \uparrow y$ **in** -- result = 2^3

$result = power(2, 3)$

This expression is local to the let statement.

Free variables are also possible:

> **let** $y = 2$ **in**
> **let** $f = \lambda\, x : \mathbb{N} \bullet x - y$ **in**
> $result = f(5)$ -- result = 5 - 2

and curried expressions:

> **let** $power = \lambda\, x : \mathbb{N} \bullet \lambda\, y : \mathbb{N} \bullet x \uparrow y$ **in**
> $result = power(3)(2)$ -- result = 2^3

In **VDM-SL** Lambda expressions cannot be polymorphic.

Exercise 5.13: A value *i* held in memory can be increased or decreased by one by pressing an appropriate button. We represent the buttons as an enumerated set

$$Button = \text{INCREMENT} \mid \text{DECREMENT}$$

Using lambda expressions how could we write a single operation which given the button pressed would either increase or decrease the value appropriately?

5.15.7 Iota expressions

Operator	Text	Mathematical
iota	iota	ι

Iota expressions are similar to lambda expressions except that for any definition there must be a unique assignment of values for the expression. An iota expression has the form:

$$\iota\text{Bd} \bullet \text{E}$$

where Bd is either a set or type bind, and E is a Boolean expression. For example, the iota expression:

$$\iota x : \mathbb{N} \bullet x{\uparrow}2 = 4$$

has the value 2, but the expression:

$$\iota x : \mathbb{Z} \bullet x{\uparrow}2 + x - 2 = 0$$

generates two values 1 and -2 for *x* and is therefore undefined.

5.16. MODULES

Modules allow **VDM** specifications to be defined in self-contained units each having an interface which defines the external properties of the module, and a set of definitions defining its operations and state.

The use of modules has been withdrawn and reintroduced many times during the development of the **VDM** standard. During this development their structure and use have changed considerably, and is likely to do so in the future. The notation introduced for such structures in this section is therefore likely to represent only a rough approximation of current developments in this area and has been included only to give the reader a general idea of their structure and use.

If you are seriously considering using such structures it is important that you consult the current standardisation work in the area. Until a sufficiently stable notation has developed they are probably best avoided. However, you may come across specifications containing such structures and it is therefore important that you be aware of them. A module has the form:

module Identifier
parameters
...
imports
...
exports
...
instantiations
...

definitions
types
...
state
...
operations
...
end Id

where Id is the name of the module (which is the same at both the beginning and end of the module).

The parameters section defines the parameters for a parameterised module. A parameter being a type, value or function signature.

The interface of the module defines the external properties of the module and it's relation to the outside world. This can contain **imports** from and **exports** to other modules.

The import section has the form:

imports
from Id_1 S_1,
....
from Id_n S_n

and the export section the form:

exports S_M

where Id_1 ,..., Id_n are the names of the modules from which imports are being made and S_1,..., S_n are the signatures of the types and operations being exported from these modules. The keyword '**all**' can be used instead of the signatures if we wish to import all the defined constructs of the module. S_M is the module signature giving the signatures of the operations exported by the module. The export section is used to make constructs visible to other modules.

The import section describes types and signatures of functions and operations being imported and used by the module. The export section describes the types and signatures of operations and signatures defined in and exportable from the module. Both the export and import sections are optional and can be omitted if not needed.

The rest of the module is taken up defining the type, state and function and operations of the module. As with a normal specification only those sections of the definition section necessary for the specification need be defined.

```
-- module to add the ability to calculate tangents using operations
-- and types imported from another module called 'scientific'.
module mathematical
import from scientific
   types Sci_Num
   functions
        cos, sin, divided_by: Sci_Num × Sci_Num → Sci_Num
exports
    types Num
    operations
       tan: Sci_Num → Sci_Num
definitions
      types
operations
         tan(x : Sci_Num) result : Sci_Num
         post divided_by(sin(x), cos(x))
end mathematical
```

Here we import the operations *sin, cos* and *divided_by* from a module called *scientific*. We also import the type *Sci_Num* used by these functions (this type might, for example, hold high-precision values). The module *mathematical* exports an operation for calculation of tangents. The signatures of these also use the *Sci_Num* type, so we have to declare this in the export section as well as the signatures. Because we define a single function we have no need of a state definition so this is omitted. In this case we have defined only one function. In most cases a module will contain a series of types, operations and other definitions connected in some way by a relationship between them, for example, in defining the type definitions and operations on a particular data type or construct.

As well as defining modules for specific types, they can also be defined as generic templates, allowing the module to be used with many different types and values. This is similar in many ways to **VDM-SL**'s ability to define polymorphic functions, but allows us to define values as well as types in this way. We define such a module by including a parameter section in our module in the form:

parameters S_M

In the example on the next page only one type, called 'Element', is given as a parameter (though any number of types may be given). Functions can also be given as parameters. For example:

parameters
  types *Key, Element, Product*
  functions
    $quantity : Product \rightarrow \mathbb{N}$
exports
  ...

When we call the module in another module we instantiate the module to the particular types we wish to use. We do this with an instantiation section:

instantiation
  Index **as** *Ext_List*(*Element* → *DataString*)
  types *List*
  functions
    $unique : List \rightarrow \mathbb{B}$
    $inlist : Element \times List \rightarrow \mathbb{B}$
    $disjoint : List \times List \rightarrow \mathbb{B};$

Here we are instantiating the module *Ext_List* as Index, and the parameter *Element* to be of type *DataString*. We also list the types and functions we will use from the module by giving the function signatures.

The Instantiation of *Ext_List* to Index has the effect of instantiating the type *List* to *Index`List*, and the functions *unique*, *inlist* and *disjoint* to *Index`unique*, *Index`inlist* and *Index`disjoint* respectively. Whenever we refer to these in the calling module we use the new instantiated names.

-- This module extends the operations for sequences

module *Ext_List*
  parameters
    types *Element*
  exports
    types *List*
    functions
      $inlist : Element \times List \rightarrow \mathbb{B};$
      $sublist : List \times List \rightarrow \mathbb{B};$
      $disjoint : List \times List \rightarrow \mathbb{B};$
      $unique : List \rightarrow \mathbb{B};$
      $last : List \rightarrow Element;$
      $reverse : List \rightarrow List$
definitions
  types $List = Element^{+}$
  functions
    -- true if element is in list
    $inlist : Element \times List \rightarrow \mathbb{B}$
    $inlist(x, lst) \triangleq \exists i \in \mathbf{inds}\ lst \bullet x = lst(i);$
    -- true if list1 is subsequence of list2
    $sublist : List \times List \rightarrow \mathbb{B}$
    $sublist(l1, l2) \triangleq \exists i \in \mathbf{inds}\ l2 \bullet l2(i,..., \mathbf{len}\ l1 + i - 1) = l1;$
    -- true if two lists are disjoint
    $disjoint : List \times List \rightarrow \mathbb{B}$
    $disjoint(l1, l2) \triangleq \forall i \in \mathbf{inds}\ l1 \bullet \forall j \in \mathbf{inds}\ l2 \bullet l1(i) \neq l2(j);$
    -- true if no value is repeated in a list
    $unique(lst) \triangleq \forall i,j \in \mathbf{inds}\ lst \bullet lst(i) \neq lst(j) \vee i = j;$
    -- gives the value of the last element of a list
    $last : List \rightarrow Element$
    $last(lst) \triangleq lst(\mathbf{len}\ lst);$
    -- returns a list with its elements reversed
    $reverse : List \rightarrow List$
    $reverse(lst) \triangleq \lambda\ i \in \mathbf{inds}\ lst \bullet i \mapsto lst(1 + (\mathbf{len}\ lst - i))$
end *Ext_List*

The instantiation section is placed just after the export section. It is important to note that when we instantiate a module, we do not place its definitions in the import section. For example:

```
module DataStore
  parameters
    types DataString
  exports
    types Index`List
    functions
      position : DataString × List → ℕ
      insert_names : List × List → List;
      delete_repeats : List × List → List
  instantiation
      Index as Ext_List(Element → DataString)
      types List
      functions
        unique : List → 𝔹
        inlist : Element × List → 𝔹
        disjoint : List × List → 𝔹;
definitions
    types Index : DataString⁺
    functions
      -- returns position of name in sequence
      position(name : DataString, lst : Index`List) i: ℕ
      pre Index`inlist(name, lst)
      post lst(i) = name;
      -- adds a list of names to another list
      -- only adds  names not already in list
      insert_names : Index`List × Index`List → Index`List
      insert_names(lst, nms) ≜
      if Index`disjoint(lst, nms)
      then lst ⁀ nms
      else lst ⁀ delete_repeats(nms, ls);
       -- removes elements from list X that are in list Y
      delete_repeats : Index`List × Index`List → Index`List
      delete_repeats(l1, l2) ≜
      if X = [] then []
      else if Index`inlist(hd l1, l2)
      then delete_repeats(tl l1,  l2)
      else hd X ⁀ delete_repeats(tl l1,  l2);
end DataStore
```

We can instantiate any number of the types declared in the parameter list of the module by including them within the parentheses:

$$\text{Id } \mathbf{as} \text{ Inst\_Id}(\text{Id}_1 \rightarrow \text{I}_1, \text{Id}_2 \rightarrow \text{I}_2, \ldots, \text{Id}_n \rightarrow \text{I}_n)$$

where Id is a type or function given in the parameter list and I is it's instantiated name. For example:

instantiation
Vectors **as** *Lists*(*List* → *Vector*)
operations
reverse : *Vector* → *Vector*;
Matrices **as** *Arrays*(*Array* → *Matrix*)
functions
add : *Matrix* × *Matrix* → *Matrix*;

5.16.1 Using

When we use an operation declared in a module within another module we encounter a problem if the operation uses any state variables declared in the called module. A way of overcoming this when calling the operation is to employ the using statement which has the form:

Operation() **using** Id

where Id is the name of the state variable in the original module referred to by the operation. If we declare the following module:

module *store*
parameters
types *Unit*
exports
types *List*
operations
ADD : *Unit* $\xrightarrow{o}$ ()
definitions
state store **of**
list : $Unit^+$
init *mk*_store(*lst*) $\triangleq$ *lst* = []
end
operations
ADD(*x*: *Unit*)
ext wr *list*
post *list* = $\overleftarrow{list}$ ⌢ [*x*]
end *store*

then use the module's operation ADD in another module:

```
module Database
instantiation
   namestore as store(Unit → Name)
   operations
       ADD : Unit -o-> ()
parameters
     types Name
     exports
       types namestore`List
       operations
          ADD : Name -o-> ();
definitions
state Database of
      list : Unit+
      init mk_Database(db) ≜ db = []
  end
types Name : char*
operations
  ADD : Name -o-> ()
  ADD(val) ≜
      namestore`ADD(val) using list
end Database
```

the module thus instantiates the parameter *Unit* as *Name* and the operation *ADD* to that of the store module.

5.17. PUTTING IT ALL TOGETHER

We now need to examine how we write specifications. We will look at some small examples of routines that are generally useful when defining formal specifications and see how they can be derived.

5.17.1 Example 1 – The missing data type

One of the data types missing from **VDM-SL** is bags. A bag as stated in Chapter 2 records the number of times an element has been placed in it, but like a set does not have any order.

First, we define bag to consist of a set of mappings from some element to a number representing the numbers of times it occurs:

types

$$Bag = X \xrightarrow{m} \mathbb{N}_1$$

We have called the data type of the domain X, leaving it free to decide what the type is.

Operations and functions defined on a data type normally fall into four main categories:

- *Constants*: Functions which have no input parameter and always return the same value,
- *constructors*: Operations or functions which build up the datatype by either creating or adding elements,
- *destructors*: which reduce or destroy the data type by removing or subtracting elements,
- *selectors*: Operations or functions which extract components, or values, held in the data type but usually do not alter the state of the data type.

When defining a data type we should consider these four areas and consider what functions we require in each.

First we need an initial state for a bag. The initial state of any bag would be empty:

values

$$empty\_bag = \{\mapsto\}$$

This is an example of a constant; *empty_bag* will always return the same value. We also require a function which is able to insert an element in a bag:

functions

bag_insertion(x : X, bg : *Bag*) *newbag* : *Bag*
post *newbag* = $bg \dagger \{x \mapsto bag\_count(x, bg) + 1\}$;

bag_insertion is an example of a constructor function.

Conversely, we also need to be able to remove elements from a bag. The function *bag_deletion* deletes an element, if present, from a bag:

bag_deletion : X × *Bag* ⟶ *Bag*
bag_deletion(x, bg) $\triangleq$
if $x \notin$ **dom** bg **then** bg -- if x not in bag return bag unchanged
elseif $bag\_count(x, bg) = 1$
then $\{x\} \triangleleft bg$ -- deleting x will make count=0 so remove from bag
else $bg \dagger \{x \mapsto (bag\_count(x, bg) - 1)\}$;

bag_deletion is an example of a destructor function. We may also wish to see if an element of type X is in the bag:

$$in\_bag : X \times Bag \to \mathbb{B}$$
$$in\_bag(x, bg) \triangleq x \in \textbf{dom}\ bg;$$

which is true if the element is in the bag.

We would also want to be able to interrogate the data type to see how many times the element is present in the bag. The function *bag_count* would do this, returning the number of times an element appears in a Bag:

$$\begin{array}{l} bag\_count : X \times Bag \to \mathbb{N} \\ bag\_count(x, bg) \triangleq \\ \textbf{if}\ x \in \textbf{dom}\ bg \\ \textbf{then}\ bg(x) \\ \textbf{else}\ 0; \end{array}$$

This is an example of a selector functor. It selects a particular element from the data type and returns the value held there.

The function *bag_sum* combines two bags into a single bag with the new bag containing the sum of occurrences in the two bags:

$$\begin{array}{l} bag\_sum(bg1, bg2 : Bag)\ newbag : Bag \\ \textbf{post}\ newbag = \{\, x \mapsto (bag\_count(x, bg1) + bag\_count(x, bg2)) \mid \\ \qquad\qquad x \in (\textbf{dom}\ bg1 \cup \textbf{dom}\ bg2)\}; \end{array}$$

Again, this is a constructor function in that it builds up the data type.

Another useful function we can define is *bag_common* which takes two bags and returns a bag which includes for each element occurring in both bags the minimum number of times it occurs in either but not both bags, thus giving only those elements common to both bags:

$$\begin{array}{l} bag\_common(bg1, \mathrm{bg2} : Bag)\ newbag : Bag \\ \textbf{post}\ newbag = \{\, x \mapsto min(bag\_count(x, bg1), bag\_count(x, bg2)) \mid \\ \qquad\qquad x \in (\textbf{dom}\ bg1 \cap \textbf{dom}\ bg2)\}; \end{array}$$

This requires the additional function *min* giving the minimum of two numbers:

-- returns minimum value of 2 numbers

$$\begin{array}{l} min(x, y : \mathbb{N})\ minnum : \mathbb{N} \\ \textbf{post}\ (minnum \le x) \wedge (minnum \le y) \wedge (minnum \in \{x, y\}); \end{array}$$

min is an example of an *auxiliary function;* a function used by another function to make it more readable. We could simply have included the properties defined in *min* in the *bag_common* routine, but this would have made it less understandable and more complex. Auxiliary functions allow functions and operations to be split into more manageable chunks. They can also be called by a number of functions, thus reducing the need to reiterate the same section of text again.

It would also be useful to be able to convert sequences into bags. We define a constructor called *items* which turns a sequence into a bag:

$$
\begin{array}{l}
items : X^* \rightarrow Bag \\
items(sq) \triangleq \\
\textbf{if } sq = [] \textbf{ then } \{\} \\
\textbf{else let } x = \textbf{hd } sq \textbf{ in} \\
bag\_insertion(x, items(\textbf{tl } sq))
\end{array}
$$

This is an example of a recursive function. The function will continue to recursively call itself until the empty sequence is reached.

Although an overall functional style has been used in the specification of the bags, the functions themselves have been a mixture of implicit and explicit. This is often the case. If possible try to define the property of the function implicitly. However, as can be seen in the above, this is not always possible.

Using a functional style the operations defined are independent of the state. It is therefore fairly easy to plug them into another specification. Functional specifications are often more concise and clearer than their state-based counterparts and far easier to prove correct.

5.17.2 Example 2 – Bits and bytes

A numeric representation which can prove useful is binary. We can define data types *Bit* and *Byte* for use with this number base. We have already defined these data types earlier in this chapter as:

values

$$Byte\_Size : \mathbb{N} = 8$$

types

$$
\begin{array}{l}
Bit = \mathbb{N} \\
\textbf{inv } Bit \triangleq Bit \in \{0, 1\} \\
\\
Byte = Bit^+ \\
\textbf{inv } Byte \triangleq \textbf{len } Byte = Byte\_Size
\end{array}
$$

We need routines able to convert decimal values to this form:

functions

decimal_to_binary : $\mathbb{N} \to Bit^*$
decimal_to_binary$(n) \triangleq$
let *divisor* = *n* **div** 2, *remainder* = *n* **mod** 2 **in**
if *divisor* $\neq 0$
then *decimal_to_binary*(*divisor*) $\frown$ [*remainder*]
else [*remainder*];

and vice versa:

binary_to_decimal : $Bit^+ \to \mathbb{N}$
binary_to_decimal$(n) \triangleq$
let *length* = **len** *n* **in**
if *length* = 1
then hd *n*
else hd $n \times 2 \uparrow$ (*length* - 1) + *binary_to_decimal*(**tl** *n*);

These functions are defined in an explicit style. It is important to realise that the steps described in each of these functions may not necessarily be the best way of implementing them in a programming language. An explicit specification should be seen as an example of a way of carrying out the process. The actual implementation might, and can, be realised in a different way, as long as it produces the same results as the specification. For example, these two functions might actually be implemented using the computer's built-in routines for carrying out these processes.

Now we are able to construct bytes and their values, we can define operations on them. We can create bitwise *not, and, or* and *xor* functions. These would be similar to the logic operators given in Chapter 2 except that instead of true and false they would use and return bit values of zero and one:

byte_not(*x* : *Byte*) *z* : *Byte*
post $\forall_i \in$ **inds** $z \bullet z(i) = (x(i) + 1)$ **mod** 2;

byte_and(*x*, *y* : *Byte*) *z* : *Byte*
post $\forall_i \in$ **inds** $z \bullet z(i) = (x(i) + y(i))$ **div** 2;

Byte_or is slightly more complicated in that we first have to define the auxiliary function *bit_or* for a single bit:

$bit\_or : Bit \times Bit \rightarrow \mathrm{Bit}$
$bit\_or(x, y) \triangleq$
if $(x = 1 \vee y = 1)$
then 1
else 0;

We can then use this in an operation for or-ing two bytes:

$byte\_or(x, y : Byte)\ z : Byte$
post $\forall_i \in$ **inds** $z \bullet z(i) = bit\_or(x(i), y(i));$

An additional operation is required for exclusive or, which is similar to the normal OR operation except that it returns zero if both bits are set to one.

a	b	a **xor** b
0	0	0
0	1	1
1	0	1
1	1	0

XOR table

Exclusive or allows one or the other but not both the bits to be set to one. This is described in the following function:

$byte\_xor(x, y : Byte)\ z : Byte$
post $\forall_i \in$ **inds** $z \bullet z(i) = (x(i) + y(i))$ **mod** 2

5.17.3 Example 3 – Sorting

The third specification we look at is a sorting routine which takes a list of numbers and sorts them into ascending order.

First we need to define what type of numbers are to be sorted. In this example we shall use integers. We will therefore define the operation to take and return a sequence of integers.

We also need to decide what is the smallest sequence of numbers that need sorting. Obviously, the sort should work for all situations, but, there is little point in sorting an empty list.

We therefore state that the type of the operation is non empty sequences:

$$sort(list : \mathbb{Z}^+)\ slist : \mathbb{Z}^+$$
$$\textbf{post}\ sorted(slist) \wedge perm(list, slist);$$

The operation *sort* requires that the result of the operation is that the list is sorted and that the new list is a permutation of the old list. We now need to define these two operations.

The first operation, *sorted*, checks to see if the list sent to it has its numbers in ascending order, and returns the Boolean value true if this is the case:

$$sorted(list : \mathbb{Z}^+)\ result : \mathbb{B}$$
$$\textbf{post}\ \forall_{i,j} \in \textbf{inds}\ list \bullet i < j \Rightarrow list(i) \leq list(j) \wedge result = \textbf{true};$$

The second operation checks whether a list is a permutation of another list. That is, they both contain the same number of elements and each element occurs the same number of times in the list, though not necessarily in the same order.

$$perm(list1, list2 : \mathbb{Z}^+)\ \text{result} : \mathbb{B}$$
$$\textbf{post}\ \ items(list1) = items(list2) \wedge result = \textbf{true}$$

To do this we use the items operation defined previously in our bags routines. By converting both the lists into bags before we compare them, we remove the ordering, only comparing the elements and their frequency.

You will have noticed in the sorting operations, how the operation is carried out is not expressed, only the required result (the post-condition). This allows freedom to the implementor in choosing the most appropriate type of sorting routine.

5.18. OBSOLETE CONSTRUCTS

A number of constructs were removed from **VDM-SL** before standardisation and should no longer be used. However, you may come across them in early **VDM** specifications and therefore they will be noted briefly.

One construct that was removed was the McCarthy statement. This construct was a hybrid of the **if** ... **else** and **case** statements and had the form:

$$(B_1 \rightarrow E_1, B_2 \rightarrow E_2, \ldots, B_n \rightarrow E_n, \textbf{others} \rightarrow E)$$

Using this construct the example of a *max* function we gave using the **if...else** statement would be defined in the form:

-- returns maximum value of 3 numbers x,y and z

$((y \leq x) \wedge (z < x) \rightarrow max := x,$

$(x < y) \wedge (z < y) \rightarrow max := y,$

others $\rightarrow max = z)$

Since the McCarthy statement performed the same function as the **if...else** construct it was deemed unnecessary. Some readers might recognise it as being similar to Dikjstra's guarded command statements[10] and similar constructs are used in many formal languages.

Early **VDM-SL** allowed incomplete type definitions, in the form:

Type-name **is not yet defined**

where the type-name was the name of the type to be defined. This statement stated that the specification of the type was at this stage incomplete, but would be filled in at a later stage. However, the construct was open to abuse and was therefore removed.

VDM-SL also had an additional error handling operator, called the error command. This was equivalent to a return in which no value had been given:

error

The command also implicitly extended the pre-condition of an operation which contained it, in such a way that it excluded any values of parameters and state variables which would cause an attempt to execute it. For example:

-- Square of x

$SQUARE : \mathbb{N} \xrightarrow{o} \mathbb{N}$

$SQUARE(x) \triangleq$

if $x < 0$ **then error**

else return $x \times x$

would prevent values of x which were less than zero being passed to this statement. This is equivalent to:

-- Square of x

$SQUARE : \mathbb{N} \xrightarrow{o} \mathbb{N}$

$SQUARE(x) \triangleq$

return $x \times x$

pre $x \geq 0$

---

[10] Dijkstra E.W. *A Discipline of Programming*, Prentice Hall 1976.

5.19. PRESENTATION

It is important to consider the readability of your specifications. Liberal use of indenting and spacing is recommended to improve layout.

VDM-SL specifications are normally displayed using a set format to aid readability. Keywords are presented in bold, user-defined names in italics and enumerated types in capitals. The only exception to this is in the case of the *is_* and *mk_* operators which are normally represented in italics.

The font used for comments is not important, but it is advisable to use one which distinguishes the comments from the rest of the specification; this allows the reader to easily separate the specification from its surrounding text.

5.20. PROGRAM DEVELOPMENT IN VDM

As stated at the beginning of this chapter **VDM** incorporates not only a specification language but also a methodology for deriving programs from specifications. This section briefly explains the concept behind this methodology.

We can think of the process of deriving program code from an abstract specification in **VDM** as involving two processes:

1) **Refinement**. An algebraic process by which we produce a more concrete level of specification. Where the original abstract specification may consist of pre and post-conditions, the final stage of refinement results in code showing explicitly how to carry out the operations necessary to fulfil these conditions. Refinement only produces a more concrete specification, the final refinement is still described in the formal specification language and is not a program or system that can be run in the programming language chosen.

2) **Translation**. After the specification has been refined it is necessary to *translate* the final specification into the required programming language's notation making it suitable for compiling and running on a computer. This requires converting the specification written in the specification language to programming code written in the programming language.

5.20.1 Refinement

Each stage of refinement produces a more concrete level of specification. For a refinement step to be correct the new, more concrete, model must adequately reflect the previous stage. Since the process is algebraic, the proof of this correctness can be shown using rules and axioms which govern the properties of the objects in the specifications. As such, proof of correctness is fundamentally rule based, each stage of refinement able to be verified using formal logic techniques.

A formal specification can be thought of as consisting of two components: data types and operations. Refinement can therefore be seen to consist of two distinct processes: the conversion of abstract data types into concrete data structures (*data reification*) and the transformation of functions and operations into concrete algorithms (*operation decomposition*).

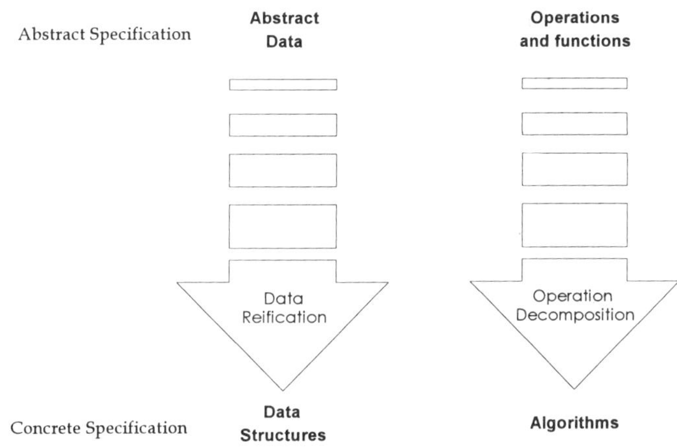

Figure 5.1: Refinement

5.20.1.1 Data reification

Data reification is the process of transforming abstract data types such as sets, sequences and maps into concrete data structures such as arrays, structures (records) and lists. Take for example the abstract data type Directory given in the telephone directory example:

$$Directory = Name \xrightarrow{m} TelephoneNo$$

This could be represented on a more concrete level as a set of records:

types

map :: *name* : *Name*
telno : *TelephoneNo*

Directory = **map-set**

The process of reification may occur many times before the final specification is defined. For example, the previous data structure could be further reified to a sequence of records:

$$\begin{aligned}&\mathit{Directory} = \mathit{map}^{+}\\&\textbf{inv-}\mathrm{Directory(dir)} \triangleq\\&\qquad \forall_{i,\,j} \in \textbf{dom}\ \mathit{dir} \bullet i{=}j \vee \mathit{dir}(i).\mathit{name} \neq \mathit{dir}(j).\mathit{name}\end{aligned}$$

We have an invariant on this data type that the same name should not occur twice in the list. This type of invariant is known as a *data-invariant*. It is a property of the original data type being a set, and therefore containing no duplicates. It is important that the data-invariant is not violated by the operations acting upon the data. If you look at the ADD operation in our telephone directory example which is an operation acting upon this data set:

$$\textbf{post}\ \mathit{dir} = \overleftharpoon{\mathit{dir}} \dagger \{\mathit{name} \mapsto \mathit{telno}\}$$

you will see that the post-condition fulfils this invariant in that only one mapping from a particular name will ever exist in the set. The new name is either added to the list if not present, or replaces the previous mapping if it is already present. If, however, we had defined the operation as:

$$\textbf{post}\ \mathit{dir} = \overleftharpoon{\mathit{dir}} \cup \{\mathit{name} \mapsto \mathit{telno}\}$$

then we would require a pre-condition:

$$\textbf{pre}\ \mathit{nm} \notin \mathit{dir}$$

to ensure that no duplicate names are added to the directory, and thus maintain the data-invariant. Care should be taken when refining the operations into more concrete form that the new form of the operation still maintains the data type invariant.

During reification we need to check that the transformation from an abstract data type to a more concrete one is correct. The term we use to describe this is *adequacy*;. For the new data structure to be *adequate* every element of the old data type must have at least one representation in the new data structure; that is, every value in the abstract state is represented by at least one value in the concrete state.

To prove that a new data structure is an adequate realisation of the old (more abstract) one we can create a function called a *retrieve* function such that:

$$\forall_a \in A \bullet \exists_c \in C \bullet \mathit{retrieveA}(c) = a$$

where A is the abstract data structure and C the more concrete one. If using this we can prove that for every element a in A (the abstract original) there is an element c in C (the new reified structure) such that *retrieveA*(c) = a, then we have proved that the new structure is an adequate representation of the old one.

5.20.1.2 *Operational and functional decomposition*

Operations and functions are usually initially written in an *implicit* form, describing what they are required to accomplish rather than how the task is to be carried out. Refinement involves making them more *explicit*. Refinement can thus be seen as ideally starting with a set of assertions (in the form of pre- and post-conditions) and the gradual translation of these into functional specifications which at some stage in the process change from specifying what you want to how to go about it.

For a more concrete operation to be a correct implementation of a more abstract one it must be able to accept the same range of values as the original abstract one, and upon accepting these values return the same results as the original would. These two criteria, known as the *domain* and the *result rules*, are dependent to the pre- and post-conditions of the operation since these determine respectively the input range and the resultant output of the operation.

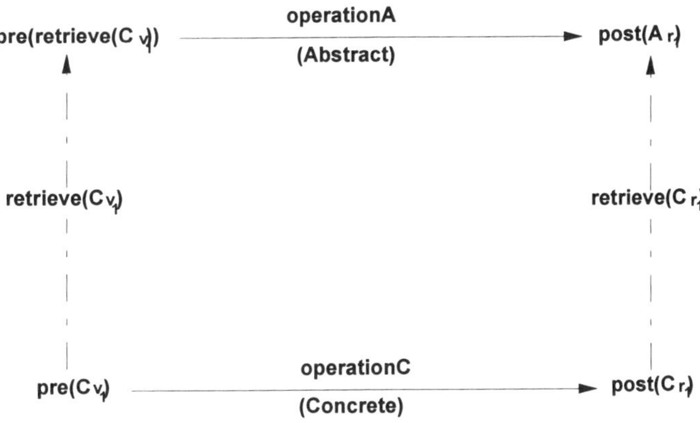

Figure 5.2: Use of retrieve functions

We can check the first part of this requirement, the *domain rule*, by reusing the *retrieve* function defined in the previous section. If we take a value in the more concrete form (C) and using the retrieve function convert it to its abstract form (A), then if the retrieved value is within the pre-condition of the abstract operation then the corresponding concrete value should also be in the pre-condition of the new more concrete specification.

In order to be a correct conversion *all* values accepted by the old abstract operation must, in their more concrete form, be accepted by the new operation (Fig. 5.2). We define this formally as:

$$\forall_c \in C \bullet \text{preconditionA}(\text{retrieve}(c)) \rightarrow \text{preconditionC}(c)$$

where c is a value in the new concrete form, preconditionA is the pre-condition of the abstract operation and preconditionC is the pre-condition of the concrete operation.

The second requirement, the *result rule*, is that an operation returns the same results as the original for those values accepted. This again uses the *retrieve* function. If we take a value accepted by the concrete operation and use the operation upon it:

$$\text{operationC}(C_{v1}) \rightarrow C_{r1}$$

it will give the result C_{r1}.

If we then use the retrieved value of the original argument C_{v1} with the abstract operation:

$$\text{operationA}(\text{retrieve}(C_{v1})) \rightarrow A_{r1}$$

this will return the result A_{r1}. If the two operations are equivalent the retrieved form of C_{r1} should be the same as A_{r1}; that is, the *retrieved result* of the concrete operation should fulfil the post-condition of the abstract operation.

$$\text{retrieve}(C_{r1}) = A_{r1}$$

5.20.2 **Translation**

Translation is the conversion of the final concrete refinement, still in the formal language's notation, into code in a specific programming language capable of running on a computer. Unlike refinement, the conversion from the specification notation to an implementation in the programming language cannot normally be formally proved in **VDM**. The difficulty arises because, in order to translate, we have to go from the specification language's semantic environment to that of the programming language's.

One solution is to have the semantics of the programming language defined in the specification language being used. This allows a correspondence to be made between the specification and implementation. Whilst this method represents a significance step towards formally proving the translation stage, sadly few programming languages have been formally defined in this way.

5.21. SUGGESTIONS FOR EXERCISES

1. Extend the telephone directory example so that it can also hold a person's address as well as their telephone number. This may require the use of a different composite type and the reworking of a number of the operations.
2. A construct commonly used in specifications is a stack. This consists of a collection of elements all of the same type in which the last element put on the stack is the first element to be taken off. Such a structure uses two main operations; *push* which places an element on the top of the stack, and *pop* which takes the top element off the stack. Define this type and its associated operations. As well as these operations you should also define the initial state of the stack. Consider also the possibility of any error conditions and write additional code to cope with these. If you get stuck there is a structure similar to a stack described as one of the examples in the next chapter of this book.
3. Examine how you might generalise the bag construct so that it could be used with elements of any type.
4. Create two additional functions sub_bag and bag_card where sub_bag checks if a bag is a sub-bag of another bag, and bag_card gives the sum of *all* the occurrences of each element in the bag. Hint: use range not domain.
5. Try refining the bag data type into a construct suitable for implementation in a programming language. Create and use a retrieve function to prove your refinement correct.

6

The Z notation

Z is a formal notation based on standard set theory, and uses a stylised mathematical notation to express the properties of a system. A small example of a Z specification has already been given in Chapter 3 showing an electronic telephone directory. Parts of this specification are used here to introduce some of the aspects of Z in this section. It is therefore suggested that you revisit the example before starting this chapter. Z specifications are structured using schemas. For example:

```
┌── Add ─────────────────────────────
│ ΔDIR
│ name? : NAME
│ no? : NUM
├────────────────────
│ dir' = dir ⊕ {name? ↦ no?}
└────────────────────────────────────
```

A specification document written using the Z specification language usually consists of a mixture of natural language narrative text interspersed with the formal description. Schemas encompass the formal parts of the description and, as well as fulfilling other properties, help to separate the formal description from the surrounding informal text.

The Z language consists of two parts: a base language, and a standard library or toolkit which is defined in terms of the base language. This library contains definitions concerned with areas such as set operations, sequences, ordered pairs, bags, numbers, relations and functions; these are all defined in terms of the base language. This means that Z only has a minimal set of built-in constructs from which many more constructs are derived. The mathematical library can be thought of as a set of useful macros built from the minimal constructs of **Z**. In this chapter the difference between operators in the basic language and those in the mathematical library will not be defined.

Z allows extensibility, making it possible to define your own operations and definitions and allows generic definitions. Unless you are involved in this type of specification it is unlikely that the distinction between basic and library operations will be important.

The formal text of a **Z** specification is usually divided into a number of units, or blocks:

- **Basic type definitions** defining the values which constants and variables may take,
- **global constant and variable definitions** within the system and any constraints on them,
- **schemas** defining the state and operations of the system.

New global constants may be introduced throughout the specification by the use of **axiomatic** and **abbreviation definitions**.

6.1. THE INTERCHANGE LANGUAGE

Before examining the **Z** language itself, we need to first briefly introduce **Z**'s interchange language. **Z** has three notations, one using special 'graphical' symbols (and referred to as the mathematical notation) and two others which are entirely text based. The interchange language forms one of the two text-based notations. Being entirely text-based it represents a portable notation which can be transmitted between different machines.

In many cases the graphical symbol used in **Z** is replaced on a one-to-one basis by a textual string in the text-based notation. For example, the symbol:

$$\Leftrightarrow$$

is simply replaced by the textual string:

iff

Where a symbol is used within the interchange notation, an ampersand is placed before it to show it is an operator.

a &iff b

All operators must have an ampersand placed before them in the interchange language, even where the interchange notation does not vary from the graphical notation. For example, the operator for range in both the **Z** graphical notation and interchange language is defined as:

ran

When used in the interchange language, however, it is always prefixed by an ampersand:

&ran x

The ampersand helps differentiate **Z** operators from variables, schemas names and user-defined types. Structures are defined in the interchange language by surrounding them by markers, or tags defining the structure. These have the form:

<structure_name> structure </structure_name>

where the forward slash denotes the end of the structure. The angular opening and closing brackets in this case are actually written, they do not represent placeholders. For example, to define a user-defined set of types:

[NAME, NUM]

we would use the notation:

<givendef> NAME, TEL_NO </givendef>

The first marker may in some cases also contain arguments defining particulars about the structure.

A **Z** specification, written in the interchange language, must also be enclosed in similar structures to show that it is a **Z** specification.

```
<Z>
...Z specification...
</Z>
```

For example, the following is a definition of the Add schema given at the beginning of this chapter:

```
<Z>
<givendef> NAME, NUM </givendef>
<schemadef style=vert purpose=operation> Add
<decpart>
&Delta DIR
 name?: NAME
 no?: NUM
 <axpart>
 <predicate>
dir' = dir &oplus &lcub name? &map(no?) &rcub
 </schemadef>
 </Z>
```

In some cases, depending on the context, the end markers of certain structures may be omitted, as can be seen in the previous example. The example is given merely so that you can gain an idea of the structure of interchange specifications. Do not look at it too closely at this stage as the notation will become clearer as we progress through this chapter.

Finally, where subscripts or superscripts are used in the interchange language they are defined with the enclosing:

_{...}

for subscripts, and:

^{...}

for superscripts. For example:

x_2 and y^3

would be represented as:

x ₂
y ³

respectively.

The interchange language is designed to replace an earlier notation used to transfer **Z** specifications. This was based upon a special set of macros written for a text based editor called LaTeX, which converted the text notation into a graphical format. Unfortunately, this notation has been widely used, particularly in tool development. The interchange language conforms to current standardisation work in **Z**, and in the future the interchange language should gradually replace the earlier notation. The **Z** standard contains a comprehensive description of the semantics and layout of the interchange language.

6.2. USER-DEFINED IDENTIFIERS

User-defined words in **Z**, such as value, type and schema names, follow certain conventions. They must always start with and consist of at least one letter (upper or lower case). This may be followed by any sequence of characters including letters, digits and Greek letters. The Greek characters[1] Ξ and Δ have special significance in the case of schemas in that they may be

---

[1] Greek characters are represented in the interchange notation by their written names. Thus Ξ is represented by the word 'Xi'. If the lower case version of the symbol is required then the first letter of the name is in lower case; for example, the text 'delta' represents 'δ'. If the first letter of the word is a capital then this represents the upper case version of the symbol; for example, 'Delta' represents the symbol 'Δ'.

prefixed to the schema name. They indicate whether the operation of the schema alters the state of the system, and will be explained in greater detail later.

The underscore character can be used to separate compound words. For example:

This_is_a_user_defined_word

Spaces, dashes and **Z** symbols cannot be used in a user-defined word, and keywords (except as part of a compound word) should be avoided. Letter case in **Z** is significant, so:

User_defined_word
user_defined_word

are both different identifiers and are not related.

By convention the question mark '?' and exclamation mark '!' are used to denote input and output respectively when postfixed to an identifier. We have seen this in the telephone directory example where the schema LookUp referred to the input variable *name*? and an output variable *no*!.

```
___ LookUp ________________________________
| ΞDIR
| name? : NAME
| no! : NUM
|__________________________
| name? ∈ dom(dir) ∧
| no! = dir(name?)
|__________________________________________
```

Exercise 6.1: Which of the following names are valid **Z** user-defined identifiers?

First_name, airport?, report!, b_3, alphaβ, 1st_field, _data, last-name

6.3. DATA TYPES

All types in Z are maximal sets. They consist either of a basic type, or a complex type made up from the basic types; there is no subtyping in the language[2].

[2] Types are not defined over subsets of values in **Z**. Whenever subsetting is used, as, for example, with ranges in the form 1 .. x, the type of the associated variable is an integer with a predicate asserting the range restriction.

There are essentially four kinds of types in the language:

- Basic types
- Set types
- Product types
- Schema types

Other complex types (such as bags) are defined in the mathematical toolkit, but are built from the basic sets and their operations.

Each type in **Z** has associated with it a set of operators specific to it. These have a variety of applications, from defining type invariants to manipulating data in functions and operations. All expressions in **Z** have a decidable type. It is thus possible to statically check that all expressions in a specification are well typed[3]. We declare a variable to be of a certain type using the format:

Variable_name : Type

For example, stating the variable *number* to be of type integer:

$$number : \mathbb{Z}$$

We can also declare a variable to be in a range of values[4]

Constructor	Text	Mathematical
Range	_ nldr _	$x_1 .. x_n$

For example:

$$day : 1 .. 7$$

which declares that *day* can take on a value in the range 1 to 7. This, as we shall see later, is equivalent to:

$$day : \mathbb{Z}$$

$$day \geq 1 \land day \leq 7$$

[3] This means that the definition of 'correctly typed' is far more liberal than in some other formal languages such as **VDM**.

[4] The number range operator (denoted by two dots ..) is not limited in its use to just type definitions, but can be used in other areas, such as defining sequences. The numbers in the range are, by default, integers.

A number of variables may be declared to be of same type using the format:

$$\text{var}_1, \text{var}_2, .., \text{var}_n : \text{Type}$$

For example:

$$x, y : \mathbb{N}$$

Semicolons can be used to separate different type declarations:

$$positive : \mathbb{N} ; negative : \mathbb{Z}$$

Alternately, within schemas, newlines may be used to separate type definitions:

```
┌── Value ─────────────────────────────
│ positive : ℕ
│ negative : ℤ
├──────────────────
│ negative < 0
└──────────────────────────────────────
```

6.4. BASIC TYPES

The bounds of a specification are defined in terms of the basic or atomic sets. These sets consist either of the predefined basic sets, or user-defined given sets. Starting with these objects more complex objects, or types, can be put together.

6.4.1 Predefined types and sets

Z has only integer as a predefined basic type:

Type	Text	Mathematical
Integers	int	$\mathbb{Z}$

It also has a number of subsets of this type[5]:

Set	Text	Mathematical
Natural	nat	$\mathbb{N}$
Positive integers	nat1	$\mathbb{N}_1$

The natural numbers form part of the mathematical toolset, and are defined in terms of the integer set. Although we use the symbols $\mathbb{N}$ and $\mathbb{N}_1$ to declare objects to be natural numbers or positive integers, it is important that we realise that when we do, we are in fact really declaring an object of type integer, which is constrained to the set of natural or positive integers by a predicate. Thus if we declare x as:

$$x : \mathbb{N}$$

we are, in reality, declaring an object x of type integer constrained by a predicate to only positive numbers. The symbol $\mathbb{N}$ can thus be considered shorthand for:

$$\{x : \mathbb{Z} \mid x \geq 0\}$$

For most purposes this distinction is unimportant, and in the rest of this chapter we refer to natural numbers, somewhat loosely, as a type. Only when we come to areas such as *normalisation* and *type checking* and the building of *complex types* does the distinction become important.

Both the type integer and its predefined subsets represent infinite sets. Unlike many other formal methods **Z** does not include types such as Reals, Booleans or Characters.

6.4.2 Given types

Given types, or basic sets as they are sometimes called, are user-defined atomic types. Such types are introduced by a name given in square brackets. For example, we may define a type called USERTYPE as:

[USERTYPE]

Such types are written without concern for their internal elements, though the elements of the type must be assumed to be uniquely identifiable in some way.

By convention the name used to identify such a type should consist of a singular noun and be written in CAPITALS.

---

[5] A **Z** type is a *maximal set*, there are therefore no subtypes in **Z**, only subsets.

Several types can be described in a single line, for example the two types used in the schema given at the beginning of this chapter:

[NAME, NUM]

This represents the set of all uniquely identifiable names and all uniquely identifiable telephone numbers respectively.

Given types are defined in the interchange language by enclosing them in the markers:

<givendef> user_names </givendef>

For example, the previous types would be defined as:

<givendef> NAME, NUM </givendef>

6.4.3 Free types

Free types represent a way of defining enumerated types and of building recursive types such as trees and lists. A free type definition consists of a series of constants and/or constructors. Constants are atomic elements, and constructors are functions delivering a value of the type. A free type has the form:

$$\text{FreeType} ::= \text{Element}_1 \mid \text{Element}_2 \mid \ldots \mid \text{Element}_n$$

where each element is either a single constant or a single constructor. Each element represents a possible branch.

A free type consisting simply of constants is equivalent to an enumerated set, for example[6]:

DIGIT ::= '0' | '1' | '2' | '3' | '4' | '5' | '6' | '7' | '8' | '9'

is equivalent to:

DIGIT == {'0', '1', '2', '3', '4', '5', '6', '7', '8', '9'}

Each of the values in the free type must be a disjoint value (i.e. be a distinct literal). Often identifiers are simply used to represent the elements of the type, rather than constant values. For example:

---

[6] Single or, less commonly, double quotes surrounding text are often used to represent textual strings, though this is only a convention and not part of the Z standard. Z has no predefined character or string types.

$$\text{SWITCH} ::= \mathit{off} \mid \mathit{on}$$

where *off* and *on* are identifiers for each of the elements of the type SWITCH. Note that from this expression we know nothing about *off* or *on* apart from the fact that they are distinct from each other.

Constructors, like functions, define the types they receive. These are placed within chevrons:

Name	Text	Mathematical
Bar	verbar	$\mid$
Left chevron	lchev	$\langle\!\langle$
Right chevron	rchev	$\rangle\!\rangle$

in the form:

$$\text{constructor\_name}\langle\!\langle\text{arguments}\rangle\!\rangle$$

where the arguments are the types taken as input. If we use constructors in the definition we can create more complex structures. For example, a binary tree could be defined as:

$$\text{TREE} ::= \text{leaf} \mid \text{node}\langle\!\langle \mathbb{N} \times \text{TREE} \times \text{TREE} \rangle\!\rangle$$

which holds natural numbers in its nodes (Fig. 6.1).

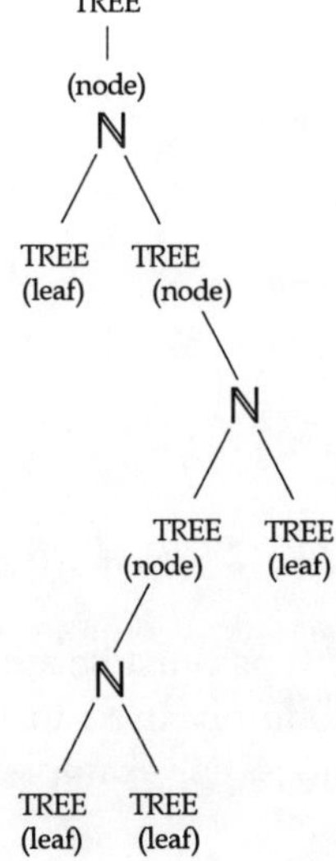

Figure 6.1: Example of binary tree structure

Free types differ from compound types in that compound types are always built from other simpler types. With free types we can build new types from the elements of the type itself in a recursive manner.

Care must be taken when defining such structures to ensure that recursion is not infinite, and so ensure the consistency of the type. Free types are a purely syntactic notational aid in **Z** and as such are not really necessary. Their main use is to simplify the construction of certain structures. However, they should be used cautiously because of restrictions in their use.

Exercise 6.2: One of the main uses for free types in **Z** is in the outputting of messages. Since **Z** has no character or string type how would we go about representing a type of which a variable of that type would be capable of outputting the messages 'name in list', or 'name not in list'?

6.4.4 Basic type operators

Z contains all the normal Boolean operators:

Operator	Text	Mathematical
Negation	not	$\neg$
And	and	$\wedge$
Or	or	$\vee$
Implies	rArr	$\Rightarrow$
Equivalent	iff	$\Leftrightarrow$
Universal quantifier	forall	$\forall$
Existential quantifier	exist	$\exists$
Unique identifier	exist1	$\exists_1$
Separator	bull	$\bullet$
Truth value	true	**true**
Falsehood	false	**false**

Although **Z** does not have Boolean as a built-in type it does have the literals **true** and **false** describing truth and falsehood.

Logic statements in **Z** follow the normal layout and conventions of standard logic. For example:

$$\forall x, y : \mathbb{N} \bullet \exists z : \mathbb{N} \bullet (x \ \mathbf{mod} \ z = 0) \wedge (y \ \mathbf{mod} \ z = 0)$$

The following numeric operators are also provided in Z:

Operator	Text	Mathematical
Multiplication	*	*
Unary minus	uminus	-
Addition	+	+
Subtraction	bminus	-
Integer division	div	div
Integer modulus	mod	mod
Successor	succ	*succ*
Equals	=	=
Not equals	ne	≠
Less than	lt	<
Less than or equal to	le	≤
Greater than	gt	>
Greater than or equal to	ge	≥

Z's use of these operators is consistent with their normal usage in standard arithmetic and logic. The minus operator varies in its text form: the unary minus applies only to single values, whereas the binary minus applies to two values, thus -6 uses the unary operator, whereas 6 - 6 = 0 uses the binary operator.

The successor function *succ* can only be used with values of type natural and gives the next natural number in ascending order. It is equivalent to adding one to the previous value. For example:

$$\mathit{succ}\ (n) = n + 1$$

The parentheses are optional.

Z also has the operators *min* and *max* which give the minimum value and maximum value respectively from a non-empty *set* of integers.

$$\mathit{min}\ \{1,5,4,3,2\} = 1$$
$$\mathit{max}\ \{1,5,4,3,2\} = 5$$

6.5. COMPOUND TYPES

There are three main composite, or compound, types in **Z**, which can be created using the built-in type constructors in the language; set types, product types and schema types. More complex types can be created using a combination of these types, and the mathematical toolkit contains a number of additional types constructed in this way including bags and sequences.

6.5.1 Sets

Types and sets in **Z** are in many cases one and the same. A user-defined type such as:

[NAME]

represents the set of all possible uniquely identifiable elements of that type. The type $\mathbb{Z}$ and the subsets of this type $\mathbb{N}$ and $\mathbb{N}_1$ represent the set of integers, natural numbers and positive natural numbers respectively. We can thus see in these cases that the definition of set or type is interchangeable. Only when we come to construct complex types does the distinction become more acute.

Type	Text	Mathematical
Powerset	pset	$\mathbb{P}$
Non-empty subsets	pset1	$\mathbb{P}_1$
Finite subset	fset	$\mathbb{F}$
Non-empty finite subset	fset1	$\mathbb{F}_1$

The power set represents the set of all subsets of set S:

$$\mathbb{P}\, S$$

and is placed before the set. To see the value of powersets in defining types we need, by way of an example, to define the type:

[NAMES]

This represents the set of all possible names (in the universe). If we now take a telephone directory containing a set of names of people whose telephone numbers we know, then this set of known names consists of names which are part of the set of all possible names (NAMES). At any one time the set of names in our telephone directory consists of one of the elements of the powerset of NAMES. If we look at part of the powerset of NAMES we might see:

$$\mathbb{P}\ \text{NAMES} = \{...\{Fred\}, \{Fred, John\}, \{Fred, John, David\}, \{...\}...\}$$

The powerset of NAMES is equivalent to the set of all possible collections of names we might have in our phonebook. Conversely, our collection of names has the potential of consisting of any one of the elements of the powerset of NAMES. Our set of phonebook names will therefore be in the powerset of NAMES. We can therefore describe our set of names as being of the type powerset of NAMES.

```
── Phonebook ─────────────────────────────
│ names : ℙ NAME
│ dir : NAME ⇸ NUM
├──────────────────
│ names = dom dir
└─────────────────────────────────────────
```

The powerset of a set will always have the empty set as one of its elements; there may be circumstances, however, when we may not wish to allow the empty set. **Z** allows us to define this constraint. When a subscripted 1 is placed next to the powerset symbol:

$$\mathbb{P}_1\ S$$

this represents the set of all non-empty subsets of S.

All sets are by default potentially infinite in **Z**. Sometimes it is useful to restrict a set to a finite size. This can be done using the finite set operator, so:

$$\mathbb{F}\ S$$

represents the set of all finite subsets of S, and:

$$\mathbb{F}_1\ S$$

represents the set of all non-empty finite subsets. For example:

$$\mathbb{F}_1\ \mathbb{Z}$$

represents the set of all non-empty finite subsets of integers. By making a set finite we can carry out operations that would be impossible on an infinite set, such as determining the size of the set.

6.5.1.1 *Set values*

Symbol	Text	Mathematical
Left set bracket	lcub	$\{$
Right set bracket	rcub	$\}$
Empty set	empty	$\{\}$ or $\varnothing$

Sets are enclosed in curly brackets in **Z**. As in most formal notations sets can be defined explicitly by their members, or implicitly by some property. Explicit sets follow the normal notation. For example:

$$\{1, 2, 3, 5, 8, 13\}$$

The format for set comprehension, however, differs slightly from that in normal set notation:

{Declaration | Predicate • Expression}
← Schema text → ← Term →

A set comprehension in **Z** consists of three parts; a declaration which introduces any bound local variables, a constraint (the predicate) restricting the values of the declared variables and a term (the expression) defining the form and construction of the elements of the set. For example, the first 10 squares:

$$\{i : \mathbb{N} \mid 1 \le i \land i \le 10 \bullet i * i\}$$

Both the predicate and the expression are optional and can be omitted. For example, omitting the predicate in the above:

$$\{i : \mathbb{N} \mid i * i\}$$

gives the set of all squares. If we omit the expression, or term:

$$\{i : \mathbb{N} \mid 1 \le i \land i \le 10\}$$

we obtain a set consisting of the numbers 1 .. 10.

We can also use schema names in place of the declaration and predicate. For example, if we defined a schema InRange1to10:

```
__ InRange1to10 ________________________
| i : ℕ
|_______________________
| 1 ≤ i ∧ i ≤ 10
|________________________________________
```

We could equally state:

$$\{\text{InRange1to10} \bullet i * i\}$$

6.5.1.2 Set operators

Z has the basic set membership operators:

Operator	Text	Mathematical
Member	isin	$\in$
Non-member	notin	$\notin$
Cardinality	num	#

to determine whether a value is an element of a set. For example:

$$a \in \{a, b, c\}$$
$$x \notin \{a, b, c\}$$

Z also has the cardinality operator # giving the number of elements in a set. For example:

$$\#\{\} = 0$$
$$\#\{a, b, c\} = 3$$

This operator only applies to finite sets.

Relations between sets are defined by equality, inequality, proper subset and subset:

Operator	Text	Mathematical
Equality	=	$=$
Inequality	ne	$\neq$
Proper subset	sub	$\subset$
Subset	sube	$\subseteq$
Empty set	empty	$\varnothing$ or $\{\}$
Non empty subsets	pset1	$\mathbb{P}_1$

For example:

$$\{a, c, d, b\} = \{a, b, c, d\}$$
$$\{a, b, d\} \neq \{a, b, c\}$$
$$\{a, b\} \subset \{a, b, c\}$$
$$\{a, b\} \subseteq \{a, b, c\} \subseteq \{a, c, b\}$$

Z also has the standard set operators union, relative complement (also called set difference) and intersection.

Operator	Text	Mathematical
Union	cup	$\cup$
Difference	sdiff	$\setminus$
Intersection	cap	$\cap$

For example:

$$\{a, b, c\} \cup \{d, e, f\} = \{a, b, c, d, e, f\}$$
$$\{a, b, c, d, e, f\} \setminus \{a, b\} = \{c, d, e, f\}$$
$$\{a, b, c, d\} \cap \{c, d, e, f\} = \{c, d\}$$

as well as the prefix operators distributed union and intersection:

Operator	Text	Mathematical
Distributed union	Bigcup	$\bigcup$
Distributed intersection	Bigcap	$\bigcap$

For example:

S == {{London, Paris}, {Paris, Tokyo, London}, {Washington, London}}
$\bigcup$S = {London, Paris, Tokyo, Washington}
$\bigcap$S = {London}

Exercise 6.3: Given the set [NAME] which consists of the set of all uniquely identifiable persons names, and a building consisting of two rooms 'A' and 'B', where room 'A' can only be entered via room 'B'.

a) How could we represent the set of individuals who are in each of the rooms?
b) If we wished to restrict the individuals allowed in Room A we could introduce a set called *allowed_people* giving the names of those people allowed. How could we express the fact that at any time the people in room A should only be from this set?
c) How could we express the condition that a person cannot be in both rooms at once (as could be the case if room A was inside room B)?
d) Knowing the previous property, how could we find the total number of people in the building?

6.5.2 Products

Z allows Cartesian products to be defined:

Constructor	Text	Mathematical
Cartesian product[7]	times	$\times$

For example:

$$NAME \times ADDRESS \times TEL\_NO$$

is the set of all three tuple subsets of NAME, ADDRESS, TEL_NO.

6.5.2.1 *Tuple values*

Cartesian products are composed of a finite set of tuples, where each tuple consists of a set of elements $x_1,...,x_n$. To represent a tuple in **Z** the component values of the tuple are enclosed in round brackets, or parentheses:

Constructor	Text	Mathematical
Tuple	$(x_1,..., x_n)$	$(x_1,..., x_n)$

For example, for the Cartesian product type:

$$NAME \times ADDRESS \times TEL\_NO$$

we can define one of its elements, or tuples, of the type to consist of:

(Fred Smith, 176 Park Street, 44987)

To select one of the elements of the tuple, we use the *tuple selection operator*[8]:

tuple.index

where index is the number of the element we wish to select. For example, if the previous tuple is referred to as *t*:

t == (Fred Smith, 176 Park Street, 44987)

---

[7] The interchange keyword for Cartesian products was 'prod' in earlier versions of the standard and this may still be used in some tools.

[8] Tuple selection was only introduced in the first draft standard and is not available in earlier versions of the language, which were limited to obtaining components of ordered pairs only.

Then we can select the *components* of the tuple in the following way:

$t.1$ = Fred Smith
$t.2$ = 176 Park Street
$t.3$ = 44987

or:

(Fred Smith, 176 Park Street, 44987).1 = Fred Smith

The components of a tuple may be expressions as well as values.

Exercise 6.4: The Federal Aviation Authority needs to keep a record of what airports serve which destinations. Given two sets; [AIRPORT] and [DESTINATION] which represent the set of all possible airport names and the set of all possible destinations define a set called *HasFlightsTo* which consists of a set of tuples associating airports with destinations. Having created this set place in details saying Heathrow airport has flights to Paris and New York, and that Charles de Gaulle has flights to London.

6.5.3 Ordered pairs

Ordered pairs have two operators which give either the first element and the second element of the ordered pair:

Operator	Text	Mathematical
first second	first second	*first* *second*

For example:

$$first(a, b) = a$$
$$second(a, b) = b$$

With the introduction of tuple selection these two operators may become obsolete in the next version of the standard but at the time of writing were still available.

6.5.4 Bags

One of the constructs that Z has built into its mathematical toolkit is bags. Bags can be thought of as sets in which duplicates are allowed, and where the number of times duplicate elements occur is significant. Like sets the order of the elements is not significant. We use the prefix bag to describe a bag type in Z:

Constructor	Text	Mathematical
Bag	bag T	bag T

where T represents a type. Bags can be finite or infinite.

6.5.4.1 Bag values

Bags are expressed in double square brackets:

Symbol	Text	Mathematical
Left bag bracket	lbag	$[\![$
Right bag bracket	rbag	$]\!]$

For example:

$$[\![1, 1, 2, 3, 2, 4, 5]\!]$$

Bags are a useful tool for keeping a count or tally of items. They do not necessarily have to be finite in size.

6.5.4.2 Bag operators

Constructor	Text	Mathematical
Bag membership	in	$\in$
Sub bag	sqsubseteq	$\sqsubseteq$
Bag union	uplus	$\uplus$
Bag difference	uminus	$\cup\!\!\!\!-$
Count	count	*count*
Cardinality	num	#
Bag scaling	otimes	$\otimes$
items	items	*items*

The items operator allows a bag to be created from a sequence, for example:

$$items\langle a, b, c, d\rangle = [\![a, b, c, d]\!]$$

The Bag membership operator '⋿' is used to determine if an item is in a bag. For example:

$$Paintings == [\![Monet, Renoir, Picasso, Degas, Monet, Cezanne]\!]$$
$$Monet \sqsubset Paintings$$

The count operator determines how many times the item occurs in the bag, and has the format:

count B item

where B is the Bag and item the object being counted. For example:

$$count\ Paintings\ Monet = 2$$

The subbag operator determines if the elements of one bag form part of another bag. The subbag operator is similar in many ways to the subset operator for sets, and like the subset operator the order of the elements is unimportant. However, the number of times an element occurs in a bag is significant; a bag is only a subbag of another if the elements of the bag do not occur more often than in the bag being compared with. Thus:

$$[\![a, b, c]\!] \sqsubseteq [\![a, b, b, c, c, d]\!]$$

and:

$$[\![d, a, b, c]\!] \sqsubseteq [\![a, b, b, c, c, d]\!]$$

are both true, whereas:

$$[\![a, b, b, c]\!] \sqsubseteq [\![a, b, c, d]\!]$$

is not since the element b occurs more often in the first bag than the second. The size or length of a bag can be determined by the cardinality operator:

$$\#Paintings = 6$$

Bags can be combined using bag union:

$$[\![a, b, c, d]\!] \uplus [\![d]\!] = [\![a, b, c, d, d]\!]$$

We can also obtain the difference of two bags:

$$[\![a, a, a, b, b, c]\!] \uminus [\![a, a, b, c, c, d]\!] = [\![a, b]\!]$$

The result is the number of times an element appears in the first set, minus the number of times it occurs in the second set. If, as in the example, an element appears more often in the second set than in the first, or does not occur at all in the first set, then it does not appear in the result. We can also scale up a bag using the bag scaling operator:

$$n \otimes B$$

where n is a natural number and B a bag. This results in a bag in which there are n times as many elements as there were in the original. For example:

$$2 \otimes [\![a, b, b, c]\!] = [\![a, a, b, b, b, b, c, c]\!]$$

Each element thus occurs n times as many times as it did in the first bag.

Exercise 6.5: A network has a number of services available to users. Unfortunately, the amount of storage is almost exceeding requirements and the system administrator wants to remove services which are never or rarely used. To determine this the administrator needs to know how many times each process is accessed. In order to do this each service is given a unique identifying number represented by a natural number, and every time a person uses the process this number is logged. At the end of the day the number of times each service is used is recorded. How could we model this using bags?

6.5.5 Sequences

Constructor	Text	Mathematical
General sequence	seq T	seq T
Non-empty sequence	seq1T	seq_1 T
Injective sequence	iseq T	iseq T

Here T represents a type.

The general sequence type allows empty sequences, whereas a non-empty sequence must contain at least one element.

Injective sequences contain no duplicates; therefore, no value can appear more than once in the sequence.

6.5.5.1 *Sequence values*

Angular brackets are used to describe sequences in **Z**:

Symbol	Text	Mathematical
Left sequence bracket	lang	$\langle$
Right sequence bracket	rang	$\rangle$

For example:

$$\text{Squares} == \langle 1, 4, 9, 16, 25 \rangle$$

An empty sequence is written as empty brackets $\langle\rangle$. All sequences in **Z** are finite. Sequence comprehension is not defined in **Z**, only sequence enumeration.

6.5.5.2 *Sequence operators*

There are a number of sequence operators:

Constructor	Text	Mathematical
Head	head	*head*
Front	front	*front*
Tail	tail	*tail*
Last	last	*last*
Reverse	rev	*rev*
Domain subtraction	dsub	$\lhd\!\!\!-$
Domain restriction	dres	$\lhd$
Range subtraction	rsub	$\rhd\!\!\!-$
Range restriction	rres	$\rhd$
Extraction	extract	$\upharpoonleft$
Filtering	filter	$\upharpoonright$
Compaction	squash	*squash*
Concatenation	frown	$\frown$
Distributed concatenation	dcat	$\frown/$
Prefix	prefix	prefix

Constructor	Text	Mathematical
Suffix	suffix	suffix
Membership	in	in
Disjoint	disjoint	disjoint
Partition	partition	partition
Cardinality	num	#
Domain	dom	dom
Range	ran	ran

A sequence can be regarded as a partial function mapping from the natural numbers to the elements of the sequence. Thus the value one maps to the first element, the value two to the second, the value three to the third etc.

$$Seq: \mathbb{N} \rightarrow\!\!\!\!\!+ X$$

So, for example, if we had the sequence:

$$Square == \langle 1, 4, 9, 16, 25 \rangle$$

then we could regard this as the mapping:

$$\{1 \mapsto 1, 2 \mapsto 4, 3 \mapsto 9, 4 \mapsto 16, 5 \mapsto 25\}$$

It can be seen, therefore, that a sequence, just like a function, has a domain and a range. We can use these operators in **Z**:

dom S
ran S

where S is the name or a definition of a sequence. For example, in the previous case:

$$\text{dom } Square = \{1, 2, 3, 4, 5\}$$
$$\text{ran } Square = \{1, 4, 9, 16, 25\}$$

We can select an element of the sequence by function application. Thus, for example, if we want to select the third element of the sequence *Square*, we write:

$$Square\ 3$$

which returns the value nine (the third element of the list)[9].

[9] Brackets can optionally be used around the selection for clarity as, for example, in *Square* (3), but this is a matter of personal choice. Whatever style is chosen, however, it should be used consistently throughout a specification.

We stated that a sequence is a partial function mapping. This is because it is possible to apply a value which is outside the range of the sequence. For example:

$$Square\ 6$$

would be undefined since it is outside the bounds of the sequence.

We can also use the domain and range restriction operators on sequences. So, for example, if we wished to restrict a sequence to its first n elements we could state:

$$(1..n) \lhd S$$

where S is a sequence, or we could take a subrange from two to four:

$$(2..4) \lhd \langle 1, 4, 9, 16, 25 \rangle = \langle 4, 9, 16 \rangle$$

In such cases, however, the result will not be a sequence, since the indices no longer bear any relationship to their position. For example, the result of the domain restriction given previously would be a relation of the form:

$$\langle 2 \mapsto 4, 3 \mapsto 9, 4 \mapsto 16 \rangle$$

where the first element had been the indices. In many cases, particularly with range restriction and subtraction, the result will not have a contiguous set of indices. To convert this to a sequence we use the *squash* operator which turns the result back into a sequence, renumbering the elements and 'closing the gaps'.

If we wish to select a subrange of a sequence, a better method is to use the extraction operator, which has the form:

$$\text{Set of indices} \upharpoonleft \text{Sequence}$$

For example:

$$(2..4) \upharpoonleft \langle a, b, c, d, e, f \rangle = \langle b, c, d \rangle$$

The extraction operator is analogous to domain restriction followed by a squash:

$$squash((2..4) \lhd \langle a, b, c, d, e, f \rangle)$$

and results in a new sequence containing exactly those elements of the sequence whose indices appear in the set on the left-hand side. The elements in the resultant sequence appear in the same order they were in the original sequence.

The extraction operator can perform more powerful operations than simply subranges, since the set of indices does not necessarily have to be ordered. Thus we could, for example, extract the first, third and fourth elements from the sequence:

$$(\{1, 4, 3\}) \upharpoonleft \langle a, b, c, d, e, f \rangle = \langle a, c, d \rangle$$

or define some property of the set, using this to determine which elements are extracted.

Like sets, we can take the cardinality, or number of elements, of a sequence, so, for example:

$$\#\text{Square} = 5$$

Sequences can be joined, or concatenated together using the concatenation operator to give a new sequence:

$$S_1 \frown S_2$$

For example:

$$\langle \text{c, o, n, c} \rangle \frown \langle \text{a, t, e, n, a, t, e} \rangle = \langle \text{c, o, n, c, a, t, e, n, a, t, e} \rangle$$

A distributed concatenation operator also exists which allows a sequence of sequences to be concatenated together:

$$\frown/SS$$

where SS is a sequence of sequences. For example:

$$\frown/\langle\langle a, a, b, b\rangle, \langle c, c, d\rangle, \langle d, e, e, f\rangle, \langle f\rangle\rangle = \langle a, a, b, b, c, c, d, d, e, e, f, f\rangle$$

The reverse operator reverses a sequence, thus:

$$rev\ \langle a, b, c, d, e, f \rangle = \langle f, e, d, c, b, a \rangle$$

The head operator returns the first element of a list:

$$head\ \langle a, b, c, d, e, f \rangle = a$$

Note that the result is an element, not a sequence. The tail operator returns the sequence with its head removed:

$$tail\langle a, b, c, d, e, f \rangle = \langle b, c, d, e, f \rangle$$

The result in this case is another sequence. Tail is undefined on an empty sequence. The *last* operator returns the last element in a sequence

$$last\langle a, b, c, d, e, f\rangle = f$$

and the *front* operator returns the sequence with the last element removed:

$$front\langle a, b, c, d, e, f\rangle = \langle a, b, c, d, e\rangle$$

Note that the *last* operator will return undefined for an empty sequence.

Z contains an operator called *filter* which is analogous to range restriction, followed by a squash. Filtering produces a sequence whose elements are members of the specified set. It has the format:

$$\text{Sq} \upharpoonright \text{St}$$

where Sq is a sequence and St a set. For example, given:

$$Colours == \langle Yellow, Magenta, Cyan, Red, Indigo\rangle$$
$$Primaries == \{Red, Yellow, Blue\}$$

then:

$$Colours \upharpoonright Primaries = \langle Yellow, Red\rangle$$

Thus the resultant sequence contains those elements of the original sequence that are also elements of the set. Note that the ordering of the elements is as in the original sequence. **Z** allows us to see if a sequence is contained within another sequence:

$$\langle c, d, e\rangle \text{ in } \langle a, b, c, d, e, f, g\rangle$$

The membership (in) operator tells us if the sequence on the left of the operator forms a contiguous part of the sequence on the right. **Z** also allows us to see if the sequence forms the first part of the sequence:

$$\langle a, b, c\rangle \text{ prefix } \langle a, b, c, d, e, f, g\rangle$$

or the final part of the sequence:

$$\langle e, f, g\rangle \text{ suffix } \langle a, b, c, d, e, f, g\rangle$$

Z also has a number of operators for comparing sequences made up of sets. The first of these, the disjointness operator, compares the sets in a sequence to see if they are disjoint (have no elements in common). For example:

$$\text{disjoint}\langle\{a, b, c\}, \{d, e, f\}, \{g, h, i\}\rangle$$

is true, but:

$$\text{disjoint}\ \langle\{a, b, c\}, \{c, d, e\}, \{e, f, g\}\rangle$$

is not, since the sets share common elements.

Z has a second operator, partition, which checks if a sequence of sets partitions another. A sequence of sets partitions another larger set if they are disjoint and their distributed union forms the entire larger set. So:

$$\text{disjoint}\langle S_1, S_2, \ldots S_n\rangle \wedge \bigcup\{S_1, S_2, \ldots S_n\} = LS$$

where $S_1, S_2, \ldots S_n$ is the sequence of sets and LS the larger set consisting of them, for example:

VEGETABLES == {*lettuce, cucumber, parsnip*}
FRUITS == {*apple, orange, pear*}
FLOWERS == {*tulip, rose*}
PLANTS == {*lettuce, cucumber, parsnip, apple, orange, pear, tulip, rose*}

$$\langle VEGETABLES, FRUITS, FLOWERS\rangle \text{ partition } PLANTS$$

Exercise 6.6: Define a textfile as a sequence of ASCII characters.

a) Initialise it as empty.
b) Write an operation to append text to the end of the file.
c) Define an operation to insert a piece of text at a given position in the file.
d) Given the start and end positions of a piece of text write an operation to delete the text from the file.

6.5.6 Abbreviation definitions

An abbreviation definition, as seen in some of the earlier examples, can be used to introduce new global constants. It has the form:

Identifier == Expression

The double equals sign serves as a 'textual equivalence' operator stating that the identifier on the left-hand side is textually equivalent to the expression on the right-hand side. The identifier on the left-hand side is thus an abbreviation, or shorthand, for the expression on the right hand side. We can use such shorthand to build up global types, for example stating that *Text* consists of a sequence of ASCII characters, which are themselves made up of natural numbers:

$$ASCII == \mathbb{N}$$
$$Text == \mathbf{seq}\ ASCII$$

Once such an identifier has been declared it can then be used anywhere in the specification from the point at which it has been declared. Abbreviation definitions are encoded in the interchange language in the form:

<abbrevdef> ... <body> ... </abbrevdef>

For example:

$$x == y + z$$

would be defined in the interchange language as:

<abbrevdef> x <body> y + z </abbrevdef>

The textual equivalence sign is also used in **let** statements, introduced later in this chapter, which perform a similar purpose, but where the identifier is local to the statement immediately following the **let** statement.

Exercise 6.7: Using the textual equivalence for Text/ASCII given previously, use this to alter the Insert operation given in the previous exercise.

6.6. SCHEMAS

Although we introduced the concept of schemas earlier in this chapter we now need to look at them in more detail.

Schemas form the backbone of **Z** specifications, helping to structure and modularise specifications and allowing us to describe states, operations, types, predicates and theorems. A schema describes a set of variables whose values are constrained. The general format of a schema is:

```
┌── SchemaName ──────────────────────
│ Declarations
├────────────────────
│ Predicate
└────────────────────────────────────
```

This is referred to as vertical format. Schemas may also be represented by the alternative, horizontal format:

$$\text{SchemaName} \triangleq [\ \text{declarations} \mid \text{predicate}\ ]$$

The symbol '≙' representing textual equivalence:

Type	Text	Mathematical
Schema definition	is	≙
Left square bracket	lsqb	[
Right square bracket	rsqb	]

There is a similarity between schema definition and set comprehension. The two indeed relate, though schema calculus is far more powerful. As with set comprehension the declaration part defines the names and types of the variables, and the predicate the properties, or constraints on the variables.

The types used in the variables must be either the standard built-in types, or have been declared earlier in the specification[10]. If we take one of the schemas given in the phone book example:

```
┌── Add ─────────────────────────────
│ ΔDIR
│ name? : NAME
│ no? : NUM
├──────────────────
│ dir' = dir ⊕ {name? ↦ no?}
└────────────────────────────────────
```

the types NAME and NUM would have had to be declared previously by the declaration:

$$[\text{NAME}, \text{NUM}]$$

Semicolons can be used to terminate and separate declarations in schemas. For example:

$$\text{Add} \triangleq$$
$$[\Delta\text{DIR};\ name?\text{: NAME};\ no?\text{:NUM} \mid dir' = dir \oplus \{name? \mapsto no?\}\ ]$$

[10] Z does not allow forward referencing. The scope of a type is only in that area of the specification following its declaration.

However, if a schema contains several lines in the declaration then each line is regarded as being terminated by a newline and so a semicolon is unnecessary in this case.

If the predicate is laid out over several lines, the lines are considered as being joined by conjunction operators. Thus:

```
 ___ LookUp ________________________________
| ΞDIR
| name? : NAME
| no! : NUM
|_____________________
| name? ∈ dom(dir)
| no! = dir(name?)
|___________________________________________
```

is equivalent to:

LookUp ≙
  [ΞDIR; *name*?: NAME; *no*!: NUM | *name?* ∈ dom(*dir*) ∧ *no*! = *dir*(*name*?)]

A newline break can thus be considered as representing termination of a variable declaration in the declarations, and forming a conjunction in the predicate.

Schemas can be declared as generic over one or more of their types, parameterising them and allowing reusable templates to be created. For example, we could create the following *generic schema* for a database:

```
 ___ Database[KEY, DATA] ___________________
| database : KEY ⇸ DATA
|___________________________________________
```

By associating the types STOCK_NO and ITEMS with KEY and DATA this can be used to build a directory of stock information in which there are a series of mappings from stock number to item description:

Stockinfo ≙ Database[STOCK_NO, ITEM]

As a generic schema, Database represents a family of schemas, each with its own private state variables, but with different KEY and DATA sets. We could equally well create generic schemas for the operations upon these databases, though this would normally be done in conjunction with the *renaming* of the database (see later).

We can also define *generic constants*. These have no schema name given, only parameters, and are distinguished from normal schemas by a double line on the upper part of the box. They can be used to introduce generic objects such as:

$$[X]$$

$$head : \mathrm{seq}_1\, X \rightarrow X$$

$$\forall s : \mathrm{seq}_1\, X \bullet head\ s = s(1)$$

which defines a family of constant functions named '*head*' that take the first element from any sequence of values. This example states that for all elements s of type seq_1 (a non-empty sequence) *head* s is the first element of that sequence. The type of X can be stated explicitly when the object is used:

$$head[\mathbb{N}]\ \langle 1, 2, 3, 4, 5 \rangle$$

or can be left implicit:

$$head\ \langle 1, 2, 3, 4, 5 \rangle$$

if there is enough context to deduce it uniquely as being of a certain type.

Using such generic constants allows them to be applied to many different types, thus *head* can be used with sequences of any type of element. The **Z** toolkit defines most of its operations and objects in these terms.

If we wish to represent schemas in a purely textual form using the Z interchange language we use the following tags:

<schemadef style=... purpose = ...> Schema_id
<decpart>
<axpart>
<predicate> ... <predicate>
</schemadef>

style can be *vert* (for vertical) or *horiz* (for horizontal). This defines whether the schema is in its vertical or horizontal format.

purpose can be defined as *state, operation* or *data type* and is an optional parameter which can be left out.

There can be one or more predicates, in which case each predicate must be prefixed by the <predicate> tag.

If we go back to the example we gave at the beginning of this chapter, we can represent it in a horizontal format, without its purpose being explicitly stated:

```
<schemadef style=vert> Add
<decpart>
&Delta DIR
name?: NAME
no?: NUM
<axpart>
<predicate>
dir' = dir &oplus &lcub name? &map(no?) &rcub
</schemadef>
```

Generic definitions are of a similar format except that they begin with the <gendef> tag:

```
<gendef style=...> Schema_id
<decpart>
  ...
<axpart>
<predicate>
  ...
</gendef>
```

though for functions and relations this has been replaced by the use of fixity paragraphs which we shall come across later.

Exercise 6.8: Define a generic operator to add an element to the *front* of a sequence of the same type, then define a generic operator to determine how many times this element occurs in a list.

6.6.1 Scope of variables in schemas and axiomatic definitions

Any variables declared in a schema are local to that schema, thus *name*? and *no*? were local to the schema *Add* in the telephone directory example. Because of this we had to declare new variables corresponding to the two variables each time they were used in other schemas (for example, in Update and LookUp). Each of these variables is local to the schema in which it is declared and is distinct from variables of the same name in the other schemas.

However, if a declaration is declared external to any schema, then it is global to any part of the specification declared after it. It is accessible throughout the specification from the point at which it has been declared, and does not need to be declared within a schema which uses it.

We can use predicates to constrain the value of *global* variables, by declaring *axiomatic definitions* in the form:

| *declaration*
|---
| *predicate*

For example:

| $range : \mathbb{N}$
|---
| $0 \leq range \land range \leq 10$

introduces a global variable *range* whose value must lie between 0..10. We can also declare constants. For example:

[STATUS]
| $on, off : STATUS$
|---
| $on \neq off$

Here the set STATUS consists of two distinct constants *on* and *off*. Such constants, introduced by a global declaration, may be used from their point of declaration onwards[11]. Declarations like these are also useful for declaring numeric constants, such as:

| $array\_size : \mathbb{N}$
|---
| $array\_size = 8$

The predicate part of an axiomatic declaration is optional, and can be left out, for example where we do not wish to state the value, only the type:

| $global\_constant : TYPE$

More than one constant can be given in the declaration. For example:

[11] In many cases these definitions can alternatively be given by abbreviation definitions.

[AIRPORT, DESTINATION]

| *Heathrow, Charles_de_Gaulle, Narita* : AIRPORT
| *London, Paris, Japan* : DESTINATION

Although we have not given these a value, they cannot be changed and are constants which cannot be altered by any system operation.

We can also use such definitions to define mathematical operators. For example, since **Z** does not have a built-in power operator, we can define one ourselves in the following definition:

$$\_\uparrow\_ : \mathbb{N} \times \mathbb{N} \rightarrow \mathbb{N}$$

$$\forall p : \mathbb{N} \bullet p \uparrow 0 = 1$$
$$(\forall n : \mathbb{N}_1 \bullet p \uparrow n = p * (p \uparrow (n - 1)))$$

which states the property of a power. We can then use this like a normal mathematical operator:

$$2 \uparrow 8$$

This schema has been declared as a recursive definition using an infix notation (where the operator is placed between its arguments). Do not worry if you do not understand the definition, it will become clearer as you progress through this chapter.

Axiomatic declarations are defined in the interchange language in the form:

<axdef> *id*
<decpart>
....
<axpart>
<predicate>
...
</axdef>

For example, if we wished to define the previously defined axiomatic definition of *array_size*:

```
<axdef>
<decpart>
array_size : &Nat
<axpart>
<predicate>
array_size = 8
</axdef>
```

An axiom *id* is optional, and in this case has not been included. If there is more than one predicate, then each predicate must start with the <predicate> tag.

Exercise 6.9: Define a global variable *digit* which represents a number between 1 and 9.

6.6.2 Using schemas to define state

In our example in Chapter 3, we defined the telephone directory as:

$$\mathrm{DIR} \mathrel{\hat=} [dir : \mathrm{NAME} \mathrel{\ooalign{$\rightarrow$\cr\hidewidth$+$\hidewidth}} \mathrm{NUM}]$$

We can see that this can be represented as a schema without a predicate:

```
┌── DIR ─────────────────────────────
│ dir: NAME ⇸ NUM
└────────────────────────────────────
```

We could additionally add a predicate constraining the DIR, for example limiting the size of the directory:

```
┌── DIR ─────────────────────────────
│ dir: NAME ⇸ NUM
├──────────────────
│ #(dom dir) < 1000
└────────────────────────────────────
```

This uses the cardinality operator '#' to specify that the dir should not contain more than 1000 entries.

6.6.3 Defining operations as schemas

If we wish to describe an operation in terms of a schema we need to be able to specify how the state of the system is affected by the schema. We need to determine the inputs to the schema, the effect of the schema on these inputs and the resultant output. We declare the inputs and outputs to a schema by adding question marks '?' to the names of the variables being input and exclamation marks '!' to variables being output . Thus *name*? is an input to the schema LookUp and *no*! the output.

```
┌── LookUp ─────────────────────────────
│ ΞDIR
│ name? : NAME
│ no! : NUM
├───────────────────
│ name? ∈ dom(dir)
│ no! = dir(name?)
└───────────────────────────────────────
```

In addition, with operations which change the state of variables we need to define whether we are talking about the state of the variable before or after it has been changed by the operation. We do this by using the name of the variable terminated with a prime character ' to represent the value of the variable *after* the operation[12]. Thus in the operation:

```
┌── Add ────────────────────────────────
│ ΔDIR
│ name? : NAME
│ no? : NUM
├───────────────────
│ dir' = dir ⊕ {name? ↦ no?}
└───────────────────────────────────────
```

dir represents the old state of the variable, and *dir'* represents the new state after the operation. We are therefore saying that the new state of the directory consists of the old directory overridden with the name-to-number mapping.

It is important to note that in a **Z** schema only components that are specifically constrained have a particular value. In operations where there are before and after values if the components are not specifically related, the after state can be any arbitrarily allowed value; it will not necessarily be the same as the before value by default.

---

[12] When a variable or schema name has a symbol such as the prime attached to it it is said to be 'decorated'.

For example, suppose we had defined the state:

```
POSITION ____________________
| x , y : ℕ
|_____________________________
```

which gave the position of an object. We might wish to define an operation to increment 'x' by one:

```
IncX ________________________
| ΔPOSITION
|____________
| x' = x + 1
|_____________________________
```

Simply stating this, however, means that 'y' can take on any natural number value after the operation; it has not been constrained to it's previous value. If we wish 'y' to remain unchanged we would need to state this in the operation:

```
IncX ________________________
| ΔPOSITION
|____________
| x' = x + 1
| y' = y
|_____________________________
```

We have thus stated that the new value of 'y' is equal to the old value of 'y'. That is, it remains unchanged. We have to be particularly careful with this property when using arrays. For example, if we had defined the *add* operation for our address book as:

```
Add _________________________
| ΔDIR
| name? : NAME
| no? : NUM
|____________
| dir' (name?) = no?
|_____________________________
```

then we would have constrained only one particular element of the array *dir*, but not the rest of the elements in the array which would be free to take on any permissible value. We therefore used the override operator to give an operation where *dir* has the same value as it did before the operation apart from the element pointed to by *name?* which is overridden.

6.6.3.1 The Delta and Xi conventions

Every time a data type is declared, two operations:

```
── ΔState ────────────────────────────
│ State
│ State'
└──────────────────────────────────────
```

and:

```
── ΞState ────────────────────────────
│ State
│ State'
├──────────────────
│ State' = State
└──────────────────────────────────────
```

are considered to be declared implicitly for the data type. For example, in our telephone book example the data type DIR would have the two schemas:

$$\Delta \text{DIR} \mathrel{\widehat{=}} [\text{DIR}, \text{DIR}']$$

and:

$$\Xi \text{DIR} \mathrel{\widehat{=}} [\Delta \text{DIR} \mid dir' = dir]$$

declared implicitly. The first of these (prefixed by the Delta 'Δ' symbol) allows the directory to be modified, with *dir*' being the result of this modification. The second operation (prefixed by Xi 'Ξ') states that no modification is allowed by declaring that the new state of the directory *dir*' must be equal to the old state of the directory *dir*.

There is no need to declare these operations explicitly, as by convention they are considered to be implicitly created. Whilst these schemas can be overridden by explicit definitions (as indeed can many of the operations in the toolset), normally we can consider any data type prefixed by the Delta 'Δ' symbol to mean that the operation can change the state (or value) of the data type, whereas with any data type prefixed by the Xi decoration 'Ξ' the operation will *not* alter the state of the data type. We can use these conventions whenever we declare an operation, as for instance in the telephone book LookUp operation, where we would wish to state that we are not altering the state of the directory, only examining it by using 'ΞDIR'.

```
___ LookUp ________________________
| ΞDIR
| name? : NAME
| no! : NUM
|__________________
| name? ∈ dom(dir)
| no! = dir(name?)
|___________________________________
```

We can also use the prime symbol ' on schemas. Priming the schema name indicates that the corresponding values, within the schema, are also primed.

Exercise 6.10: A queue is a data structure in which elements can be added (enqueued) and extracted (dequeued). Queues are FIFO (First In, First Out) structures where the first element to be put on the queue, is the first element to be taken from it.

a) Define *queue* as a state variable.
b) Define the initial state of the queue as empty.
c) Define the operations *Enqueue* and *Dequeue* which add and remove elements from the queue respectively. State a pre-condition on *Dequeue* that it will work only on non empty lists.

6.6.4 Pre-conditions of schemas

Z has a pre-condition operator which extracts the precondition of an operation from the schema. A pre-condition being a condition that must be satisfied if the operation is to yield a correct result. The pre-condition operator is used in the form:

pre Schema_Name

The pre-condition operator effectively hides the result and output variables of the schema so that it contains only the components of the schema which correspond to the state before the operation and its input[13]. So, for example:

PreLookUp ≙ **pre** LookUp

[13] It does this by existentially quantifying the primed and output variables and moving them to the predicate part of the schema.

would give:

```
PreLookUp
DIR
name? : NAME
----------------
name? ∈ dom(dir)
```

This has effectively removed the output variables (those symbols postfixed with an exclamation mark). If the schema contained any after states (postfixed with the prime symbol ') these too would be hidden.

Exercise 6.11: State the pre-condition of the following schema:

```
Logon
SYSTEM
name? : NAME
report! : STATUS
----------------
name? ∈ allowed
name? ∉ logged_on
#logged_on < max_capacity
logged_on' = logged_on ∪ {name?}
report! = ok
```

6.6.5 Combining and negating schemas

New schemas can be created by combining previously defined schemas, or by negating their properties by use of the negation operator.

6.6.5.1 Schema inclusion

Schemas can be combined by a process known as *schema inclusion*. If the name of a schema or schemas, declared previously in the specification, is included in the declaration part of a new schema then all the declared variables and predicates of the previously declared schemas are made available to the new schema. Their declarations are effectively merged and their predicates conjoined with those of the new schema.

For example, if we are given the following two schemas:

Bookings

$flight? : FLIGHT\_NO$
$passengers : NAME \pfun FLIGHT\_NO$
$number\_of\_bookings : \mathbb{N}$

$number\_of\_bookings = \#(\mathrm{dom}\ (passengers \rhd \{flight?\}))$

Aircraft_seating

$flight? : FLIGHT\_NO$
$number\_of\_seats : FLIGHT\_NO \pfun SEATING\_CAPACITY$
$max\_seating\_capacity : \mathbb{N}$

$max\_seating\_capacity = number\_of\_seats(flight?)$

---

a new schema can be created which uses the properties of these two schemas to define a new property; that the *number_of_bookings* is less than or equal to the *max_seating_capacity* of the plane:

Booking_limit

Bookings
Aircraft_seating

$number\_of\_bookings \leq max\_seating\_capacity$

This is equivalent to the following schema:

Booking_limit

$flight? : FLIGHT\_NO$
$passengers : NAME \pfun FLIGHT\_NO$
$number\_of\_seats : FLIGHT\_NO \pfun SEATING\_CAPACITY$
$max\_seating\_capacity, number\_of\_bookings : \mathbb{N}$

$number\_of\_bookings = \#(\mathrm{dom}\ (passengers \rhd \{flight?\}))$
$max\_seating\_capacity = number\_of\_seats(flight?)$
$number\_of\_bookings \leq max\_seating\_capacity$

6.6.5.2 Operations on schemas

The propositional logic operators can be used to negate or combine schemas to create new schemas or define new properties. Given two schemas S_1 and S_2 it is possible to write $S_1 \wedge S_2$, $S_1 \vee S_2$, $S_1 \Rightarrow S_2$ or $S_1 \Leftrightarrow S_2$ providing that any variable names common to the two schemas share the same base type. The negation operator $\neg S$ can also be used to reverse or negate the predicate part of a schema.

In conjunction the declarations of the two schemas are merged and their predicates conjoined. We can use conjunction to build up operations adding properties in a similar way to schema inclusion. The only real difference between schema inclusion and conjunction is that we are not adding any additional properties not already stated in the schemas being combined.

In disjunction the declarations of the two schemas are again merged but their predicates are 'or-ed' together instead of conjoined. For example, given:

LessThan

$x, y : \mathbb{N}$

$x < y$

EqualTo

$x, y : \mathbb{N}$

$x = y$

then:

$$\text{LessThan\_or\_Equal} \mathrel{\widehat{=}} \text{LessThan} \vee \text{EqualTo}$$

would give:

LessThan_or_Equal

$x, y : \mathbb{N}$

$x < y \vee x = y$

which is equivalent to:

```
┌── LessThan_or_Equal ─────────────────
│ x, y : ℕ
├──────────────────────
│ x ≤ y
└──────────────────────────────────────
```

Disjunction of schemas is particularly useful when we wish to give a series of alternative options depending on a condition, for example in the case of error handling and exceptions. We could, for example, declare that:

$$\text{Ticket\_status} \mathrel{\widehat{=}} \text{Booking\_limit} \vee \text{Overbooked}$$

where Overbooked is a schema indicating that we have exceeded the plane's seating capacity.

The negation of a schema results in the predicate part of the schema being negated. For example, suppose we defined a schema:

```
┌── AboveZero ─────────────────────────
│ temperature : ℕ
├──────────────────────
│ temperature > 0
└──────────────────────────────────────
```

which determines whether the temperature is above freezing, then we can use the negated form in the form:

$$\begin{aligned} &\text{Check} \mathrel{\widehat{=}} \\ &\quad (\ \text{AboveZero} \wedge [\text{report!:TEXT} \mid \text{report!} = \text{OK}]) \vee \\ &\quad (\neg\text{AboveZero} \wedge [\text{report!:TEXT} \mid \text{report!} = \text{Frozen}]) \end{aligned}$$

The schema ¬AboveZero gives us a check for temperatures below or equal to zero. The negation of a schema has the same signature as the original schema. However, its properties are true on just those bindings where the properties of the original schema are not true.

Care must be taken when using negation, however, as it often does not give the result we expect. For example, we could be tempted to define the schema Overbooked given in the disjunction example as simply the negation of Booking_limit:

$$\text{Overbooked} \mathrel{\widehat{=}} \neg\text{Booking\_limit}$$

This would, however, not give the correct result since *all* the predicates of Booking_limit (including implicit ones) would be negated, including those in the included schemas and those relating to types.

In schema implication the declarations of the two schemas are again merged and their predicates combined using the implies operator. For example, given:

Condition1
$$a, b, c : \mathbb{Z}$$
$$a = b \land b = c$$

and

Condition2
$$a, c : \mathbb{Z}$$
$$a = c$$

then:

$$\text{Transitive} \mathrel{\widehat{=}} \text{Condition1} \Rightarrow \text{Condition2}$$

would give:

Transitive
$$a, b, c : \mathbb{Z}$$
$$a = b \land b = c \Rightarrow a = c$$

Schema equivalence, similarly uses the equivalence operator. For example, given:

Condition1
$$a, b : \mathbb{Z}$$
$$a = b$$

and

Condition2
$$a, b : \mathbb{Z}$$
$$b = a$$

then:

$$\text{Equivalence} \mathrel{\widehat{=}} \text{Condition1} \Leftrightarrow \text{Condition2}$$

would give:

```
┌── Equivalence ──────────────────────
│ a, b : ℤ
├──────────────────
│ a = b ⇔ b = a
└─────────────────────────────────────
```

In all these operations the two schemas must have type compatible signatures.

Exercise 6.12: In a previous exercise we created an operation for removing an element from a queue.

a) Create a schema which can be used to check if a queue is empty, and if so output a message stating this.
b) Using one of the schema operators combine this new schema with the dequeue operation so that if an attempt is made to remove an element from an empty queue an error message is displayed.

6.6.5.3 Normalisation

We have already stated that to combine schemas, any variables common to the two schemas must be defined as being of the same base type. For example, if we take two schemas:

```
┌── S1 ───────────────────────────────
│ x, y : ℤ
├──────────────────
│ x < y
└─────────────────────────────────────
```

```
┌── S2 ───────────────────────────────
│ y, z: ℤ
├──────────────────
│ y < z
└─────────────────────────────────────
```

and combine them:

$$\text{Combined} \triangleq S_1 \wedge S_2$$

we can merge the occurrence of 'y' in the schemas to give:

```
┌─ Combined ──────────────────────────
│ x, y, z : ℤ
├──────────────────
│ x < y ∧ y < z
└─────────────────────────────────────
```

This is because the variable 'y' shares a common type in both the schemas. If, however, one of the schemas had 'y' defined as a natural number:

```
┌─ S2 ────────────────────────────────
│ y : ℕ
│ z : ℕ
├──────────────────
│ y < z
└─────────────────────────────────────
```

it should still be possible to combine the two schemas, because natural numbers are a subset of integers, therefore there is still a common type. We use a process known as '*normalisation*'. If we take S_2 we can '*normalise*' it so that it's 'y' shares the same type as that of S_1, whilst ensuring that it still retains its original properties. This involves changing 'y' from a natural to an integer in the declaration part of the schema, and then adding an additional condition to the predicate part of the schema constraining the property of 'y' to that of natural numbers:

```
┌─ S2 ────────────────────────────────
│ y : ℤ
│ z : ℕ
├──────────────────
│ (y < z) ∧ (y ∈ ℕ)
└─────────────────────────────────────
```

In this way 'y' now has the same type in both schemas, but still retains the type constraints of the original schema, that of being a natural number.

Normalisation is only possible when one of the instances of the common variable has a type that is a subset of the other, or when the two types have a non-null intersection. It involves changing the type of the variable whose type is a subset of the others and the adding of a predicate to its schema defining the properties of the subset.

Another example, by way of illustration, would be if S_1 and S_2 had been defined as follows:

S_1

$x, y : \mathbb{N}$

$x < y$

S_2

$y : 0..9$
$z : \mathbb{N}$

$y < z$

In this case the common base type would be natural numbers. S_2 could therefore be normalised to:

S_2

$y : \mathbb{N}$
$z : \mathbb{N}$

$y < z \land y < 10$

with the second occurrence of 'y' being considered a subset of the natural numbers.

Normalisation may also be necessary when we negate a schema. For example, if we take the schema:

AboveZero

$temperature : \mathbb{N}$

$temperature > 0$

and we wished to negate the schema to ¬AboveZero first, we would have to normalise the schema:

AboveZero

$temperature : \mathbb{Z}$

$temperature > 0 \land temperature \in \mathbb{N}$

Only then could we negate the formula, to give:

```
 ___ ¬AboveZero ______________________
| temperature : ℤ
|______________________
| ¬(temperature > 0 ∧ temperature ∈ ℕ)
|_____________________________________
```

which is equivalent to:

```
 ___ ¬AboveZero ______________________
| temperature : ℤ
|______________________
| temperature ≤ 0 ∨ temperature ∉ ℕ
|_____________________________________
```

It can be seen that in the negated schema it is necessary for *temperature* to be able to take on negative values and therefore it could not stay as type 'natural'.

6.6.6 Quantifying over schemas

As well as using propositional logic, the predicate logic quantifiers $\forall$, $\exists$ and $\exists_1$ can also be used to express properties using schemas. For example, we can use the previously defined schema ¬S to state that there is some number that is a temperature that is less than zero, or not a natural number.

$$\exists\ temperature : \mathbb{Z} \bullet \neg\ \text{AboveZero}$$

Exercise 6.13: Given a schema *Prime* which states the properties of being a prime, state that some natural numbers have this property.

6.6.7 Hiding

Hiding is a technique for removing components from the declarative part of a schema and turning them into local variables of existential operators in the predicate part of the schema. It is thus a form of existential quantification.

Type	Text	Mathematical
Hiding operator	hide	\

The syntax is of the form:

Schema \ (name of components in schema to be hidden)

For example, given the schema:

```
┌── Equal ──────────────────────
│ x, y : ℕ
├───────────────
│ x = y
└───────────────────────────────
```

then:

$$\text{Property} \mathrel{\widehat{=}} \text{Equal} \setminus (y)$$

would give the following schema:

```
┌── Property ───────────────────
│ x : ℕ
├───────────────
│ ∃ y : ℕ • x = y
└───────────────────────────────
```

This is equivalent to existentially quantifying over 'y' within the schema. The variable 'y' is therefore no longer one of the variables of the schema and has become a local variable of the existential quantifier.

Any number of variables, separated by commas, can be given in the brackets after the hiding operator.

Hiding can be used to obtain the precondition of a schema by hiding all the variables that correspond to after states (e.g. x') and all outputs (e.g. $x!$).

6.6.8 Schema projection

Schema projection is the antithesis of the hiding operator in that all the variables *except* those named in the second argument are hidden.

Type	Text	Mathematical
Projection	proj	$\upharpoonright$

It has the syntax:

$$\text{Schema}_1 \upharpoonright \text{Schema}_2$$

Only those components which occur in the domains of both the schemas are not hidden, thus:

$$\text{Property} \mathrel{\widehat=} \text{Equal} \upharpoonright [x : \mathbb{N}] \equiv \text{Property} \mathrel{\widehat=} \text{Equal} \setminus (y)$$

Projection is more convenient than hiding when a large number of variables have to be hidden.

Exercise 6.14: Given the schema:

```
 ── Is_sum_of ──────────────────────────
│ a, b, c : ℤ
├───────────────────
│ a = (b + c)
 ───────────────────────────────────────
```

a) What would be the result of:

$$\text{HSchema} \mathrel{\widehat=} \text{Is\_sum\_of} \setminus (b, c)$$

b) How would this compare with:

$$\text{HSchema} \mathrel{\widehat=} \text{Is\_sum\_of} \upharpoonright (a)$$

6.6.9 Schema renaming

The renaming operation allows a variable name to be replaced with a new name. It has the form:

Schema[newname/oldname]

where 'Schema' is the name of the schema on which the replacement is to take place, 'oldname' is the old name of the variable and 'newname' the name to be substituted. Any number of substitutions can be given in the square brackets as long as they are separated by commas. For example:

Schema[*new1*/*old1*, *new2*/*old2*, *new3*/*old3*]

Renaming is useful when combined with generic instantiation. For example, given the generic definition of a database defined previously:

```
 ── Database[KEY, DATA] ────────────────
│ database : KEY ⇸ DATA
 ───────────────────────────────────────
```

We can clarify specific instantiations of this by renaming the variables in the schema as well as instantiating the types:

Stockinfo ≙
    Database[STOCK_NO, ITEM][*stockdata*/ *database*]

which would be equivalent to:

```
 ┌── Stockinfo ─────────────────────────
 │ stockdata : STOCK_NO ⇸ ITEM
 └──────────────────────────────────────
```

Exercise 6.15: Given the state:

```
 ┌── Position ──────────────────────────
 │ x, y : ℕ
 └──────────────────────────────────────
```

rename the two variables in this schema as column and row respectively in a new schema Coordinates.

6.6.10 Selection

It is possible to select the value of an element used in a schema by using binding selection. This has the form:

Binding.variable_name

where the Binding is a schema and the variable name is in the domain of the signature from which the schema is constructed. For example, given the schema:

```
 ┌── Init ──────────────────────────────
 │ ΔState
 │ a', b' : ℕ
 ├──────────────────
 │ a' = 1 ∧ b' = 2
 └──────────────────────────────────────
```

then:

Init.a' = 1

The operation can be used in a way similar to record selection. For example, if we created the schema:

```
── DETAILS ─────────────────────────
│ name : NAME
│ address : ADDRESS
│ tel_no : TEL_NO
└──────────────────────────────────
```

and had defined the *dir* in our electronic telephone directory to map to it:

$$\text{DIR} \mathrel{\widehat{=}} [dir : \text{NAME} \mathrel{+\!\!\!\!\rightarrow\!\!\!\!\rightarrow} \text{DETAILS}]$$

we could select particular details in the same way we would from a record:

```
── Lookup_address ──────────────────
│ ΞDIR
│ name? : NAME
│ address! : ADDRESS
├──────────────────
│ name? ∈ dom(dir)
│ address! = (dir(name?)).address
└──────────────────────────────────
```

6.6.11 Sequential composition

Sequential composition, or forward relational composition, allows two operation schemas which define changes in state to be combined into a single 'composite' schema.

Type	Text	Mathematical
Schema composition	scomp	⨟

In order to do this all variables common to the two schemas must be of the same basic type. For example, given the schema:

```
── Increment ───────────────────────
│ ΔState
├──────────────────
│ counter' = counter + 1
└──────────────────────────────────
```

which increments a counter defined in a State schema, we can describe:

$$Increment\_twice \mathrel{\hat=} Increment \mathbin{;} Increment$$

a new schema which increments the counter twice. Sequential composition can be used in conjunction with other logical operators. If we redefine two schemas we gave earlier in this chapter to report their status:

```
┌── Booking_limit ─────────────────────────
│ Bookings
│ Aircraft_seating
│ report! : REPORT
├──────────────────────
│ number_of_bookings ≤ max_seating_capacity
│ report! = valid_booking
└──────────────────────────────────────────
```

```
┌── Overbooked ────────────────────────────
│ Bookings
│ Aircraft_seating
│ report! : REPORT
├──────────────────────
│ number_of_bookings > max_seating_capacity
│ report! = invalid_booking
└──────────────────────────────────────────
```

and add an additional schema to increment the number_of_bookings:

```
┌── Add_booking ───────────────────────────
│ flight?: FLIGHT_NO
│ name?: NAME
│ passengers, passengers': NAME ⇸ FLIGHT_NO
├──────────────────────
│ passengers' = passengers ⊕ {name? ↦ flight?}
└──────────────────────────────────────────
```

we can define a schema:

$$Add\_and\_Report \mathrel{\hat=} Add\_booking \mathbin{;} (Booking\_limit \lor Overbooked)$$

which adds a new booking, thereby increasing the number of bookings by one, and then reports whether the booking limit has been exceeded.

Effectively the variables describing the after state of the first schema and the equivalent variables describing the before state in the second schema are merged and the schemas conjoined yielding a single schema describing the overall initial and final states, and inputs and outputs when the first operation is followed by the second. In order for the variables to be merged they must both be of the same type.

It should be noted that all inputs and outputs shared by the schemas are identical. If any output is shared by both schemas then a single value for that output is created; the outputs are effectively merged. Thus:

```
── Increment ──────────────────────────
│ ΔState
│ output! : ℕ
├──────────────────
│ counter' = counter + 1
│ output! = counter'
└───────────────────────────────────────
```

if used in the previous 'Increment_twice' example would yield only one output value, not two. Such situations should be avoided.

Exercise 6.16: Using two state definitions *XPosition* and *YPosition* and two schemas IncX and IncY which increment x and y respectively:

```
── XPosition ──────────────────────────
│ x : ℕ
└───────────────────────────────────────

── YPosition ──────────────────────────
│ y : ℕ
└───────────────────────────────────────

── IncX ───────────────────────────────
│ ΔXPosition
├──────────────────
│ x' = x + 1
└───────────────────────────────────────

── IncY ───────────────────────────────
│ ΔYPosition
├──────────────────
│ y' = y + 1
└───────────────────────────────────────
```

Using sequential composition how could we create a new schema *Diagonal* which moves diagonally by one position?

6.6.12 Piping

Piping is similar to sequential composition, except that instead of the outputs being merged, the output of the first schema becomes the input of the second schema, with the states being merged.

Type	Text	Mathematical
Piping	>>	>>

It offers a way of combining two schemas, with input→output relationships, into a single schema whilst treating the output of the first schema as the input of the second. In order to use this operator the types of the two components must be the same, as must the types of any 'shared' variables in the schemas. For example, taking the schema:

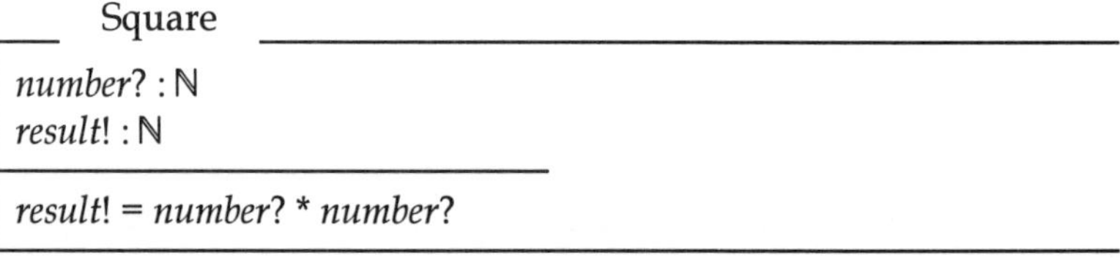

we could create a new schema *Power_4* giving $number^4$ by a combination of piping and renaming:

$$Power\_4 \mathrel{\widehat{=}} Square \gg Square[result?/number?, final\_result!/result!]$$

Effectively, the outputs of the first schema are made to correspond to the inputs of the second schema and the schemas conjoined.

Exercise 6.17:

a) Create a schema which given the number of minutes that have occurred since midnight converts this into hours and minutes in 24-hour format, and outputs the number of hours and minutes resulting, i.e. 785 minutes would convert to 13 hours 5 minutes.

b) Create a second schema which given the number of hours since midnight converts this into 12-hour format, i.e. 14 hours would become 2 o'clock.

c) Using piping create a new schema which given the number of minutes since midnight outputs the time in 12-hour format, i.e. 785 minutes would convert to 1 hour 5 minutes.

6.6.13 Relations

We looked at relations briefly in Chapter 2. In **Z** the concept of a relation is much more detailed and we need to look at the operators given in **Z** for such structures.

A relation consists of a set of ordered pairs of elements made up from two other sets. For example, if we had two sets X and Y, then a relation between these two sets $X \leftrightarrow Y$ can be described as a set of pairs (x, y) where x is an element of the set X, and y is an element of the set Y.

In **Z** a relation consists of a subset of all the possible pairs. For example, given the binary relation less_than '<' the binary relation would be the set of all ordered pairs of numbers where x is less than y.

Constructor	Text	Mathematical
Ordered pair	(x, y)	(x, y)
Maplet	map	$\mapsto$
Relation	rel	$\leftrightarrow$

The relation between two sets is equivalent to the powerset of the Cartesian product of the two sets, thus:

$$X \leftrightarrow Y \text{ is equivalent to } \mathbb{P}(X \times Y)$$

Any element, or ordered pair, of the relation can be described as a mapping from one element to another. So the ordered pair (x, y) can alternatively be described as a mapping from x to y, or vice versa:

$$(x, y) \text{ is equivalent to } x \mapsto y$$

Suppose we take the relation KnownTo[14]:

$$\text{KnownTo: PERSON} \leftrightarrow \text{PERSON}$$

where:

PERSON == {*Anne, John, Peter, David, Carol, Philip*}

[14] 'KnownTo' is an example of a *homogeneous* relation in that the relation uses the same type on both sides of the relation. Where the types differ the relation is referred to as *heterogeneous*.

Then we can represent the relation as a series of mappings, e.g.

$$\{Anne \mapsto John,\ Anne \mapsto Peter,\ John \mapsto Anne,\ John \mapsto Carol,$$
$$John \mapsto Philip,\ Peter \mapsto Anne,\ Peter \mapsto Philip,\ David \mapsto Carol,$$
$$Carol \mapsto David,\ Carol \mapsto John,\ Philip \mapsto John\}$$

Note that with relations there are no restrictions requiring the values of the sets to be paired one-to-one. Relations pair many-to-many.

Z allows relation names to be used as infix symbols. So, for example, we can turn the previously defined relation into an infix notation:

PERSON KnownTo PERSON

allowing us to write statements such as:

Anne KnownTo *John*

to determine if the relationship holds between Anne and John.

When defining the type of infix relations (and operations) we use the underscore to represent place holders for arguments. Thus if we wished to redefine the type for KnownTo as an infix operator we would state:

_ KnownTo _ : PERSON ↔ PERSON

The underscores tell us that one argument, of type PERSON, appears on each side of the relation name.

If we wish to define a relation as prefix, infix or postfix using the interchange language we have to state it with an operator type declaration before the operator is declared. This has the format:

<opdec optype = *format*> *relation_id* </opdec>

where the *format* can be set to either *inrel* (infix relation), *prerel* (prefix relation), *ingen* (infix generic) or *pregen* (prefix generic). For example, if we had defined the relation _ *IsSquareOf* _:

IsSquareOf: ℕ ↔ ℕ
$\forall x, y{:}\mathbb{N} \bullet x \text{ IsSquareOf } y \Leftrightarrow (x = y * y)$

then we would declare its operation type in the form:

```
<opdec optype=inrel> IsSquareOf </opdec>
<axdef>
<decpart>
_IsSquareOf_: &Nat &rel &Nat
<axpart>
<predicate>
&forall x,y:&Nat &bull x IsSquareOf y &iff x = y * y
</axdef>
```

The opdec declaration was superseded in draft 1.2 of the Z standard by the use of 'fixity paragraphs' which will be covered when we look at functions.

Since a relation consists of a set of ordered pairs we can use the domain and range operators:

Operator	Text	Mathematical
Domain	dom	dom
Range	ran	ran
Domain restriction	dres	◁
Range restriction	rres	▷
Domain subtraction	dsub	⩤
Range subtraction	rsub	⩥

In a relation $X \leftrightarrow Y$, the domain would be in $\mathbb{P}X$ and the range $\mathbb{P}Y$. Given the relation:

$HasFlightsTo$: AIRPORT $\leftrightarrow$ DESTINATION

$HasFlightsTo = \{Heathrow \mapsto Paris, Heathrow \mapsto New\_York,$
$Charles\_de\_Gaulle \mapsto London, Charles\_de\_Gaulle \mapsto Newark,$
$Chicago\_OHare \mapsto London, Chicago\_OHare \mapsto Paris\}$

and the set EUROPE:

EUROPE == $\{Paris, London, Athens\}$

then

$\mathrm{dom}\ HasFlightsTo = \{Heathrow, Charles\_de\_Gaulle, Chicago\_OHare\}$
$\mathrm{ran}\ HasFlightsTo = \{Paris, New\_York, London, Newark\}$

$$\{Heathrow\} \lhd HasFlightsTo = \{Heathrow \mapsto Paris, \\ Heathrow \mapsto New\_York\}$$

$$\{Heathrow\} \ntriangleleft HasFlightsTo = \{Charles\_de\_Gaulle \mapsto London, \\ Charles\_de\_Gaulle \mapsto Newark, \\ Chicago\_OHare \mapsto London, \\ Chicago\_OHare \mapsto Paris\}$$

$$HasFlightsTo \rhd \{d : \text{DESTINATION} \mid d \in \text{EUROPE}\} = \\ \{Heathrow \mapsto Paris, Charles\_de\_Gaulle \mapsto London, \\ Chicago\_OHare \mapsto London, Chicago\_OHare \mapsto Paris\}$$

$$HasFlightsTo \ntriangleright \{d : \text{DESTINATION} \mid d \in \text{EUROPE}\} = \\ \{Heathrow \mapsto New\_York, Charles\_de\_Gaulle \mapsto Newark\}$$

In addition to these standard operators **Z** has a number of other relational operators, built into the mathematical toolset1[15]:

Operator	Text	Mathematical
Identity relation	id	id
Iteration[16]	*iter k* _	$\_^k$
Forward composition	rcomp	$\fatsemi$
Backward composition	compfn	$\circ$
Overriding	oplus	$\oplus$
Relational inversion	_tilde	$\_^\sim$
Left relational image bracket	limg	$\_\llparenthesis$
Right relational image bracket	rimg	$\rrparenthesis$
Transitive closure	tcl	$\_^+$
Reflexive transitive closure	rtcl	$\_^*$

If we wish to discover the set of values in the range of a relation that are related by the relation to a given set of values we can use the relational image operator. This has the format:

---

[15] In the table the underscore represents a placeholder (where a relation name would be given), and does not appear in the notation. It has been used here to show that the symbols occur after the relation name.

[16] *k* is a number representing the number of iterations.

$$\text{Relation}⦇\text{set}⦈$$

For example, if we take the previously defined relation *KnownTo*:

$$KnownTo⦇\{Anne, Carol, Philip\}⦈ = \{John, Peter, David\}$$

The elements of the set do not necessarily need to be in the domain of the relation, so:

$$KnownTo⦇\{Anne, Richard\}⦈ = \{John, Peter\}$$

is still valid.

Every relation has an inverse obtained by reversing the ordered pairs in the relation. To obtain the inverse of a relation we use relational inversion[17]:

$$\text{Relation}^{\sim}$$

For example, suppose we wished to find out what airports serve certain countries. We could define:

$$ServedBy : \text{DESTINATION} \leftrightarrow \text{AIRPORT}$$

$$ServedBy = HasFlightsTo^{\sim}$$

which would give the set of mappings:

$$\begin{aligned} ServedBy = \{&Paris \mapsto Heathrow, New\_York \mapsto Heathrow, \\ &London \mapsto Charles\_de\_Gaulle, Newark \mapsto Charles\_de\_Gaulle, \\ &London \mapsto Chicago\_OHare, Paris \mapsto Chicago\_OHare\} \end{aligned}$$

We could then find out which airports serve, for example, London:

$$ServedBy⦇\{London\}⦈ = \{Charles\_de\_Gaulle, Chicago\_OHare\}$$

ServedBy is the inverse of HasFlightsTo.

If two relations have the same type, we can form a new relation having the properties of the first relation, except in those mappings where the domain coincides with those of the second relation. In these cases the first relation is 'overridden' by the second relation's mappings. For example,

---

[17] Sometimes R^{-1} is used instead of $R^{\sim}$ to represent the inverse.

suppose in our airports scenario Charles_de_Gaulle had to divert all its flights to London. We can state:

$$HasFlightsTo' = HasFlightsTo \oplus \{Charles\_de\_Gaulle \mapsto London\}$$

then *HasFlightsTo* would become:

$$HasFlightsTo' = \{Heathrow \mapsto Paris, Heathrow \mapsto New\_York, Charles\_de\_Gaulle \mapsto \mathbf{London}, Charles\_de\_Gaulle \mapsto \mathbf{London}, Chicago\_OHare \mapsto London, Chicago\_OHare \mapsto Paris\}$$

We can also use the override operator to add new elements, for example adding a new airport:

$$HasFlightsTo' = HasFlightsTo \oplus \{Narita \mapsto London\}$$

giving the mappings:

$$HasFlightsTo' = \{Heathrow \mapsto Paris, Heathrow \mapsto New\_York, Charles\_de\_Gaulle \mapsto London, Charles\_de\_Gaulle \mapsto Newark, Chicago\_OHare \mapsto London, Chicago\_OHare \mapsto Paris, \mathbf{Narita} \mapsto \mathbf{London}\}$$

Most of the set operators can also be used with relations, since relations are sets of ordered pairs. We could, for example, do the previous operation of adding an airport by the use a union:

$$HasFlightsTo' = HasFlightsTo \cup \{Narita \mapsto London\}$$

Certain relations have the property of being *transitive*. Suppose we have the relation OlderThan:

$$OlderThan == \{Peter \mapsto John, John \mapsto Carol, Carol \mapsto Philip\}$$

We can see intuitively that Peter must be OlderThan Philip. We say such a relation is transitive where the second element of a mapping relates to the first element of another mapping in the relation. That is:

$$\{x_1 \mapsto x_2, x_2 \mapsto x_3\}$$

from which we can say:

$$\{x_1 \mapsto x_3\}$$

We can form the *transitive closure* of a homogeneous relation:

$$OlderThan^{+} = \{Peter \mapsto John, John \mapsto Carol, Carol \mapsto Philip, \\ Peter \mapsto Carol, Peter \mapsto Philip, John \mapsto Philip\}$$

The transitive closure consists of all the mappings in the relation where the second element of a mapping can be reached from the first by following one or more intermediate mappings. The transitive closure of a relation R results in a new relation obtained by relating each member of the domain of the original relation R to its images under R and to anything related to any of its images under R by any number of steps of application of R.

The identity relation allows us to create a relation in which every member of the set maps onto itself. For example, given:

$$X = \{1, 2, 3, 4, 5\}$$

we can use the identity relation to give the relation:

$$\mathsf{id}\ X = \{1 \mapsto 1, 2 \mapsto 2, 3 \mapsto 3, 4 \mapsto 4, 5 \mapsto 5\}$$

The *reflexive transitive closure* operator extends the *transitive closure* operator by the identity relation. Thus, given:

$$\mathrm{Relation} : X \leftrightarrow X$$

then:

$$\mathrm{Relation}^{*} = \mathrm{Relation}^{+} \cup \mathsf{id}\ X$$

or conversely:

$$\mathrm{Relation}^{+} = \mathrm{Relation}^{*} \setminus \mathsf{id}\ X$$

To understand the difference between transitive and reflexive transitive closure let us define a relation FlightConnections:

$$FlightConnections : \mathrm{DESTINATION} \leftrightarrow \mathrm{DESTINATION}$$

$$FlightConnections = \{London \mapsto Paris, Paris \mapsto Germany, \\ Germany \mapsto London, Paris \mapsto Amsterdam\}$$

Using either *transitive closure* or *reflexive transitive closure* we could create a relation giving all the possible destinations we can reach, including those via flights through other cities, There would be circularity of some of the possible connections:

$$\text{London} \rightarrow \text{Paris} \rightarrow \text{Germany} \rightarrow \text{London}$$

which would give mappings such as:

$$\text{London} \rightarrow \text{London}$$

showing we can get from London to London via some of the other airports (which could be useful to know). However, using *reflexive transitive closure* we would also get Amsterdam mapping onto itself:

$$\text{Amsterdam} \rightarrow \text{Amsterdam}$$

which would give a false impression that we could return to Amsterdam via some other airports. We would not get this mapping using *transitive closure*. In this case *transitive closure* would therefore seem to be the better operator to use.

There are, however, situations where we might wish to show that the relation also applies to the objects with themselves, as well as between the various other entities.

Suppose, for example, we wished to set up a secure network. We allow data to be passed only in one direction and set up the following list of one-way connections between sites:

[SITE]

| $A, B, C, D, E : \text{SITE}$

| $Connected : \text{SITE} \leftrightarrow \text{SITE}$
|---
| $Connected = \{A \mapsto B, A \mapsto E, B \mapsto C, C \mapsto D, C \mapsto E\}$

We can create a relation which additionally states which sites can be communicated with via other sites using these one way pathways. For example, site A can communicate with D via sites B and C. We can obtain this relation using transitive closure:

$$Can\_communicate = Connected^{+}$$

This relation allows us to see all possible flows of information. So we can see, for example, that site B can only communicate, directly or indirectly, with sites C, D and E whilst it can only receive from site A.

If we used this relation to define who we can send messages to, we could run into trouble if a person on the same site wished to communicate with another person at the same site (for example, via electronic mail). The relation does not say that a site can communicate with itself. Assuming we wished to allow this, we need to use reflexive transitive closure to allow this property:

$$Can\_communicate = Connected^{*}$$

By using reflexive closure we additionally include identity relations in the relation allowing sites to communicate with themselves.

Given a relation we can create new composite relations from it by composing it with itself a number of times using *iteration*. In many ways this is similar to transitive closure except that we are stating the number of intermediate mappings required. For example, if we take the relation mappings given for a secure network that we gave earlier we can find out how many connections between sites require an intermediate site (and therefore need *two* pathways) by stating:

$$\text{Connected}^2$$

If we examine the set of mappings it can be seen that there are only a limited number of mappings which can compose with each other:

$$A \rightarrow B \text{ and } B \rightarrow C \text{ (giving } A \rightarrow B \rightarrow C)$$
$$B \rightarrow C \text{ and } C \rightarrow D \text{ (giving } B \rightarrow C \rightarrow D)$$
$$B \rightarrow C \text{ and } C \rightarrow E \text{ (giving } B \rightarrow C \rightarrow E)$$

Such an iteration would therefore result in the new relation:

$$\text{Connected}^2 = \{A \mapsto C, B \mapsto D, B \mapsto E\}$$

If we wished to know how many connections require two intermediate sites (and therefore need *three* pathways) we could state:

$$\text{Connected}^3$$

which would give:

$$\text{Connected}^3 = \{A \mapsto D, A \mapsto E\}$$

since:

$$\begin{array}{lll} A \rightarrow B & & \\ & B \rightarrow C & \\ & & C \rightarrow D \end{array}$$

and:

$$A \rightarrow B$$
$$B \rightarrow C$$
$$C \rightarrow E$$

compose with each other

We can now, if we wish, state properties such as that A and D are connected by two sites (i.e. there are 3 paths).

$$(A, D) \in Connected^3$$

which would equal true. Alternatively we can use transitive closure:

$$(A, D) \in Connected^+$$

to state that there is a repeated composition of Connected which relates A to D. This can be used to say that a connection exists between A and D (which may or may not involve intermediate sites).

It should be noted that iteration and closure are only possible if the relation is homogeneous; that is, the domain and range of the relation are of the same type.

Relations can be combined by the use of composition operators to form new relations. Given the relations R_1:X $\leftrightarrow$ Y and R_2:Y $\leftrightarrow$ Z, these can be combined to form a new relation R_3:X $\leftrightarrow$ Z. The forward composition operator '$⨾$' combines all the members of the relation R_1 that map to members of the domain of R_2. So, for example, if:

$$LivesIn == \{Joyce \mapsto London, Henri \mapsto Amsterdam, Uchiyama \mapsto Nagoya, Steve \mapsto Toronto\}$$

$$CapitalOf == \{London \mapsto England, Amsterdam \mapsto Netherlands, Tokyo \mapsto Japan, Toronto \mapsto Canada, Paris \mapsto France\}$$

then:

$$LivesInCapitalOf = LivesIn \, ⨾ \, CapitalOf$$

would equal:

$$LivesInCapitalOf = \{Joyce \mapsto England, Henri \mapsto Netherlands, Steve \mapsto Canada\}$$

The backward compositional operator, provided in **Z**, is merely an alternative way of carrying out the same operation, with the relations being transposed in the notation:

$$R_2 \circ R_1$$

The following would result in exactly the same relation as the previous example:

$$LivesInCapitalOf = CapitalOf \circ LivesIn$$

Where a relation has a property that is immutable and can be predetermined we can express such a relation using an axiomatic definition; for example, the relationships OlderThan and YoungerThan:

$$\begin{array}{|l} \_\ \mathrm{OlderThan}\ \_ : \mathbb{N} \leftrightarrow \mathbb{N} \\ \_\ \mathrm{YoungerThan}\ \_ : \mathbb{N} \leftrightarrow \mathbb{N} \\ \hline \forall i, j : \mathbb{N} \bullet i\ \mathrm{OlderThan}\ j \Leftrightarrow i > j \\ \forall i, j : \mathbb{N} \bullet i\ \mathrm{YoungerThan}\ j \Leftrightarrow i < j \end{array}$$

Here we use the equivalence operator '$\Leftrightarrow$' to describe a property of the relation.

Exercise 6.18: Define a relationship *DividesInto* which states that one element divides exactly into the other.

6.6.14 Functions

In an earlier chapter we defined functions as being special types of relations in which each element in the domain can only map onto one element in the range. This means that functions do not allow an element in the domain to map onto multiple elements in the range, such as in the case of the HasFlightsTo relation given in the previous section (where, for example, Heathrow mapped onto a number of cities)[18]. We have seen that there are many different classes of function- injective, surjective and bijective - and that these can be total or partial functions.

---

[18] The reverse is, however, allowed in that a number of elements in the domain can map onto the same element in the range.

Z represents the signature arrow for each of these classes of function with different symbols:

Constructor	Text	Mathematical
Partial function	pfun	$\pfun$
Finite partial function	fpfun	$\ffun$
Total function	rarr	$\rightarrow$
Partial injection	pinj	$\pinj$
Finite partial injection	fpinj	$\finj$
Total injection	rarrtl	$\rightarrowtail$
Partial surjection	psur	$\psurj$
Total surjection	Rarr	$\twoheadrightarrow$
Bijection	bij	$\bij$

The way these arrows are built up in **Z** is related to the properties defined. A plain arrow represents a total function:

$$f: \mathbb{N} \rightarrow \mathbb{N}$$

Whereas if the arrow is crossed this represents a partial function:

$$f: \mathbb{N} \pfun \mathbb{N}$$

A double-crossed arrow represents a partial function that is also finite[19]:

$$f: \mathbb{N} \ffun \mathbb{N}$$

A double-headed arrow means the function is surjective:

$$f: \mathbb{N} \twoheadrightarrow \mathbb{N}$$

and an arrow with a tail means the function is injective:

$$f: \mathbb{N} \rightarrowtail \mathbb{N}$$

Other classes are made up from combinations of these structures, such as bijection:

$$f: \mathbb{N} \bij \mathbb{N}$$

[19] A function with a finite domain is known as a mapping and must itself be finite.

which is a function having the properties of being injective and surjective.

As with relations **Z** allows functions, and operations, to be declared as prefix, infix or postfix. For example, the function *plus*, which adds two natural numbers together, expressed in the prefix form would be:

$$\text{plus} : \mathbb{N} \times \mathbb{N} \twoheadrightarrow \mathbb{N}$$

in which case it would be called as follows:[20]

$$x = \text{plus}(2, 3)$$

Expressed in the infix form the function type would be declared as:

$$\_\ \text{plus}\ \_ : \mathbb{N} \times \mathbb{N} \twoheadrightarrow \mathbb{N}$$

with placeholders for the arguments, or input values, on each side of the function name. It would be called as follows:

$$x = 2\ \text{plus}\ 3$$

Postfix functions, and operations, normally have a single argument. For example, the relational inverse operator would have the type:

$$\_^{\sim} : (X \leftrightarrow Y) \rightarrowtail\!\!\!\!\twoheadrightarrow (Y \leftrightarrow X)$$

which takes an argument consisting of a relation between X and Y and returns a relation from Y to X. In this case the placeholder (or underscore) is put before the operator.

Version 1.2 of the **Z** draft standard introduced *fixity paragraphs*. These can be viewed as a picture of an operator with the argument slots (placeholders) made explicit. To declare the operator the specifier simply presents this picture. Such paragraphs can be used to augment the operator definition providing not only details of the position of placeholders but also parsing, precedence and associativity information for the operator. Fixity paragraphs have the form:

fixity [Category] Template

where category consists of either of the keyword **rel** (for a relation), **leftfun** or **rightfun** (for a function) followed, in the case of the latter two, by a precedence.

---

[20] The parentheses in this case are optional.

The template defines the operator name and its placeholders. For example, in the union operator:

fixity leftfun 30 _∪_

$$
\begin{array}{l}
[X] \\
\hline
\_\cup\_ : \mathbb{P}X \times \mathbb{P}X \rightarrow \mathbb{P}X \\
\hline
S \cup T = \{x : X \mid x \in S \vee x \in T\} \\
\hline
\end{array}
$$

and the inequality relation:

fixity rel _≠_

$$
\begin{array}{l}
[X] \\
\hline
\_\neq\_ : X \leftrightarrow X \\
\hline
\forall x, y : X \bullet x \neq y \Leftrightarrow \neg(x = y) \\
\hline
\end{array}
$$

The **leftfun** and **rightfun** keywords define the associativity of the function and together with the precedence can help resolve potentially ambiguous adjacent operator instances. For example, declaring the subtraction and multiplication operators with the following fixity paragraphs:

fixity leftfun 10 _-_ ;
fixity leftfun 11 _ * _

where 10 and 11 are the precedences, can help resolve instances such as:

1 - 2 * 3

Fixity paragraphs can also be used to build more complex definitions, such as allowing an argument slot (or placeholder) to take a comma separated list of expressions rather than a single expression. These more complicated definitions will not be covered in this book.

In the interchange language fixity paragraphs have largely replaced the previous *infundec* (infix function), *opdec* (infix relation) and *gendef* (generic definition) declarations. *infundec* was defined similarly to the *opdec* of relations having the format:

<infundec priority = ...> *function_name* </infundec>

with priority being given a value from 1 to 6, which related to the precedence of the operator. For example:

<infundec priority = 6> *plus* </infundec>

The new interchange format uses fixity paragraphs defined as:

<fixity category= firstarg= lastarg=> function name </fixity>

where category is set to either 'rel', 'leftfun' or 'rightfun' and firstarg and lastarg (first and last arguments) can be set to 'normal' or 'type'. Either or both of the arguments can be present depending on whether the operator is prefix, postfix or infix. For example:

fixity leftfun 20 *_power_*

would be declared as:

<fixity category=leftfun 20 firstarg=normal lastarg=normal>
power
</fixity>

and

fixity rel *_isodd*

would be declared as:

<fixity category=rel firstarg=normal> isodd </fixity>

Normally whatever arguments are present will be set to 'normal', unless generic instantiation is being used in which case the keyword 'type' is used. For more detail on this you should consult the standard.

6.6.15 Axiomatic declaration of functions

Many functions maintain a constant property from their input parameters to their output values. If the property of the mapping can be described in terms of an axiom, then the function can be given in an axiomatic definition. For example:

$$square: \mathbb{N} \rightarrowtail \mathbb{N}$$

$$\forall n : \mathbb{N} \bullet square\ (n) = n * n$$

Here the property is such that the output value is always equal to the square of the input parameter.

Exercise 6.19: Using an axiomatic definition, define *sum*, which given a sequence of natural numbers returns the sum of all its entries.

6.6.16 Lambda and Mu expressions

Operator	Text	Mathematical
Abstraction	lambda	λ
Mu	mu	μ
Separator	bull	$\bullet$

The Lambda operator in **Z** can be used for the specification of certain kinds of set-comprehension, in particular of ordered n-tuples. It has the form:

$$(\lambda \text{ Schema\_text} \bullet \text{Expression})$$

where the schema text introduces local variables, and possible constraints on these variables, whose scope is the expression. The parentheses are mandatory. An example of the use of the lambda notation would be with the square function we defined in the previous section. In the lambda notation, this could be defined as:

$$square \triangleq (\lambda n : \mathbb{N} \bullet n * n)$$

Mu-expressions define unique values. Their notation is the same, except that the expression and the separator following the schema text are optional. A Mu-expression is defined only if there is a unique assignment of values to the variables declared in the declaration which satisfy the constraint, otherwise it is undefined. An example of a Mu-expression is:

$$\text{Value} == (\mu x, y : \mathbb{Z} \mid x - y = 1 \land y = 2 \bullet x * y)$$

In the above the values assigned to x and y must be 3 and 2 respectively. The value of the expression is 6.

Exercise 6.20: Using a lambda expression define a function *decrement* which returns the value of its argument reduced by one for the set of natural numbers. Describe the equivalent set comprehension for this expression.

6.7. ADDITIONAL CONSTRUCTS

As well as the operators defined for each type, **Z** also has a set of general operators which are used to building predicates in schemas.

6.7.1 Conditional expression

The **Z** notation contains the **if** ... **then** ... **else** conditional expression familiar to most programming languages[21]:

if predicate **then** expression_1 **else** expression_2

which states that if the predicate condition holds then the expression evaluates to the first expression else the expression evaluates to the second expression. For example:

MaxInt

$x?, y? : \mathbb{Z}$
$maxi! : \mathbb{Z}$

$maxi! = \textbf{if } x? > y? \textbf{ then } x? \textbf{ else } y?$

which gives the maximum of two integers.

Use of the **if** ... **then** ... **else** construct is best avoided as it implies an explicit operation rather than a property. It is normally better to state the requirements using an implicit definition:

MaxInt

$x?, y? : \mathbb{Z}$
$maxi! : \mathbb{Z}$

$x? \leq maxi! \wedge y? \leq maxi! \wedge maxi! \in \{x?, y?\}$

Exercise 6.21: Using an **if** ... **then** construct write a schema which returns the non-negative difference of two natural numbers.

---

[21] In version 1.0 of the Z draft standard the if...then construct was temporarily changed to the format *If* predicate *Then* expression_1 *Else* expression_2 *Fi*, but was restored to its original form in draft 1.2.

6.7.2 Notational structuring expressions

Z allows local definitions within predicates by the use of the **let** statement, which has the form:

$$(\textbf{let } x_1 == E_1 \,;\, x_2 == E_2 ;\ldots;\, x_n == E_n \bullet \text{Predicate})$$

where $x_1 == E_1$; $x_2 == E_2$;...; $x_n == E_n$ represents a definition list. In the predicate immediately following the expression list all occurrences of $x_1,\ldots,x_n$ take on the value of their corresponding expressions $E_1,\ldots,E_n$. Thus x_1 represents E_1, x_2 represents E_2 etc. Within the scope of the predicate all occurrences of $x_1,\ldots,x_n$ can be thought of as being textually replaced by the expressions given in $E_1,\ldots,E_n$. The parentheses in the statement are mandatory to avoid confusion over which predicate the **let** statement applies to.

Let statements can be used to abbreviate lengthy expressions which are used more than once in an expression. For example[22]:

$$\begin{array}{l}(\textbf{let } \mathit{lsbyte} == \mathit{no?} \text{ mod } (2\uparrow 8);\ \mathit{byte2} == (\mathit{no?} \text{ div } (2\uparrow 8)) \text{ mod } (2\uparrow 8);\\ \quad \mathit{byte3} == (\mathit{no?} \text{ div } (2\uparrow 16)) \text{ mod } (2\uparrow 8);\ \mathit{msbyte} == \mathit{no?} \text{ div } (2\uparrow 24)\\ \quad \bullet\ \mathit{word} = \langle \mathit{lsbyte}, \mathit{byte2}, \mathit{byte3}, \mathit{msbyte}\rangle)\end{array}$$

Since the definitions defined on the left-hand side of each let expression are textual replacements, local to the expression, their types do not need to be defined and it is unecessary for them to be declared within the declaration part of a schema in which they are used. Thus if the previous let expression is declared within the schema:

```
── Convert ──────────────────────────────────
│ word! : seq ℕ
│ no? : ℕ
├──────────────────
│ (let lsbyte == no? mod (2↑8); byte2 == (no? div (2↑8)) mod (2↑8);
│       byte3 == (no? div (2↑16)) mod (2↑8); msbyte == no? div (2↑24)
│        • word! = ⟨lsbyte, byte2, byte3, msbyte⟩)
└─────────────────────────────────────────────
```

we would not declare *lsbyte, byte2, byte3* or *msbyte* in the declarations of the schema since these are notational replacements local to the **let** statement.

---

[22] This statement uses the power operator we declared earlier as an axiomatic definition. Z does not have a built-in power operator.

We can use a number of **let** statements to build up a complex construct in a series of steps:

```
(let rate == 15 •
    ( let tax == rate div 100 •
        ( let taxed_price == x + tax •
            if  taxed_price < 200 then
              (let  postage == 20  • taxed_price + postage)
            else
              taxed_price
)))
```

Recent versions of the draft standard (versions 1.0 and 1.2) have not included let statements, instead they have incorporated the more powerful *substitution operator* '⊙':

Operator	Text	Mathematical
Left binding bracket	lbind	⦉
Right binding bracket	rbind	⦊
Substitution operator	subs	⊙

This is used in the form:

$$⦉\, v_1{:=}E_1,\ v_2{:=}E_2, \ldots, v_n{:=}E_n\, ⦊ \odot St$$

where $⦉\, v_1{:=}\ E_1,\ v_2{:=}\ E_2, \ldots, v_n{:=}\ E_n\, ⦊$ is a binding list[23], and St the predicate, expression, declaration or schema to which it applies. Each bind represents an association of a variable name with a value. For example:

$$⦉\, a := x + 2,\ b := 3 ⦊ \odot a + b$$

The result in all cases is to replace occurrences of the variables in the statement on the right-hand side of the substitution operator by the appropriate expressions given in the binding list. Thus in the previous example the '*a*' on the right-hand side would be replaced with $x + 2$ and the '*b*' with 3 giving:

---

[23] The symbol '⇝' was considered as being used instead of the ':=' operator but was dropped in favour of the latter symbol.

$$x + 2 + 3$$

Whilst substitutions are more powerful than let statements and can be used in areas where let statements cannot, such as declarations, let expressions are so ingrained within the language that it is difficult to see them being replaced entirely by this new construct and there may be some resistance to this by the user community. It seems likely from the current standards work that the construct will be reintroduced (version 1.2 of the draft makes mention of the possibility of this). They are also still used in many of the tools available for Z. For this reason let expressions, rather than substitutions, are used in the rest of this chapter.

Exercise 6.22: How might the following schema which squares the value of the top of a sequence be better expressed using a let statement?

SquareTop

numlist, numlist': **seq** ℕ

---

numlist' = ⟨*head numlist* * *head numlist*⟩ ⁀ *tail numlist*

6.7.3 Theta expressions

Theta expressions can be used to bind variables to distinct values in expressions.

Operator	Text	Mathematical
theta	thetas	Θ

The Theta expression is used in a binding formation:

ΘSchema_name

to form a binding whose type is constructed from the signature of the schema and whose value is the binding constructed from the mapping of the names of the signature to their values in the environment. The binding associates with each variable $x_1,\ldots,x_n$ in the Schema, denoted by the schema_name, the value of that variable currently in scope.

For example, given the compound terms:

```
___ Company_details ______________________
| company: NAME
| contact: NAME
| telno :TELNO
|__________________________________________

___ Person_details _______________________
| name: NAME
| telno :TELNO
|__________________________________________
```

DETAILS ::= pd⟨⟨Person_details⟩⟩ | cd⟨⟨Company_details⟩⟩

we can declare:

```
| mk_details1: (NAME × TELNO) → DETAILS
|__________________________________________
| ∀name:NAME; telno:TELNO •
|       mk_details1(name, telno) = pd(θPerson_details)
```

and:

```
| mk_details2: (NAME × NAME × TELNO) → DETAILS
|__________________________________________
| ∀company : NAME; contact : NAME; telno : TELNO •
|    mk_details2(company, contact, telno) = cd(θCompany_details)
```

which can be used to put values into these compound terms. A Theta expression can thus be used in a way similar to the record constructor (*mk-*) in **VDM**, instantiating a type with particular values. It is important to note that the binding formation does not itself declare any variables; all the names referenced in the Schema_name must be in the scope. The Theta operator is also sometimes used with decorated schema names:

θSchema_name'

In this context the binding denotes a binding which is the same as that of the undecorated schema, but the value of which is determined by the decorated variables (x') currently in scope.

An example of its use in this context is given in the **Z** standard which defines the Ξ schema convention as:

```
    ΞState  ________________________________
   | State
   | State'
   |________________________
   | θState = θState'
   |____________________________________________
```

which asserts that the binding *State* is the same as *State'*.

A Theta expression is a way of identifying a binding. Such a binding can only be constructed from the variables in the scope if for each named element in the binding there is the same name in the environment denoting the same element. Theta expressions, though useful, are not commonly used in **Z** specification and there are normally other ways of expressing their properties.

6.8. PUTTING IT ALL TOGETHER

Having looked at the constructs available in **Z** we now need to examine how to develop specifications. We will look at a number of small **Z** specifications which should help clarify the processes involved in developing them.

6.8.1 Example 1 - Date

One useful data structure to define is DATE, giving the day, month and year. We first have to define what format we require our date in. Suppose we decide upon dd mm yyyy where each of these represents a number; for example, 12th April 1994 would be represented as:

12 4 1994

We decide also that whether or not we have trailing zeroes is unimportant as this can be determined in the output. Our initial suggestion for DATE might be:

```
    DATE  ________________________________
   | day : 1 .. 31
   | month : 1 .. 12
   | year : 1900 .. 9999
   |____________________________________________
```

This, though, would allow invalid dates such as 30th February. We require constraints on the day type. If the month is January, March, May, July, August, October or December then the range of day type is correct.

However, if the month is April, June, September or November then the day type must be restrained to thirty days. February is even more difficult in that it is 28 days normally and 29 days every leap year.

Our first statement can declare that providing the month is not one of those with less than 31 days we can leave the day field alone:

$$month \notin \{2, 4, 6, 9, 11\}$$

If the month is one with thirty days we need to constrain the day type to this range:

$$month \in \{4, 6, 9, 11\} \wedge day \leq 30$$

Finally, we need to define two predicates stating the number of days in February depending on whether it is or is not a leap year:

$$\begin{aligned} month &= 2 \wedge \neg leap\_year(year) \wedge day \leq 28 \vee \\ month &= 2 \wedge leap\_year(year) \wedge day \leq 29 \end{aligned}$$

This requires an additional schema *leap_year* which returns true if it is a leap year:

$$leap\_year\_ : \mathbb{P}(\mathbb{N})$$

$$\forall year{:}1900..9999 \bullet leap\_year(year) \Leftrightarrow (year \ \mathbf{mod}\ 4 = 0) \wedge (year \ \mathbf{mod}\ 100 \neq 0 \vee year \ \mathbf{mod}\ 400 = 0)$$

We can now define DATE again, this time with our alterations:

DATE

$day : 1 \mathrel{..} 31$
$month : 1 \mathrel{..} 12$
$year : 1900 \mathrel{..} 9999$

$month \notin \{2, 4, 6, 9, 11\} \vee$
$month \in \{4, 6, 9, 11\} \wedge day \leq 30 \vee$
$month = 2 \wedge \neg leap\_year(year) \wedge day \leq 28 \vee$
$month = 2 \wedge leap\_year(year) \wedge day \leq 29$

This example shows the importance of considering all eventualities when defining schemas.

6.8.2 Example 2 – Radiation safety interlock system

We specify part of a safety interlock system designed to prevent radiation exposure of personnel. An interlock system:

a) ensures that all appropriate radiation areas are clear of personnel prior to the use of radiation sources,
b) prevents personnel from entering areas where radiation levels exceed certain limits, and
c) ensures that should anyone enter an area where there is significant radiation their exposure is minimal.

It is necessary to control entry not only to the experimental areas where radiation is produced, but also to adjoining areas where the levels of radiation may be significant due to leakage.

We will look at the first of these requirements, building a hypothetical system capable of determining whether rooms are clear of personnel before activation of the radiation source, and preventing activation if they are not. We assume there is some way of determining when people enter or exit a room. For example, personnel might carry magnetic badges which can be used to determine if a person has entered or exited a room. The doors would not allow access to anyone without such a badge.

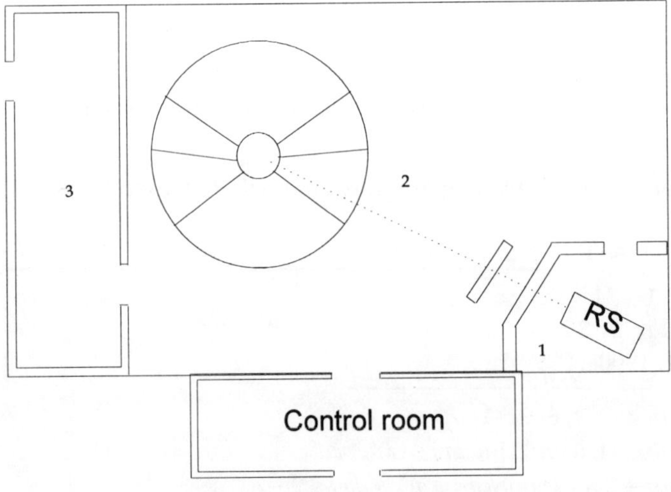

Figure 6.2: Plan of building

The radiation source goes through four phases:

1) Switched off: The radiation source (RS) is switched off and personnel are allowed to access any of the rooms.
2) Power up. The source is powered up and room 1 must contain no personnel, and the door must be locked.
3) Discharge. A beam is discharged into room 2. Rooms 1 and 2 must contain no personnel, and door access to room 2 denied.
4) Full activation. Rooms 1 and 2 and the adjoining room 3 must be free of personnel.

In order to ensure that all appropriate radiation areas are clear of personnel prior to the use of radiation sources we need to keep a record of the number of people in each room. We also need to know what the status of the system is to prevent access to particular rooms depending on the status of the system. We can define the status of the radiation source as a free type:

STATUS ::= Switched_off | Power_up | Discharge | Fully_activated

We also define the status of the doors which are either Open (allowing access) or Locked. When a door is Locked it prevents access to the room, even with a badge, but does not prevent someone leaving the room:

DOORS ::= Open | Locked

We define a constant representing the number of roooms:

$$\begin{array}{|l} number\_of\_rooms : \mathbb{N}_1 \\ \hline number\_of\_rooms = 3 \end{array}$$

We now define the state of the system, defining a sequence of elements *number_in_room* holding the number of people present in each room, and a sequence *doors* representing the set of doors associated with each room. We also need to define the status of the radiation source:

State

$$\begin{array}{|l} number\_in\_room : \mathbf{seq}_1\,\mathbb{N} \\ doors : \mathbf{seq}_1\,\mathrm{DOORS} \\ status\_of\_system : \mathrm{STATUS} \\ \hline \#number\_in\_room = number\_of\_rooms \\ \#doors = number\_of\_rooms \end{array}$$

Notice that although there may be a number of doors associated with each particular room we have not stated individual doors at this stage. Since the state of the system is that either *all* the doors associated with a room are open, or they are all locked there is no need to compose to the lower level of abstraction of individual doors. In fact, doing so at this stage would add unwanted detail.

The initial state of the system will be that all the rooms are empty, the system is switched off and all doors open:

```
── Init ──────────────────────────────
│ State
├──────────────────
│ ran number_in_room = {0}
│ ran doors = {Open}
│ status_of_system = Switched_off
└──────────────────────────────────────
```

If a person enters a room the number of people in that room is incremented:

```
── Enter_room ────────────────────────
│ ΔState
│ room_no? : ℕ
├──────────────────
│ doors(room_no?) = Open
│ number_in_room' = number_in_room ⊕
│         {room_no? ↦ number_in_room(room_no?) + 1}
│ doors' = doors
│ status_of_system' = status_of_system
└──────────────────────────────────────
```

The schema states that a person can only enter a room if the relevant doors are open. This allows us to add error conditions such as the situation where someone enters a room that is supposed to be sealed, for example because the door has jammed open.

Note that we have to define that the status of the system and the doors are unaffected by this schema. If we did not do this, the value of the system status or the doors could change to any arbitrary value. An alternative way of overcoming this problem is to define two state schemas; one for the status of the rooms and doors (*RoomState*) and one for the status of the system (*SystemState*). We would then include only the relevant state(s) used by a schema and would not need to define the state of variables not used by the schema. For example, the previous schema would only include the *RoomState* in its declarations.

If a person leaves a room then the number of people in that room is decremented:

Leave_room

$\Delta State$
$room\_no?: \mathbb{N}$

$number\_in\_room' = number\_in\_room \oplus$
$\quad \{room\_no? \mapsto number\_in\_room(room\_no?) - 1\}$
$doors' = doors$
$status\_of\_system' = status\_of\_system$

Note that the state is changed by the schemas so it is prefixed by a Delta in both cases.

We can now describe the operations of changing the status of the radiation source. In order for the unit to go from switched off to power up room 1 must be clear of personnel and the appropriate door locked:

Phase1

$\Delta State$

$status\_of\_system = \text{Switched\_off} \land number\_in\_room(1) = 0$
$doors' = doors \oplus \{1 \mapsto \text{Locked}\}$
$status\_of\_system' = \text{Power\_Up}$

In order for the unit to go from Power_Up to Discharge room 2 must be clear of personnel and the appropriate door(s) locked:

Phase2

$\Delta State$

$status\_of\_system = \text{Power\_Up} \land number\_in\_room(2) = 0$
$doors' = doors \oplus \{2 \mapsto \text{Locked}\}$
$status\_of\_system' = \text{Discharge}$

Note that we do not have to declare that room one is empty. In order to have reached Power_Up the room must already have been cleared and the doors locked.

Finally, in Phase3 we have to ensure that the adjoining room 3 is empty.

Phase3

$\Delta State$

$status\_of\_system = \text{Discharge} \wedge number\_in\_room(3) = 0$
$doors' = doors \oplus \{3 \mapsto \text{Locked}\}$
$status\_of\_system' = \text{Fully\_activated}$

On switching off the system we can make access freely available to all rooms:

Deactivate

ΔState

$\text{dom } doors = \text{dom } doors' \wedge \text{ran } doors' = \{\text{Open}\}$
$status\_of\_system' = \text{Switched\_off}$

We have now specified our system control. We have, however, not taken into account error and exception conditions. What is the response of the system if we attempt to power up whilst someone is in room 1? What happens is someone enters a supposingly sealed room? Provided we have built our system well, these situations should now be fairly easy to specify using Error! schemas.

6.9. WRITING SPECIFICATIONS

It is likely that you will develop specifications from a set of informal requirements. Whilst there is no specific methodology for the derivation of formal specifications from such requirements there are suggested ways of developing them.

Begin by looking at what sets and types are required by the system. These are often expressed as nouns within the description.

Having developed your types, look at the relationships between them. This can often be established by looking for verbs in the descriptions associated with the objects. If possible build entity relation diagrams explaining the relationships between the types. If the system is overly complicated consider initially developing it at a higher level of abstraction, and then concentrating on the detail later.

Consider the style of specification required, whether it should be developed functionally or in a state-based manner. If a state is required, then examination of the relationships at this stage should help you develop it. Look for any invariants of the system that can be described in the state. Define the initial state schema, keeping it as simple as possible.

Only then should you look at what the system is to do. Identify the operations required, again by looking for verbs in the description. Initially start by defining a system with no error conditions. Identify the basic subcomponents and partition the system into a set of distinguishable components. If a particular operation seems unduly complex consider whether you can break it down into smaller, more manageable parts.

Once you have developed a reasonable system start to consider any exception and error conditions that could occur.

Finally, keep the specification simple. The purpose of a formal specification is to aid programmers and developers, not confuse them. Far too many specifications have been written with the sole purpose of showing off the writer's knowledge. The word 'elegant' is a term often used by specification writers to describe a particular bit of a specification where the writer has come up with an ingenious method of describing some operation, often in a way that is shorter than that normally used. This is fine provided it enhances the clarity of the specification. Indeed the ability to think 'laterally' can often result in a specification that is far easier to understand. Too often, however, it simply makes it abstruse, resulting in a specification that can only be read by one person, the original specifier.

6.10. SUGGESTIONS FOR EXERCISES

1. Given two sequential lists, whose data is ordered in ascending order such that $x_i < x_{i+1}$, specify an implicit definition for a routine able to merge the two arrays into a third list, which is ordered in the same way, whose elements are a combination of the original two lists. Neither the original lists nor the resultant list should contain any repeating elements. The first two lists may, however, have elements in common. You are defining this implicitly, so define a property rather than an algorithm.
2. Consider how the queue example might be turned into a set of generic operators capable of being used with sequences of any type.
3. In the interlock system the doors associated with a room and the number of people in a room were declared separately. Consider how they might be combined using binding selection, and how this might affect the operations.
4. Soon after writing the interlock system a new room was added. Like room 3 this has one door connecting it to room 2 and another door connecting it to the outside world. Like room 3 it has to be empty when the device is at full activation. Think about how you would extend the specification to cope with this new requirement.
5. Define a simple integer calculator with the operations integer add, subtract, multiply, division, power and percentage. Include the ability to

clear the entire calculation and start again by pressing ‘C’. Add a memory to the calculator with the ability to put a value in memory ‘MS’, recall the value held in memory ‘MR’, add a value to the value in memory ‘M+’ and clear the memory ‘MC’. Expand the calculator so that it can convert a number to binary, and whilst in binary can not only perform the standard operations add, subtract, multiply and divide, but can also do the logical operations NOT, OR, AND, and XOR.

7

Formal semantics

In order to carry out verification, a method of formally stating what programming code *means* is required. Unfortunately this is difficult to do in a mathematical notation. Conventional programming languages are *procedural* and rely on *state*. Such concepts are difficult to define in pure mathematics. For example, the assignment statement found in many programming languages:

$$i := i + 1;$$

means that variable i is assigned a different value in the code after the statement has been executed from the value it had before execution. It takes on a new state. If the value of i was 2 *before* the statement then i would become the value of 3 *after* the statement. The variable i to the right of the assigment symbol represents i before the assignment, whereas the i on the left of the expression represents i after the assignment.

With mathematics a variable has the same value everywhere in an expression, there are no before and after states, so that we can only express:

$$i = i + 1;$$

However, mathematically this would mean:

$$2 = 2 + 1$$
$$\text{or } 2 = 3$$

which is clearly false.

In formal semantics it is necessary to take into account *states* and this has resulted in three different types of notation; *operational, denotational* and *axiomatic,* each suited to different purposes. In this chapter we will be mainly concerned with axiomatic semantics, discussing the other two only briefly. If the reader wishes they may skip the first two sections of this chapter and go straight to axiomatic semantics. The other two notations have only been included for completeness and will not be discussed any further in this book.

Axiomatic semantics are important because they can not only be used in verifying that the code we produce is correct but can also be used in program derivation to derive code from our formal specifications. This is discussed later in this chapter.

7.1. OPERATIONAL SEMANTICS

In operational semantics we are concerned with how *states* are modified during execution. We model execution of the code as a sequence of states run on an *abstract machine,* where there is some initial state before execution (regarded as input). Each statement transforms the current state into a new one and there is a final state (regarded as output) when execution ends.

The state of the system can be thought of as a function from a set of identifiers, or variable names, to a set of values stored in the variables. It can be seen as consisting of a set of ordered pairs in the form:

(identifier, value)

The state of a specification is a particular assignment of values to all variables defined in the specification.

For each construct in the language, we can define a function σ (the Greek symbol sigma) which describes how the current *state* is transformed by it:

$$\sigma\text{: Var} \rightarrow \text{Val}$$

where Var is the set of variable names in memory and Val the values held in the variables, thus:

$$\sigma(x) = \text{current value of variable } x$$

If, for example, variable x had previously been assigned a value of 5 then $\sigma(x) = 5$, that is, the current state of x would be 5. The symbol σ on its own without a variable name represents the entire computer store of the abstract machine. That is, *all* the variables held in memory.

Given a program P we define a state transformer to be a map from one state to another:

$$\mathcal{M}(\text{P}) : \text{state} \rightarrow \text{state}$$

where:

$$\mathcal{M}(\text{P})(\sigma)\downarrow = r,$$

means executing Program P on *initial state* σ leads to termination and *final state* r (the result). This is known as *convergence* (in most cases the downward-pointing arrow is not shown). On the other hand:

$$\mathcal{M}(\text{P})(\sigma)\uparrow$$

means executing P on initial state σ *does not* terminate – this is known as *divergence*. Note $\mathcal{M}$ is the function:

$$\mathcal{M}\text{:programs} \rightarrow [\text{state} \rightarrow \text{state}]$$

The character $\mathcal{M}$ can be thought of as representing the word *Meaning*. Thus, $\mathcal{M}$ is a function which represents the effect of the operation of the program on the state of the machine. Suppose we have the following programming code:

```
if x ≥ y
then null;
else x:=-x
endif;
```

We will define the operations in this code by operational semantics. Starting with the simplest command in the code, *null,* which does nothing:

$$\mathcal{M}(\text{null})(\sigma) = \sigma$$

The state after the operation of null is the same as the state before the command. Now we define the *assignment* statement:

$$\mathcal{M}(x := e)(\sigma) = \sigma[\text{v}(e)(\sigma)/x]$$

We substitute[1] the expression e for the value in x in state σ; where v(e)(σ) is the *value* of the expression $e \in \mathbb{Z}$ in state σ.

---

[1] Substituting one value for another is represented by a forward slash '/'; thus new/old means placing the value new in old.

For example, suppose the statement x := -x had been called with the value of x set to -2, then $\sigma(x) = -2$ and $e = -x$ resulting in $v(e)(\sigma) = -(-2) = 2$. Taking another assignment statement:

$$x := x + 1$$

where the current value of x is 3, then we would get the values $\sigma(x) = 3$, $e = x + 1$ and $v(e)(\sigma) = 3 + 1 = 4$.

If we now define the two commands, null and assignment, as P_1 and P_2 respectively we can define the if ... then .. else expression in terms of them:

$$M(\text{if } b \text{ then } P_1 \text{ else } P_2 \text{ endif})(\sigma) = \begin{cases} M(P_1)(\sigma), \text{ if } w(b)(\sigma) = tt \\ M(P_2)(\sigma), \text{ if } w(b)(\sigma) = ff \end{cases}$$

where b is the Boolean condition and $w(b)(\sigma)$ is the value of $b \in \mathbb{B}$ in the current state. The result is either P_1 applied to σ or P_2 applied to σ depending on the value of b. Loops are more complex; a while loop would be defined as:

M(while b do P_0 endwhile)(σ) = σ', (where σ' represents the new state).
if there exists a sequence $s_0, s_1, \ldots, s_n \in$ *state* such that
$\sigma = \sigma_0$; (initially σ is set to σ_0)
$\sigma_n = \sigma'$;
$\sigma_i = M(P_0)(\sigma_{i-1})$, $i = 1, \ldots, n$;
$w(b)(\sigma_i) = tt$, $i = 1, \ldots, n-1$; and
$w(b)(\sigma_n) = ff$.
otherwise
$M(\text{while } b \text{ do } P_0 \text{ endwhile})(\sigma)\uparrow$

where b is some Boolean condition and P_0 the action of the loop. This is probably best shown by an example. Consider the loop:

```
z := 2;
while z > 0 do
        z:= z - 1
endwhile
```

This is represented as:

M(z:=2; while z > 0 do z:= z - 1 endwhile)(σ),
= M(while z > 0 do z:= z - 1 endwhile)(σ) M(z:=2;)(σ))
= M(while z > 0 do z:= z - 1 endwhile)(σ[2/z])
= M(while z > 0 do z:= z - 1 endwhile)(M(z:= z - 1)(σ[2/z])
= M(while z > 0 do z:= z - 1 endwhile)(σ[1/z])
= M(while z > 0 do z:= z - 1 endwhile)(M(z:= z - 1)(σ[1/z])
= M(while z > 0 do z:= z - 1 endwhile)(σ[0/z])
= σ[0/z]

So the final state is the initial state with the value of z replaced by 0.

7.2. DENOTATIONAL SEMANTICS

As with operational semantics an abstract machine representation is used with denotational semantics. Denotational semantics model execution by defining for each program a function which states the value denoted by that program (i.e. its final state) when executed on an initial state. Denotational semantics are similar to operational semantics *except there are no intermediate states - execution is functional;* the history of the program's execution is therefore not represented as it is in operational semantics. Denotational semantics are concerned *only* with the *effect* of constructs; unlike their operational semantic counterparts which are also concerned with *how* the effect is produced. The effect of a construct is seen through an association between the initial and the final states.

The function M (the meaning function) transforms a denotation (a program or program fragment) into a function from input to output:

$$M\text{:[programs]} \rightarrow \text{state} \rightarrow \text{state}$$

A program is represented by the mapping:

$$\text{Program: Input} \rightarrow \text{Output}$$

Again, *state* is seen as representing a model of the store (that is, all values held in memory in the abstract machine). Computer store can thus be modelled as:

$$\text{State} = \text{Location} \rightarrow \text{Value}$$

which given a *location* will return the value stored in it. We again represent the operation *state* by the Greek symbol sigma 'σ':

$$\sigma : \text{Location} \rightarrow \text{Value}$$

where σ represents the value of the entire store and σ(x) represents the value held at location x. Suppose we take the code:

1. x := 2;
2. y := 6;
3. x := x + y;

We define identifiers (Id) by a mapping normally called the *environment* which associates with each identifier a corresponding storage location:

$$\text{Environment} = \text{Id} \rightarrow \text{Location}$$

If we represent the operation *environment* by the Greek symbol rho 'ρ':

$$\rho : \text{Id} \rightarrow \text{Location}$$

the meaning of an identifier is its corresponding storage location:

$$M : \text{Environment}$$
$$M[\text{Id}]\rho \triangleq \rho(\text{Id})$$

where'≜' represents '*is defined as*'. It states that the *meaning of an identifier is its corresponding storage location*. Thus *M*[*x*]ρ would return *x*'s location.

Since state 'σ' represents a model of the entire store, we need to be able to access it in order to find the value held at the specified location. We can define a function called **contents** which returns the *value* of a *storage location*:

$$\textbf{contents}: \text{State}$$
$$\textbf{contents}(\text{loc})\sigma \triangleq \sigma(\text{loc})$$

Thus after execution of lines 1 and 2 of the programming code given previously **contents**(*M*[x]ρ) would equal 2 and **contents**(*M*[y]ρ) would equal 6.

The meaning of the expression x := x + y can now be expressed in the generalised description below where x is represented by id_1 and y is represented by id_2:

$$
\begin{aligned}
&M[id_1 + id_2]\ \rho\sigma \triangleq \\
&\qquad \textbf{let}\ loc\text{–}id_1 = M[\ id_1]\ \rho\ \textbf{in} \\
&\qquad \textbf{let}\ loc\text{–}id_2 = M[\ id_2]\ \rho\ \textbf{in} \\
&\qquad\quad \textbf{contents}(loc\text{–}id_1)\sigma + \textbf{contents}(loc\text{–}id_2)\ \sigma
\end{aligned}
$$

Firstly, the environment is used to give the storage location corresponding to each identifier, then the state is used to find out the value stored in each location; and finally normal arithmetic is used to add these two results together. The let notation in this expression is defined as:

let <Id> = <exp_1> **in**
<exp_2>

where *all* occurrences of Id in exp_2 are replaced by exp_1.

Denotational semantics abstract away from how the constructs are actually executed so it is easier to reason about them than operational semantics

7.3. AXIOMATIC SEMANTICS

In axiomatic semantics every construct in a language is associated with axioms which state what is true *after* a construct (or statement) has been executed, in terms of what was true *before* it was executed. The notation:

$$\{P\}S\{Q\}$$

means if execution of S is begun in a state satisfying P (i.e. P = *true*) then execution terminates in finite time in a state satisfying Q. This is termed *total correctness*. For example:

$$\{P \in \text{program}\}\ S \in \text{Compiler}\ \{Q \in \text{Compiled program}\}$$

If P is a *correctly written* program then after executing the compiler we get Q a compiled program.

The similar notation:

$$P\{S\}Q$$

means the same thing except S is not guaranteed to terminate. This is called partial correctness. Note the position of the curly brackets.

7.3.1 Axiomatic semantics in program proofs

There are a number of approaches to proving code using axiomatic semantics. In the following we will use a technique involving *weakest pre-conditions* (*wp*). Expressed in a state model this enquires that given some set of final states what are the corresponding set of initial states needed to produce these final states when transformed by a given program?

Given S and Q, where Q denotes the desired result of executing S, the predicate *wp*(S)(Q) can be defined as the set P of *all* states such that execution of S begun in $p \in P$ (p being some state in P) is guaranteed to terminate in a finite amount of time in a state satisfying Q. In this context the pre-condition is a condition that applies before S is executed.

```
                      statement S
(pre-condition P) ——————————> (post-condition Q)
```

Where *wp*(S)(Q) = P, then P must be a weakest pre-condition (*wp*) such that executing S on P will always give the required result Q in a reasonable time. This can be shown by the example:

$$wp(i := i + 1)(i \leq 1) = (i \leq 0)$$

which simply states that for the operation i:= i + 1 to give a result where $i \leq 1$ would require that the value of i be less than or equal to zero before executing the command.

You will notice that the pre-condition is $i \leq 0$ and not for example i = 0 or i = -1. This is to make the pre-condition as general as possible. It can be seen that i = 0 and i = -1 would both be contained within the pre-condition $i \leq 0$. The pre-condition we are trying to make is the set of *all* states such that execution will terminate with the correct result. Let us now take the program code:

```
if x = y
then null;
else x:=y
endif;
```

If we start with the simplest command null:

$$wp(\text{null})(Q) = Q$$

Obviously, since null does nothing the weakest pre-condition to give the resultant state Q is Q. Now taking the assignment statement, where x is a variable and E is an expression *of the same type*:

$$wp(x := E)(Q) = Q[E/x]$$

Here we are saying for the execution of the assignment statement x := E to guarantee the post-condition Q, the predicate Q with all *free occurrences* of x *simultaneously* replaced by E must have held directly before the assignment was executed (represented by Q[E/x]). This idea is probably best explained in a graphical representation (Fig. 7.1).

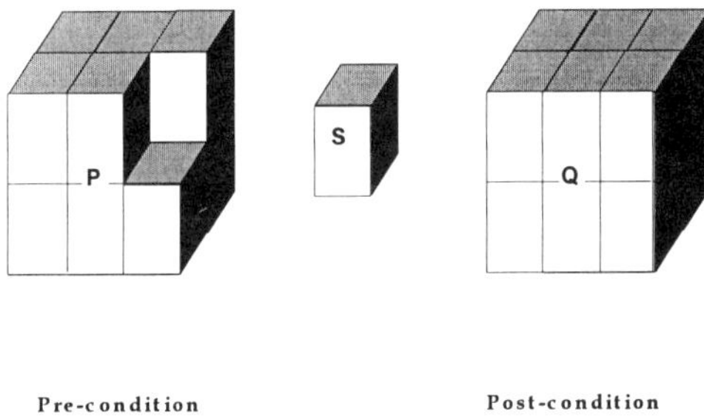

Figure 7.1: Example of pre-condition

If after being given one cube (S – the statement) you have exactly 12 cubes (Q – the post-condition) what is the weakest pre-condition necessary for you to obtain this state? Obviously, it would have been necessary for you to already possess 12 - 1 cubes; the pre-condition is the post-condition Q with the effect of S removed. Take, for example:

$$wp(x := x + 1)(x \leq 1)$$

To obtain the weakest pre-condition for an assignment statement we replace all occurrences of x in Q with the value being assigned to x (the expression part of the assignment). We therefore replace the x in the right-hand brackets (that is in Q) with the value assigned to x in the left-hand brackets:

$$wp(x := \underline{x + 1})(x + 1 \leq 1)$$

which gives a weakest pre-condition of:

$$(x + 1 \leq 1)$$

Moving the +1 over to the other side of the equation gives us:

$$x \leq 1 - 1$$

which translates as:

$$x \leq 0.$$

We now work on the if...then...else command. There are basically two conditions in the example given previously.

if x = y then null	(corresponding to the if ... then part of the statement).
if x ≠ y then x:= y	(corresponding to the else branch of the if statement)

We can therefore represent the if statement as a statement consisting of two Boolean conditions b_1 and b_2 corresponding to x = y and x ≠ y. For the operation to be complete (i.e. cover all circumstances) one of these Boolean conditions must be fulfilled. We define this with:

$$(\exists_i : 1 \leq i \leq n \bullet b_i) \text{ where } n = 2$$

which states that at least one of the Boolean conditions is fulfilled (that is, either x = y or x ≠ y).

If we now say that the command null is represented by S_1 and the assignment command x := y is represented by S_2 we can state that:

$$b_1 \rightarrow S_1 \text{ and } b_2 \rightarrow S_2$$

which states that b_1 implies S_1 and b_2 implies S_2. From this we can express the second condition:

$$(\forall_i : 1 \leq i \leq n \bullet b_i \rightarrow wp(S_i)(P))$$

which asserts that for all conditions, execution of S_i when b_i is true terminates with P true. b_i implies the weakest pre-condition for S_i.

This results in the complete condition:

$$(\exists_i : 1 \leq i \leq n \bullet b_i) \wedge (\forall_i : 1 \leq i \leq n \bullet b_i \rightarrow wp(S_i)(P))$$

We can use this generalised form to give the weakest pre-condition for the example if statement where we want x to equal y at the end:

$$(x \neq y \vee x = y) \wedge (x = y \rightarrow wp(\text{null})(x = y) \wedge x \neq y \rightarrow wp(x{:=}y)(x = y))$$

we can now substitute in:

1. $tt \wedge (x = y) \rightarrow wp(\text{null})(x = y) \wedge x \neq y \rightarrow wp(x{:=}y)(x = y)$
2. $(x = y) \rightarrow wp(\text{null})(x = y) \wedge x \neq y \rightarrow wp(x{:=}y)(x = y)$
3. $(x = y) \rightarrow (x = y) \wedge x \neq y \rightarrow wp(x{:=}y)(x = y)$
4. $tt \wedge x \neq y \rightarrow wp(x{:=}y)(x = y)$
5. $x \neq y \rightarrow (y = y)$
6. $x \neq y \rightarrow tt$
7. $\neg(x \neq y) \vee tt$
8. tt

In step 1 the rule $(x \neq y \vee x = y)$ is a *tautology* (since it is basically $a \vee \neg a$). It can therefore be replaced with the value true.

In step 2 we use a logic rule *and simplification* (discussed in Chapter 2) to eliminate the first clause.

In step 3 the weakest pre-condition for the null command such that $x = y$ after execution is that $x = y$ before the command.

In step 4 we can find the weakest pre-condition for $wp(x{:=}y)(x = y)$. This reduces to true in step 6. We use *material implication* to convert this to the formula in step 7, and use then use *or simplification* to give us the final result. What we are left with is *tt*.

Since we have been able to reduce the equation to true we have proved the code will work in *all* circumstances (all initial states) and is therefore *valid*. We now consider how we define a while loop. The loop structure is:

```
while b1 do
        S;
endwhile
```

where b_1 is some Boolean condition and *S* the body of the loop.

Suppose there is an assertion (condition) *P* such that it is true before the execution of *S* (the loop body) and is also true after the execution of *S*. Then we can state:

$$\{P\}\ S\ \{P\}$$

P is an *invariant* of the loop, its truth value is not changed by the execution of S and remains true before, during and after the execution of the loop.

If the loop terminates, it will merely execute S a finite n number of times where $n = 0, 1, 2, \ldots$. Repeated execution of S should leave P unchanged. The loop invariant will therefore often characterise the role of the variables in the loop.

For the loop to terminate b_1 must be false therefore we can add this to the post-condition:

$$\{P\} \text{ while } b_1 \text{ do S } \{P \wedge \neg b_1\}$$

For the loop to be correct the terminating condition must imply the required post-condition, therefore:

$$P \wedge \neg b_1 \rightarrow Q$$

Let us take an example loop which working with two natural numbers x and y copies the value y into x, giving the result that x is equal to y at the end of the loop. The pre-condition of this loop is that y is a non-negative number ($y \geq 0$), and the post-condition is that $x = y$.

```
{y ≥ 0}
   x := 0;
{y ≥ 0 ∧ x = 0}
   while (x ≠ y) do
         x := x + 1
   endwhile
{(x = y)}
```

The while loop also requires a pre-condition that $x = 0$ and this can be fulfilled using the assignment statement:

$$wp(x{:=}\ 0)(x = 0) = \text{true}$$

The final pre-condition for the while loop is therefore:

$$(y \geq 0 \wedge x = 0)$$

Since the procedure must return natural numbers the full post-condition should really be:

$$\{(x = y) \wedge (y \geq 0) \wedge (x \geq 0)\}$$

We can use y ≥ x as the invariant P since it encompasses both the pre- and post-conditions. The terminating condition of $P \wedge \neg b_1$ would therefore be:

$$(y \geq x) \wedge \neg(x \neq y)$$

and we can say:

$$(y \geq x) \wedge \neg(x \neq y) \rightarrow (x = y)$$

Using the rewrite rules given in Chapter 2:

$(y \geq x) \wedge (x = y) \rightarrow (x = y)$ *Double Negation*

Intuitively we can see that $(y \geq x) \wedge (x = y)$ must mean that x = y giving:

$$(x = y) \rightarrow (x = y)$$

and this can then be rewritten to true:

$\neg(x = y) \vee (x = y)$ *Implication Rule*
tt *Excluded Middle*

We have thus proved that *with a pre-condition of* y ≥ 0 on successful termination the loop will give the correct results. We now have to prove the loop will always terminate.

To ensure the loop will terminate successfully we also have to state a *variant* or *bound* function (represented by t). This function must reduce its value with every iteration of the loop ultimately reducing to a value which implies, when in conjunction with the invariant, that the loop will be exited.

In the example loop the bound function chosen is (y - x). Since x increases by 1 with each iteration this function will ultimately equal zero when x = y, which is the point at which the while condition b_1 terminates the loop. That is:

$$P \wedge t \rightarrow \neg b_1$$

as in the example:

$$(y \geq x) \wedge (y - x = 0) \rightarrow \neg(x \neq y)$$

which translates as:

$$(y \geq x) \wedge (y - x = 0) \rightarrow x = y$$

We have now shown the loop to be valid.

As well as the previous constructs we also need to know how to combine a sequence of operations. If we have two operations S_1 followed by S_2 such that:

$$wp(S_1;S_2)(Q)$$

where the semi-colon is a statement separator. We can say:

$$wp(S_1)(wp(S_2)(Q))$$

For example:

$$\begin{aligned} & wp(x:=y;\ x:=x+1)(x < 2) \\ \equiv\ & wp(x:=y)(wp(x:=x+1)(x < 2)) \\ \equiv\ & wp(x:=y)(x + 1 < 2) \\ \equiv\ & wp(x:=y)(x < 2 - 1) \\ \equiv\ & wp(x:=y)(x < 1) \\ \equiv\ & (y < 1) \\ \therefore\ & wp(x:=y\ ;\ x:=x+1)\ (x < 2) = y < 1 \end{aligned}$$

7.3.2 Proof partitioning

Up to now we have seen how to prove small pieces of code. Since many specifications are normally in the form of pre- and post-conditions[2] this suggests a way of proving specifications are correct by stating:

{pre-condition} operation {post-condition}

If the operation is small this would probably be acceptable. Take for example, the following specification for a square operation:

SQUARE(x: ℕ)
ext wr res: ℕ
post res = x * x

This could be converted to the explicit code

res := x * x

and stated in the form:

{true} res:= x * x {res = x * x}

---

[2] Or can be derived in this form, for example, in Z by using the *pre* operator.

which can then be proved

$$\begin{aligned} & wp(\text{res:= x * x})(\text{ res = x * x}) \\ \equiv\ & (\text{ x * x = x * x}) \\ \equiv\ & \text{true} \end{aligned}$$

However, with larger operations it is better to break them down, or decompose them, into smaller logical subcomponents. These in turn can be broken down again until ultimately it is easy to write and prove each component.

To carry out this decomposition a new rule for sequencing needs to be introduced. If an operation S_1 satisfies the specification:

$$\{P_1\}\ S_1\ \{Q_1 \wedge P_2\}$$

and another operation S_2 satisfies the specification:

$$\{P_2\}\ S_2\ \{Q_2\}$$

that is, part of the post-condition of S_1 is the pre-condition of S_2. Then $S_1;S_2$ satisfies:

$$\{P_1\}\ S_1\ ;\ S_2\ \{Q_2\}$$

If we therefore start with the specification:

$$\{P\}\ S\ \{Q\}$$

and can split Q into two components Q_1 and Q_2, then we can also split S into two components S_1 and S_2 such that:

$$\begin{aligned} \{ P\}\ S_1\ \{Q_1 \wedge P_2\} \\ \{P_2\}\ S_2\ \{Q_2\} \end{aligned}$$

and still satisfy the original post-condition Q.

7.3.3 Program derivation using axioms

We have seen how we can use axiomatic semantics to prove that our programs model their specifications. The use of weakest predicates can also help us to derive code from formal specifications in a methodological way, helping us to develop programming code semi-automatically.

Proof partitioning allowed us to prove a piece of code, by breaking it down into smaller, more manageable parts. We derive code in the same way, breaking a large problem down into subproblems. These subproblems can then be broken down into simpler subgoals using progressive decomposition.

We know what the goal of our code is from the post-condition. We will also probably know the pre-condition required for this piece of code to operate. We can thus define:

$$\{P\}\ S\ \{Q\}$$

with P being defined as the pre-condition, S as the code we wish to develop and Q as the post-condition required. For example, suppose we take a MAX operation[3]:

MAX()
ext wr x, y : ℕ
pre $x = X \wedge y = Y$
post $x \geq Y \wedge x \in \{X, Y\}$

which given two values x and y returns the maximum of the two values in x:

$$\{x = X \wedge y = Y\}\ S\ \{x \geq Y \wedge x \in \{X, Y\}\}$$

we need to find the operation necessary to make:

$$wp(S)(\ x \geq Y \wedge x \in \{X, Y\}) = \text{true}$$

Rather than trying to find the weakest pre-condition for this predicate we start with a slightly weaker predicate for the post-condition:

$$wp(S)(\ x \geq Y) = \text{true}$$

There are two possible conditions that x can be before execution of the operation, either $x < Y$ or $x \geq Y$:

$$x \geq Y \vee x < Y = \text{true}$$

We therefore need to satisfy both of these cases with the operation. This suggests a conditional statement, such as an if ... then ... else or a case statement.

We take the first condition that of x already being greater than or equal to Y and state:

$$x \geq Y \rightarrow wp(S)(\ x \geq Y)$$

[3] We use capital X and Y to represent the values of x and y when the operation is called.

We then repeat the process with the second condition:

$$x < Y \rightarrow wp(S)(x \geq Y)$$

We do this until all the conditions in the pre-condition have been satisfied. In the above case there are only two conditions.

Taking the first condition where x is already greater or equal to Y we need to determine what we need to do to to make $x \geq Y$. Obviously, in this case we need do nothing and so can use the null statement:

$$\{x \geq Y\}\ \mathbf{null}\{x \geq Y\}$$

We have previously proved that:

$$wp(\mathbf{null})(Q) = Q$$

so we can say:

$$wp(\mathbf{null})(x \geq Y) = x \geq Y$$

We now take the second case where $x < Y$:

$$\{x < Y\}S\{x \geq Y\}$$

In this case we need to set x to a value that is greater or equal to Y. The easiest solution seems to be simply to make x equal Y, from which we can derive the statement:

$$\{x < Y\}x := Y\{x \geq Y\}$$

We now have two statements:

$$x \geq Y \rightarrow \mathbf{null} \wedge x < Y \rightarrow x := Y$$

We now need to look at the second post-condition conjunct that of $x \in \{X, Y\}$:

$$wp(\mathbf{null})(x \in \{X, Y\}) = x \in \{X, Y\}$$

The weakest pre-condition for the **null** statement such that $x \in \{X, Y\}$ is that x is already equal to one of these values. We know this to be true since the pre-condition of the operation states that x = X. The **null** command therefore does not need strengthening. Now we take the assignment statement:

$$wp(x{:=}Y)(x \in \{X, Y\}) = x \in \{X, Y\}$$

This gives us the weakest pre-condition:

$$Y \in \{X, Y\}$$

which again is true. We do not need to strengthen the assignment statement. This may not always be the case. For example, we may have defined the assignment to say x := Y + 1. Whilst this would have fulfilled the first condition, it would not guarantee the second conjunct and so would be unsuitable. We can now derive the programming code:

```
if x ≥ y then null
elseif x < y then x: = y
endif
```

Although this is a small example it does serve to illustrate how a problem may be decomposed into smaller subproblems.

Deriving iterative statements, such as **while** and **for** loops is more difficult. We have seen in the earlier section on proofs that we need to develop a loop invariant. This can then be used for the derivation of the loop body. A loop essentially is defined as:

$$\{P\}\ \textbf{while}\ b_1\ \textbf{do}\ S\ \{P \wedge \neg b_1\}$$

where P is the loop invariant, b_1 a Boolean condition (which must be false for the loop to terminate) and S the loop body.

We have seen that given a post-condition Q, then for the loop to terminate correctly the terminating condition of the loop must imply Q:

$$P \wedge \neg b_1 \rightarrow Q$$

There is no standard method of developing a loop invariant, but there are ways to assist the developer in creating one. Most useful loop invariants are derived from the post-condition of the loop. Since the loop invariant is true both before and after execution of the loop then both the pre and post states must be contained within the invariant. One way of developing an invariant is therefore to take the post-condition state and weaken it until it encompasses the initial pre-condition state. There are three main ways of doing this:

- **Deleting a conjunct**. If the post-condition consists of $A \wedge B$ we can delete one of the conditions leaving either just A or B.
- **Replacing a constant with a variable**. If the post-condition states $x \leq 20$ we can introduce a new variable to weaken it giving $x \leq i \wedge i \leq 20$.
- **Enlarging the range of a variable**. If the post-condition states $5 < z < 30$ we can weaken it to $0 < z < 100$, or in the case of $x = y$ weakening x by turning it into $x \geq y$.

Usually the form of the post-condition will suggest which of these to apply.

Let us examine the first of these methods, that of deleting a conjunct. If we take as an example a loop which decrements a value by one each time if it is too high until it lies within the specified range, we might define the operation as:

$$\{x \geq \text{LOWER}\}\ \textbf{while}\ b_1\ \textbf{do}\ S\ \{x \geq \text{LOWER} \wedge x \leq \text{UPPER}\}$$

where UPPER and LOWER are previously defined constants. We require the number to be above the LOWER limit both before and after the operation. We can therefore use this as the invariant:

$$P = x \geq \text{LOWER}$$

If this method is employed it is also often possible to obtain the Boolean continuation condition of the loop b_1 by simply using the inverse of the deleted conjunct. Since ($x \leq$ UPPER) was the deleted conjunct, then $\neg(x \leq \text{UPPER})$ becomes the Boolean condition b_1 which can be translated to:

$$\textbf{while}\ x > \text{UPPER}\ \textbf{do}$$

We can prove this is correct since we know that:

$$P \wedge \neg b_1 \rightarrow Q$$

Thus we can state:

$$\begin{aligned}
&x \geq \text{LOWER} \wedge \neg(x > \text{UPPER}) \rightarrow x \geq \text{LOWER} \wedge x \leq \text{UPPER} \\
\equiv\ &x \geq \text{LOWER} \wedge x \leq \text{UPPER} \rightarrow x \geq \text{LOWER} \wedge x \leq \text{UPPER} \\
\equiv\ &\text{true}
\end{aligned}$$

As an example of the second method (that of replacing a constant with a variable) suppose we take a function with a pre-condition that x = 0 and a post-condition that x = VALUE which increments the x by one until it equals the required VALUE:

{x = 0} **while** b_1 **do** S {x = VALUE}

We could introduce a variable called i which encompasses both the pre- and post-conditions:

$$x = i \land 0 \leq i \leq VALUE$$

This allows us to derive our invariant.

Using this method the Boolean condition b_1 of the loop can often be obtained by using the statement that the variable is not equal to the original constant which it replaced. For example:

while v ≠ c **do**

is the continuation condition of the loop, where v is the variable and c the original constant. Thus we can obtain the loop

```
x:= 0; i := x;
while i ≠ VALUE do
   i:= i + 1;
   x := i
endwhile
```

or alternatively in a for... next loop structure:

for i:= 1 **to** VALUE **do** x:= i

We have already seen the third method of enlarging the range of the variable in the proof example of a while loop where we enlarged the range of the variable y from y = x to y ≥ x. When using this method the Boolean condition b_1 of the loop can often be obtained by using the negation of the variable within its original unexpanded range. So the continuation statement of the loop in the example became ¬(y = x), or:

while x ≠ y **do**

In many cases a number of the techniques may need to be used to obtain the invariant. The suggested methods of obtaining b_1 whilst working in many simple cases may also not always be sufficient. Insight and intuition may suggest far simpler, more elegant predicates. These methods only offer assistance, and should not be followed slavishly.

We have obtained both the invariant and the continuation condition of the loop. It is also necessary to develop the variant or bound function. This is an integer function of the program variables that is monotonically decreased by at least one with each iteration of the loop. All loops that terminate correctly will always have such a function. This function will always involve variables from the invariant and can usually be derived from it, remembering that:

$$P \wedge t \rightarrow \neg \mathrm{b}_1$$

There is no universal way of obtaining such a function but assistance can be obtained by using processes similar to those used to obtain the invariant from the post-condition, only this time obtaining it from the invariant condition.

Only after we have developed the invariant and the bound function should the process of writing the body of the function be carried out. The body of the loop should be made to fit the invariant and bound function and not vice versa.

This chapter has only touched on the processes involved in proof and program derivation and the examples have been kept fairly elementary in order to illustrate the processes clearly. To understand all the processes involved requires much more detail. There are many books on these subjects which concentrate more fully on these aspects and a number of these are recommended at the end of this book.

8

Tool support

It is unlikely that without the support of automated tools such as compilers, high-level programming languages would be as widely used as they are today. In the same way as we expect tools for programming languages we can also expect automatic assistance with the development and refinement of formal specifications.

Many formal languages were designed with tool support in mind, such as **SDL**, **LOTOS**, **Estelle** and **RAISE**. In these cases the design of the languages went hand-in-hand with the development of tools to support them.

Different formal languages tend to have tools specialising in one particular area. There is sometimes good reason for this. Some languages may have more translation tools than others because they consist of structures that are easy to translate into current programming languages. Other languages may contain higher-level constructs which are difficult to translate without some degree of refinement, but are better able to cope with proof analysis.

It is worth considering what tools are available and what you wish to do with them when choosing a specification language for an application. The range of tools is changing rapidly so it is impossible to keep account of current developments in this book. However, many organisations produce reports in this field and it is worth obtaining details from these about current tool support. User groups (particularly for specific formal methods) are a useful contact. It is best to obtain advice about these tools from an impartial source as many tools are claimed to do far more than they are capable of doing. Amongst other things it is worth looking at the amount of code that a particular tool can support and whether it can cope with the size of code necessary for industrial applications.

There are three main areas in which tool support is given: the specification, proof analysis and development of implementations. We look at the various classifications of tools, examining what they do and in some cases the reasons why they are a necessary part of formal development.

8.1. EDITORS

An editor is likely to form the focal point of any formal development process. It is therefore a good idea when developing software to use an editor specialised in the particular notation you are using. Whilst most formal languages have the option of an ASCII text-based notation, a specification is often clearer when converted into the 'graphical' notation of the language.

Most formal languages have a specialised editor available. These usually have facilities such as document formatting and pretty printing. Some allow the specification to be represented in a number of formats, including in some cases graphical representations (**SDL**, **LOTOS** and **Estelle** all having these defined within their standards). This can often assist in comprehension of the specification.

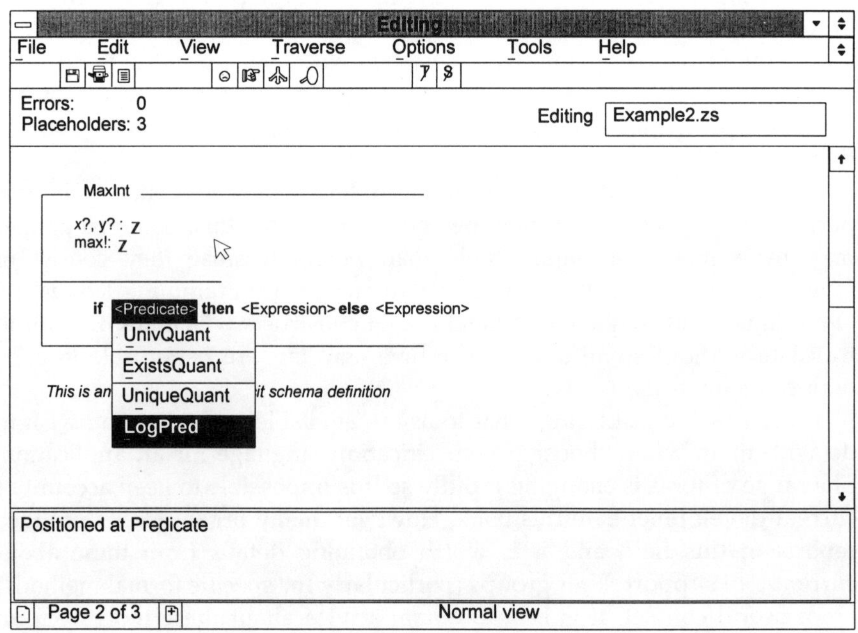

Figure 8.1: Syntax directed editor showing placeholders

Many of these editors are *syntax directed*. They have a knowledge of the language's syntax which is used to analyse text typed in, providing immediate feedback of syntactic violations. This immediate analysis allows instant reporting of errors as the specification is being edited. They can also perform other activities such as automatic formatting and indenting, removing many of the more mundane tasks in specification writing.

Such editors generally have two forms of input: the first allowing text to be typed in directly, the second providing structure editing where the user is presented with a series of templates (which provide predefined, formatted patterns for each of the constructs in the language) and placeholders. Placeholders in the templates serve as prompts, allowing further options (in the form of other templates) or text insertion. This enforces a view of the program as a hierarchical composition of structures. Specifications are created top-down by inserting new templates at placeholders in the skeleton of the previously entered templates (Fig. 8.1). In this way the user starts at the highest template and progressively refines down to the details within the program by choosing from a series of options.

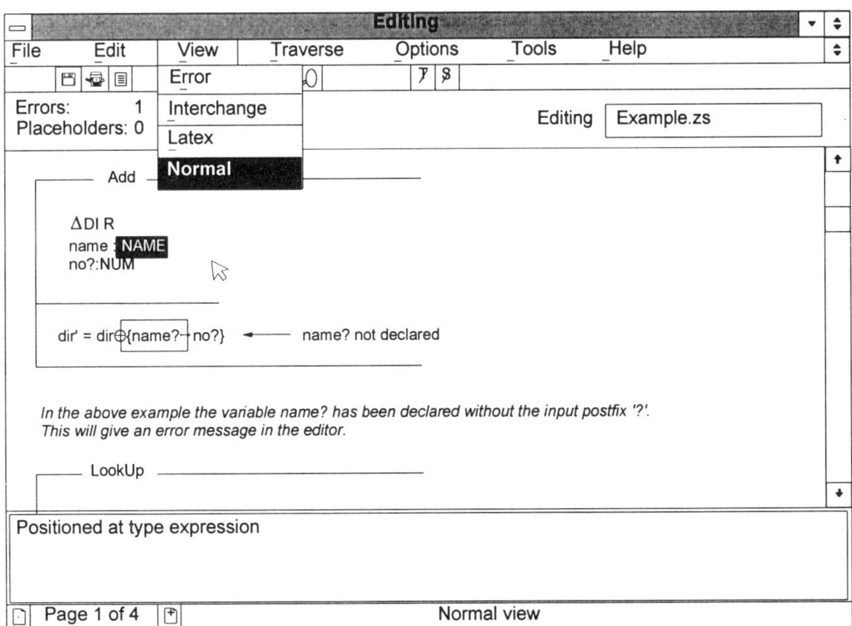

Figure 8.2: Example of a error checking with editor

Structure editing is particularly useful in the learning stage. Later on as users become proficient in the language it is quicker to type the text in directly rather than transverse the various options. The editor is still useful in preventing typing errors and mistakes checking the syntax as the text is typed in. Some editors also provide limited type checking facilities and other semantic analysis, for example making sure that a declaration is not given twice, or that a function is called without it having been declared (Fig. 8.2).

When forming part of a toolkit, the editor is likely to be able to present the specification in a way that can be used by other tools integrated with it, such as cross handlers (allowing modularisation), animators, translators, proof analysis tools and report generating tools. In the last area there has been some work on amalgamating formal specifications with *literate* programming, a programming idea by Knuth which amongst other things involves integrating code and documentation into one source file, the notion being that if the code needs to be separated from the documentation it can be extracted using purpose-designed tools. The code, however, can only be altered whilst in the original source file. The extracted code is static and unalterable. Thus you cannot update the code without updating the surrounding documentation and do not end up with documentation that is out of date as regards the source code.

8.2. PROOF ANALYSERS

It is unlikely that you will be able to carry out any degree of proof analysis without the use of proof tools. Proof analysis is very complex and for any reasonably sized program the number of transformation conditions generated is likely to be vast.

Tools in this area range from simple theorem provers to justification systems capable of applying meaning-preserving transformations to fragments of code. The latter can involve simplification and transformational tools such as algebraic simplifiers which reduce expressions to simpler forms. Confidence condition generators can also augment the process pin-pointing troublesome constructs such as division by zero.

Most proof tools are interactive, assisting rather than carrying out the full process of proof analysis. Users are therefore likely to require knowledge in both formal reasoning and detailed use of the tool. Because of the complexity of logic, fully automatic theorem provers capable of dealing with more than a few proof rules are unlikely. There are theoretical issues which seem to bear out this pessimistic view and until computers are able to have sophisticated domain-specific knowledge of logic and understand the concepts involved in an 'intelligent' way this is unlikely to change. Their use as support tools, however, is well established and a necessity for proof analysis of any but minor specifications.

8.3. SYMBOLIC SIMULATORS

Simulators, sometimes known as interpreters or animators, allow investigation of the properties of a formal description by symbolically executing the code directly. This does not involve normal 'dynamic' execution as we understand when we run a piece of software. Instead the code is statically analysed in such a way that at the end of execution the output variables are represented by expressions given in terms of symbolic values of input variables and constants. The results obtained are therefore algebraic rather than numerical values. If, for example, we took the following **Z** specification for converting a decimal value to a binary one:

```
 ___ DtoB ____________________________
| n? : ℕ
|______________________
| (let divisor == n? div 2; rem == n? mod 2 •
|     if divisor ≠ 0 then DtoB(divisor) ⁀ ⟨rem⟩
|     else ⟨rem⟩
| )
|_____________________________________
```

then animated it with a value of two as the input, it would give the result:

$$\text{DtoB}(\text{DtoB}(\langle(\text{n? } \mathbf{div}\ 2)\ \mathbf{mod}\ 2\rangle) \frown \langle \text{n? } \mathbf{mod}\ 2\rangle)$$

In order to understand how this result is obtained we have to look at how the schema would be called. In the first call n? would be equal to two:

$$\text{DtoB}(2)$$

The schema would calculate the divisor as 2 div 2 (which equals 1), and the remainder as 2 modulo 2 (which equals 0). Since the divisor is not equal to zero the schema is called again.

The remainder is concatenated onto the end of the value that will be returned by this schema call:

$$\text{DtoB}(1) \frown \langle 0\rangle$$

In the second call the value received by the schema is the divisor (which equals 2 div 2). This divided by 2 gives a divisor of zero. The remainder is therefore returned:

$$\langle 1\rangle \frown \langle 0\rangle$$

Certain specification styles, such as algebraic, lend themselves to symbolic manipulation by the use of techniques involving term rewriting, a technique involving the replacement of one equation by another. The specification languages **LOTOS** and **RAISE** both contain ways of specifying in terms of rewrite rules and are well suited to symbolic execution. However, many specification styles, such as those with pre- and post-conditions, involve constructs which are too abstract or implicit to be executed in this way since they do not provide enough information to enable animation.

Symbolic execution allows a more general form of reasoning than normal dynamic execution methods, being able to address all possible execution paths. Often they can detect redundant paths, contradictions and anomalies, and allow analysis of partial (incomplete) specifications (which has significant software development advantages allowing use in the preliminary design phases). They are also useful for generating test results, by substituting values for the symbolic values. For example, by using the equation:

$$\langle (n?\ \mathbf{div}\ 2)\ \mathbf{mod}\ 2 \rangle \frown \langle n?\ \mathbf{mod}\ 2 \rangle$$

and substituting two for the value of n?:

$$\langle (2\ \mathbf{div}\ 2)\ \mathbf{mod}\ 2 \rangle \frown \langle 2\ \mathbf{mod}\ 2 \rangle$$

We can generate the result, without actually running the program:

$$\langle (2\ \mathbf{div}\ 2)\ \mathbf{mod}\ 2 \rangle \frown \langle 2\ \mathbf{mod}\ 2 \rangle = \langle 1 \rangle \frown \langle 0 \rangle = \langle 1,0 \rangle$$

we can also calculate the required arguments to set certain bits:

first element
$x\ \mathbf{mod}\ 2 = 0$
$x\ \mathbf{mod}\ 2 = 1$
second element
$x\ \mathbf{div}\ 2\ \mathbf{mod}\ 2 = 0$
$x\ \mathbf{div}\ 2\ \mathbf{mod}\ 2 = 1$

where x is the value of the argument sent to the operation. If, for example, we wish to set the last two elements of a sequence to $\langle ...,1,1 \rangle$, we need to use a number which has the properties:

$$x\ \mathbf{div}\ 2\ \mathbf{mod}\ 2 = 1 \land x\ \mathbf{mod}\ 2 = 1$$

Values that fulfil this criterion can be generated automatically by use of a *numeric optimiser*. This is a program which given a symbolic equation automatically calculates and produces values that have the property of fulfilling the requirements of the equation. Thus an optimiser could be used to determine the possible values of x in the above equation. Such programs can be used to generate test data to investigate certain properties of a system.

Whilst symbolic methods work well for small problems, they tend to break down for problems of any significant size, producing an overwhelming amount of symbolic code.

8.4. TRANSLATORS

Translation or program synthesis tools are the compilers of the formal specification world, capable of generating programming code, or software implementations, from high-level specifications. At least that is the ideal. There are, however, theoretical and practical issues that have made it difficult to produce such tools. There is a trade-off between the generality of a specification style and its ease of compilation. Some constructs are too abstract for a machine to deal with without human assistance. For this reason most current translators require the specification to be refined to a reasonably concrete form before translation is possible, or require assistance from the operator in taking certain translation decisions.

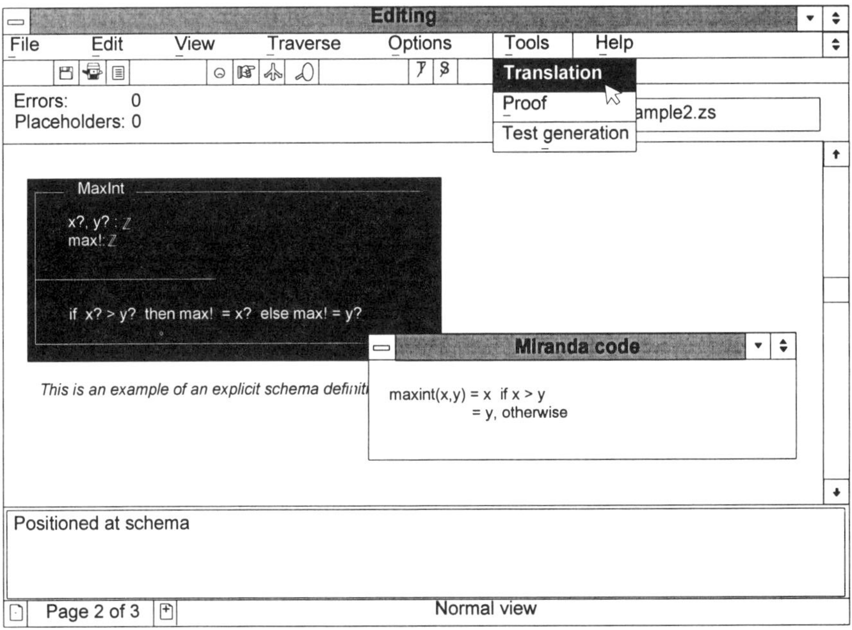

Figure 8.3: Example of code generation

It is unlikely that such tools will be able to produce code adequate enough to be commercially viable for quite some time, but they can be used to generate reference implementations or prototypes capable of being used to examine properties of the specification. This is particularly useful for verifying that a specification adequately reflects its original (informal) requirements and in the exploratory stage of design.

Automatically generating code from formal specifications could reduce the chances of errors occurring during the refinement stages, and if the rules of translation used by the tool were provably correct by formal means it would also remove the need for normal proof analysis since the resultant code would be guaranteed correct by virtue of the way it was produced (correct by construction). Currently, however, translation is still in its infancy and it is likely to be some time before adequate translation tools, let alone verified ones, are available.

8.5. TEST GENERATION TOOLS

Many protagonists of formal methods feel that testing of an implementation derived from a formal specification is unnecessary. After all, it is argued, is not the whole idea of formal methods such that the specification must be sound and therefore any implementation derived from it, using proof analysis, must necessarily also be correct?

Firstly, this attitude overlooks the fact that formal proofs only seek to prove that an implementation carries out the operations specified in the formal description. The formal specification will originally have been derived from an informal set of requirements, but because these original requirements were informal there is no way to verify using formal proof analysis that the formal specification accurately reflects the informal requirements.

Secondly, proof analysis tools are still limited in their ability to prove code. They are currently constrained by many theoretical and practical considerations. There is still difficulty in proving the translation stage where we are converting from one semantic base (the specification language's) to another (the implementation language's).

Thirdly, testing can analyse areas not encompassed in proof analysis. Normal analysis involves looking at whether an implementation of a specification carries out the operations specified. It does not check that it is not carrying out any additional (and possible subversive) activities. This is particularly relevant to security in a system. Testing, being a machine-based activity, also allows us to see the effect of the computer and software environment upon the implementation. We can thus examine areas which would not be covered by the original specification such as the effect of interrupts, exception handling, and errors due to the physical constraints of the hardware or software environment (for example, integer overflow).

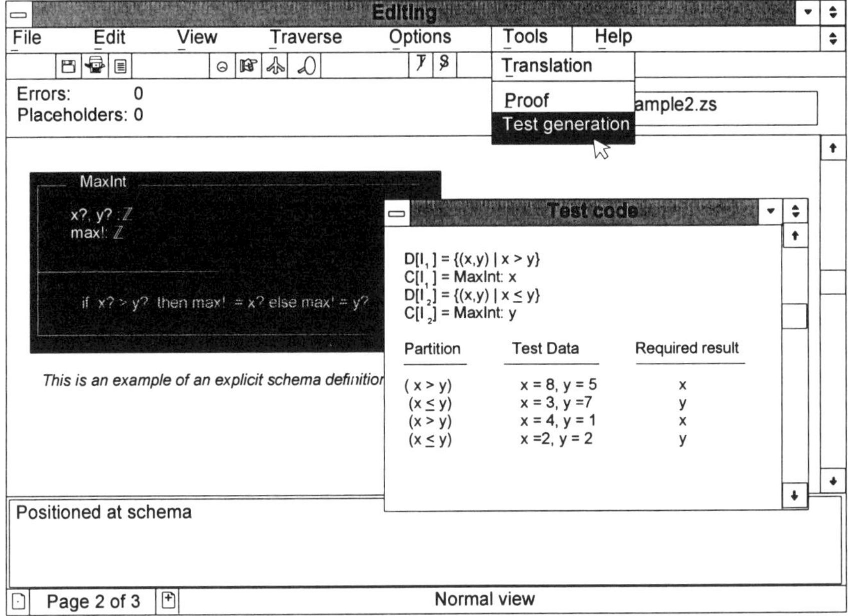

Figure 8.4: Example of test code generation

It is important not to overstate the value of testing. Testing can only be used to augment the formal process, it cannot replace it. The only dynamic testing method that would be capable of guaranteeing total validity of a program would be to create test data for every element of the input domain of the system. This is known as *exhaustive testing* and is not a practical option. With most programs the test data would be infinite or too large, and in terms of cost in memory and time requirements would be unfeasible to use. Even if we limited ourselves to an *adequate test set*, which would be large enough to span the domain, yet small enough to be of practical use, we still get problems as it has been shown that there is no way of determining the criteria necessary to produce such a set. Therefore test data can only help increase confidence in a system's correctness, not prove it totally. For test data to be useful in a formal methodology it should be derived using the original formal specification as a definitive reference. Developing data for dynamic testing involves two aspects; the selection of test input and the determination of the expected results (Fig. 8.4).

By directly animating the formal specification or producing a reference implementation that can be proven to be a correct implementation of the specification we can create an *oracle*.

An oracle is a source which for a given input description can provide a complete description of the corresponding output conditions. These referential results can be used to compare against the results from an implementation under test.

In this area simulators are particularly useful. Since the result of symbolically executing a program is an algebraic equation expressed in terms of the input values, it is fairly easy to substitute real values for the input variables and obtain actual values for the input and output. A *numeric optimiser* can then be used to determine these.

8.6. INTEGRATED ENVIRONMENTS

Many languages have fully integrated toolsets which incorporate most or all of the tools already mentioned. These are normally built around a central syntax-directed editor. Integrated development systems enforce precision and formality through the development stage. Because all the tools form part of an integrated system this assists in providing uniform documentation throughout the design, refinement and transformation stages. All the tools should also work together and on the same computer system, something you cannot always be sure of when buying separate individual tools.

8.7. EXECUTABLE SUBSETS

Although most specification languages contain constructs which cannot be made fully executable, due to their implicitness, it is possible in some cases to derive a subset of constructs which can be executed. Though this subset is generally less expressive than the language from which it was derived, due to the removal of the more abstract structures, it does allow small fragments of a code to be executed. Subsets exist for a number of languages, though generally they are seen as stand-alone languages and often contain extensions not compatible with the original specification language on which they were based.

The idea of fully executable specification languages has also been tried and there has been some success in specifying using functional and logic-based programming languages. Generally, though, fully executable specification languages suffer from a number of disadvantages over non-executable ones. Specifications have to be written explicitly and therefore tend to be more verbose (due to the extra precision required in defining explicit, rather than implicit relationships between inputs and outputs). Since functions are not defined in terms of pre- and post-conditions it is hard to determine the legality of inputs. Efficiency constraints also tend to restrict their power and they are generally less expressive with mathematical objects such as sets and lists, having to be restricted to finite representations in order to operate.

Because of their explicitness these languages tend to result in the user getting bogged down in operational detail far too early at the design stage. The result of this is that the specification is overly prescriptive and this can inhibit or prevent the development of other (possibly more efficient) implementations in the final version.

These languages (particularly functional ones) do, however, have value in prototyping. Because their level of abstraction is higher than that of normal programming languages, constructs often resemble the more explicit constructs in the higher level non-executable languages. Therefore less refinement and translation is required to convert to one of these languages than to a normal imperative one. For example, Fig. 8.3 shows an example of a piece of Z code translated into the functional language Miranda.

These languages are generally less efficient than normal programming languages and are therefore not usually suitable for providing the final implementation.

9

The future of formal methods

Formal methods at the current level of development are probably at the stage that programming languages were in the early 1960's. Such languages were cryptic, required much manual tinkering and had little tool support. Programmers were an elite group who used to talk in cryptic mathematical notations like hex and octal.

Compare this with the current situation. Most current programming languages now use structures similar to the high-level constructs of natural language. Modularisation has been incorporated with the result that code is more structured. There is also much more re-use and consequently less re-invention of the wheel. Many languages have also been standardised so that they can be easily interchanged without incompatibility problems.

In many areas, tools have been written to deal with the task of developing code for specific uses. It is unlikely anyone would now write a compiler by hand, rather they would use a compiler generator program. Nobody produces databases for a specific set of data without using a generalised database program that can be customised to fit the particular data involved.

Programming has also become a more common activity. Children are taught to program at an early stage and programming is taught on many courses from astronomy to zoology.

Now look at formal methods and we might well see similar processes developing.

There will probably eventually be standardisation of the formal notations. As the principles of formal specification are better understood this should reduce the number of notations, resulting in one or two notations becoming dominant. It is unlikely there will ever be just one formal notation, just as there is no single programming language. Different styles of languages are suited to different types of design.

As tool support improves and the cost of using formal design methods decreases it is likely that we will see formal methods used on less critical software. Anyone who has experienced the exasperation of a coffee machine giving a drink without a cup might look forward to the day when such a machine is defined formally. There are many areas which although not involving life-endangering situations could be improved with the use of formal methods, particularly of finance and commerce.

The notation used in formal methods is still very cryptic and needs improvement in presentation and style. The human brain is best at manipulating visual cues, rather than the abstract properties of mathematics. We visualise far easier than we abstract. For this reason there has been much research into ways of presenting formal methods graphically. Again we can look at program design where visual methods started with crude techniques such as flowcharts and have progressed to structured design methods incorporating many different views of the processes involved in programs (for example, entity relationship and data flow diagrams). Methods such as SSADM have developed visualisation to a fine art with a systematic development process. As similar notations become available for formal methods they should become more widely accepted and better understood.

Testing tools such as animators, editors and proof analysers may also improve with use of visual techniques. Instead of the normal animation techniques we might be able to see a visual representation of the structures running. For example, we could see values being placed on and off queues or stacks. This would allow us to better interrogate the structures we develop before turning them into programming code.

If these improvements come about, the day may come when nobody would think of writing any program without first writing a formal specification. Hopefully, you, the reader, will help to establish formal methods as part of the design methodology of software.

Appendix A

VDM-SL collected notation

The following pages gives a quick reference to the constructs of the **VDM** Specification Language (**VDM-SL**). The following shorthand is used:
S = Set, M = Map, Sq = Sequence, R = Record (composite type),
Tp = Tuple, F = Function, E = Expression, B = Boolean Expresion,
St = Statement, T = Type, N = Number, Id = Identifier,
Bd = Type or Set binding of the form Pt ∈ T or Pt : T, Pb = Pattern or Bind
Pt = Pattern (which can be an identifier, bracketed expression , set enumeration, set union, sequence enumeration, sequence concatenation, record, or tuple constructor).

Where two of these letters are placed together this infers a construct made up of the two, for example 'SS' represents a set of sets, and 'SM' a set of maps. A small 's' on the end of a construct indicates a multiple of this construct, so 'Bds' represents one or more bindings, and 'Ids' one or more identifiers. The lower case x and y represent variable names.

VDM specification

types
types definitions
values
value definitions
functions
function definitions
operations
operation definitions
state definition

Basic types

$\mathbb{B}$	Boolean
$\mathbb{N}$	Natural numbers
$\mathbb{N}_1$	Positive integers
$\mathbb{Z}$	Integers
$\mathbb{Q}$	Rationals
$\mathbb{R}$	Real
char	Character
token	Token

General type definition

Id = T
inv Pt $\triangleq$ B

Composite type definition

Id :: Id_1 : T_1
Id_2 : T_2
...
Id_n : T_n
inv Pt $\triangleq$ B

* *Composite types correspond to records.*

Product type definition

$T_1 \times T_2 \times \ldots \times T_n$

**Product types correspond to tuples.*

Union type definition

Id = $T_1 \mid T_2 \mid \ldots \mid T_n$

* *Union types correspond to enumeration types when the elements of the type are Quote types.*

Optional type definition

[T]

Literals

nil	Nil
true	Truth
false	Falsehood
"text"	Text literal
'x'	Character literal
QUOTE	Quote literal

Logic

$\neg E$	Negation
$E_1 \wedge E_2$	Conjunction
$E_1 \vee E_2$	Disjunction
$E_1 \Rightarrow E_2$	Implication
$E_1 \Leftrightarrow E_2$	Equivalence
$\forall$ Bds • B	Universal quantification
$\exists$ Bds • B	Existential quantification
$\exists!$ Bds • B	Unique quantification
ι Bd • B	Iota expression

Arithmetic

$E_1 = E_2$	Equality
$E_1 \neq E_2$	Inequality
$E_1 \times E_2$	Multiplication
$E_1 + E_2$	Addition
$E_1 - E_2$	Subtraction
E_1 / E_2	Division
E_1 **div** E_2	Integer divison
E_1 **rem** E_2	Integer remainder
E_1 **mod** E_2	Modulus
$x \uparrow N$	Power
abs E	Absolute
floor E	Floor
$x10\uparrow$	Exponent
$E_1 \leq E_2$	Less than or equal to
$E_1 < E_2$	Less than
$E_1 > E_2$	Greater than
$E_1 \geq E_2$	Greater than or equal to

Sets

T-set	
$\{E_1, E_2,...,E_n\}$	Set enumeration
$\{\}$	Empty set
$\{E \mid Bd_1,...,Bd_n \bullet B\}$	Set comprehension
$S_1 - S_2$	Set difference
$S_1 \cap S_2$	Set intersection
$S_1 \cup S_2$	Set union
$S_1 \subseteq S_2$	Subset
$S_1 \subset S_2$	Proper subset
$S_1 \in S_2$	Membership
$S_1 \notin S_2$	Non-membership
$S_1 = S_2$	Equality
$S_1 \neq S_2$	Inequality
$\mathcal{F}S$	Finite power set
card S	Cardinality
$\bigcap SS$	Distributed intersection
$\bigcup SS$	Distributed union

Maps

$T_1 \xrightarrow{m} T_2$	General map type
$T_1 \overset{m}{\leftrightarrow} T_2$	Injective map type
$E_1 \mapsto E_2$	Maplet
$\{ x_1 \mapsto y_1, ..., x_n \mapsto y_n\}$	Map enumeration
$\{ x \mapsto y \mid Bd_1,...,Bd_n \bullet B\}$	Map comprehension
$\{\mapsto\}$	Empty map
M^{-1}	Map inversion
dom M	Domain of map
rng M	Range of map
M(E)	Map application
$M_1 \overset{m}{\uplus} M_2$	Map union
merge M	Distributed map merge
$M_1 \dagger M_2$	Map override
$M_1 \circ M_2$	Map composition
$S \lhd M$	Domain restriction
$S \ntriangleleft M$	Domain subtraction
$M \rhd S$	Range restriction
$M \ntriangleright S$	Range subtraction
$M \uparrow N$	Map iteration

$M_1 = M_2$	Equality
$M_1 \neq M_2$	Inequality

Sequences

T^*	Finite sequence
T^+	Finite non-empty sequece
$[E_1, E_2,...,E_n]$	Sequence enumeration
$[E \mid Id \in S \bullet B]$	Sequence comprehension
[]	Empty sequence
$Sq(N_1,...N_n)$	Subsequence selection
Sq(N)	Sequence application
Sq † SM	Sequence modification
hd Sq	Head of sequence
tl Sq	Tail of sequence
len Sq	Length of sequence
elems Sq	Elements of sequence
inds Sq	Indices of sequence
$Sq1 \frown Sq2$	Concatenation
conc SqSq	Distributed concatenation

Composite type operators

*mk*_Id$(E_1, E_2,...,E_n)$	Record construction
R.Id	Field selection
μ(R, SM)	Record modification
$R_1 = R_2$	Equality
$R_1 \neq R_2$	Inequality

Product types

*mk*_Id$(E_1, E_2,...,E_n)$	Tuple construction
$Tp_1 = Tp_2$	Equality
$Tp_1 \neq Tp_2$	Inequality

Value definition

Pt : T = E

Function definition

Implicit

function_name (Ids_1:T_1, Ids_2:T_2, ..., Ids_3:T_3) Id:T
pre B
post B'

Explicit partial

function_name : $T_1 \times T_2 \times \ldots \times T_n \rightarrow T$
function_name (Id_1, Id_2, ..., Id_n) $\triangleq$
E
pre B

Explicit total

function_name : $T_1 \times T_2 \times \ldots \times T_n \stackrel{t}{\rightarrow} T$
function_name (Id_1, Id_2, ..., Id_n) $\triangleq$
E
pre B

**Explicit functions may be declared to be polymorphic in which case the signature is declared in the form:*

function_name[@Id_1, @Id_2, ..., @Id_n]: $T_1 \times T_2 \times \ldots \times T_n \rightarrow T$

where the identifiers in the square brackets represent the polymorphic types and some or all the types in the signature are declared in terms of these types: for example, get_element[*@type1, @type2*]: $\mathbb{N}$ × *@type1* → *@type2*.

Function operators and expressions

F(E_1, E_2,...,E_n)	Function application
$F_1 \circ F_2$	Function composition
F ↑ N	Function iteration
λ Pt_1:T_1, ..., Pt_n:T_n • E	Lambda expression
F[T_1, T_2, ..., T_n]	Function instantiation (polymorphic functions)

Operation definition

Implicit

OPERATION_NAME (Ids_1:T_1, Ids_2:T_2, ..., Ids_n:T_n) Id:T
ext rd Ids:T
wr Ids:T
pre B
post B'
errs Id_1 : $B_1 \rightarrow B_1'$
...
Id_n : $B_n \rightarrow B_n'$

Explicit

OPERATION_NAME: $T_1 \times T_2 \times ... \times T_n \xrightarrow{o} T$
OPERATION_NAME (Id_1, Id_2,..., Id_n) $\triangleq$
E
pre B

**Where there are no parameters, brackets can be used in the signature to indicate this, thus :() $\xrightarrow{o}$ () might be the signature of an operation which does not take or return any parameters, but reads and writes only to external variables.*

State definition

state Id **of**
Id_1 : T_1
Id_2 : T_2
...
Id_n : T_n
inv Pt $\triangleq$ B
init Pt $\triangleq$ B
end

State related

$\overleftarrow{Id}$	Old state

**In an assigment Id must be a state variable or a local variable introduced by a declaration preamble.*

Local binding

let Pt : T = E **in** E	Let expression
let Pt : T = E **in** St	Let statement
let Bd **be st** E in E	Let be expression
let Bd **be st** E in St	Let be statement
def $Pb_1 = E_1, \ldots, Pb_n = E_n$ **in** E	Def expression
def $Pb_1 = E_1, \ldots, Pb_n = E_n$ **in** St	Def statement

Conditionals

If expression

if B **then** E
elseif B_1 **then** E_1
elseif B_2 **then** E_2
...
elseif B_n **then** E_n
else E

If statement

if B **then** St
elseif B_1 **then** St_1
elseif B_2 **then** St_2
...
elseif B_n **then** St_n
else St

Cases expression

cases B:
$B_1 \rightarrow E_1$,
$B_2 \rightarrow E_2$,
...
$B_n \rightarrow E_n$,
others $\rightarrow$ E
end

Cases statement

cases B:
$B_1 \rightarrow St_1$,
$B_2 \rightarrow St_2$,
...
$B_n \rightarrow St_n$,
others $\rightarrow$ St
end

Loops

for Pb **in** E **do** St	Sequence for loop
for Pt **in reverse** E **do** St	Sequence for loop (reverse)
for all Pt $\in$ E **do** St	Set for loop
for Id = E **to** E **do** St	Index for loop
for Id = E **to** E **by** E **do** St	Index for loop (with increment)
while E **do** St	While loop

Assignment statements

Id := E	Assignment
dcl Id : T := E; St	Declaration preamble

Exception handing statements

always St **in** St	Always statement
trap Pb **with** St **in** St	Trap statement
tixe {$Pb_1 \mapsto St_1$,..., $Pb_n \mapsto St_n$} **in** St	Recursive trap statement
exit E	Exit expression

Miscellaneous

is-T	Is of type
$\|\|(St_1, St_2,...,St_n)$	Non-deterministic statement
skip	Identity statement
return E	Return statement
;	Separator
(St_1; St_2; St_n)	Compound statement

Comments

In-line comment

-- comment (terminated by newline)

Multi- line comment

annotations
comment
comment
...
comment
end annotations

Appendix B

VDM syntax

The following pages give the syntax for the VDM-SL notation written in a pseudo-BNF format. The grammar used to describe the syntax employs the following special symbols:

, The concatenate symbol,
| Definition separator symbol, can be seen as representing choice,
[] Options brackets, encloses optional syntactic objects,
{} Encloses syntactic objects which may occur zero or more times,
'' Single quotes used to enclose terminal symbols,
- Subtraction from a set of terminals.

Document

Definition Block, {Definition Block}

Definition Block

Type Definitions
| State Definition
| Value Definitions
| Function Definitions
| Operation Definitions

Type Definitions

'**types**' Type Definition, {';', Type Definition}

Type Definition

Identifier '=' Type, [Invariant]
| Identifier, '::', Field List, [Invariant]

Type

Bracketed Type
| Basic Type
| Quote Type
| Composite Type
| Union Type
| Product Type
| Optional Type
| Set Type
| Sequence Type
| Map Type
| Partial Function Type
| Type Name
| Type Variable

Bracketed Type

'(', Type, ')'

Basic Type

'$\mathbb{B}$' | '$\mathbb{N}$' | '$\mathbb{N}_1$' | '$\mathbb{Z}$' | '$\mathbb{Q}$' | '$\mathbb{R}$' | '**char**' | '**token**'

Quote Type

Quote Literal

Composite Type

'**compose**', Identifier, '**of**', Field List, '**end**'

Field List

{Field}

Field

[Identifier, ':'], Type

Union Type

Type, '|', Type, {'|', Type}

Product Type

Type, '×', Type, {'×', Type}

Optional Type

'[', Type, ']'

Set type

Type, '-**set**'

Sequence Type

Seq0 Type
| Seq1 Type

Seq0 Type

Type, '*'

Seq1 Type

Type, '+'

Map Type

General Map Type
| Injective Map Type

General Map Type

Type, '$\xrightarrow{m}$', Type

Injective Map Type

Type, '$\xleftrightarrow{m}$', Type

Function Type

Partial Function Type
| Total Function Type

Partial Function Type

Discretionary Type, '$\rightarrow$', Type

Total Function Type

Discetionary Type, '$\xrightarrow{t}$', Type

Discretionary Type

Type
| '(', ')'

Type Name

Name

Type Variable

Type Variable Identifier

State Definition

'**state**', Identifier, '**of**', Field List, [Invariant], [Initialization], '**end**'

Invariant

'**inv**', Invaraint Initial Function

Initialization

'**init**', Invariant Initial Function

Invariant Initial Function

pattern, '$\triangleq$', Expression

Value Definitions

'**values**', Value Definition, {';', Value Definition }

Value Definition

Pattern, [':', Type], '=', Expression

Function Definitions

'**functions**', Function Definition, {';', Function Definition }

Function Definition

Explicit Function Definition
| Implicit Function Definition

Explicit Function Definition

Identfier, [Type Variable List], ':', Function Type
Idenifier, Parameters List,
'$\triangleq$', expression,
['**pre**', Expression]

Implicit Function Definition

Identifier, [Type Variable List],
Parameter Types, Identifier Type Pair,
['**pre**', Expression]
'**post**', Expression

Type Variable List

'[', Type Variable Identifier, {',', Type Variable Identifier}, ']'

Identifier Type Pair

Identifier, ':', Type

Parameter Types

'(', [Pattern Type Pair List], ')'

Pattern Type Pair List

Pattern List, ':', Type, {',', Pattern List, ':', Type}

Parameters List

Parameters, {parameters}

Parameters

'(', [Pattern List], ')'

Operation Definitions

'**operations**', Operation Definition, {';', Operation Definition}

Operation Definition

Explicit Operation Definition
| Implicit Operation Definition

Explicit Operation Definition

Identifier, ':', Operation Type,
Identifier, Parameters,
'≙', Statement,
['**pre**', Expression]

Implicit Operation Definition

Identifier, Parameter Types, [Identifier Type Pair],
[Externals],
['**pre**', Expression],
'**post**', Expression,
[Exceptions]

Operation Type

Discretionary Type, '$\xrightarrow{o}$', Discretionary Type

Externals

'**ext**', Var Information, {Var Information}

Var Information

Mode, Name List, [':', Type]

Mode

'**rd**' | '**wr**'

Exceptions

'**errs**', Error List

Error List

Error, {Error}

Error

Identifier, ':', Expression, '→', Expression

Expressions

Bracketed Expression
| Let Expression
| Let Be Expression
| Def Expression
| If Expression
| Cases Expression
| Unary Expression
| Binary Expression
| Quantified Expression
| Iota Expression
| Set Enumeration
| Set Comprehension
| Set Range Expression
| Sequence Enumeration
| Sequence Comprehension
| Subsequence
| Map Enumeration
| Map comprehension
| Tuple Constructor
| Record Constructor
| Record Modifier
| Apply
| Field Select
| Function Type Instantiation
| Lambda Expression
| Is Expression
| Name
| Old Name
| Symbolic Literal

Bracketed Expression

'(', Expression, ')'

Let Expression

'**let**', Local Definition, {',', Local Definition},
'**in**', Expression

Let Be Expression

'**let**', Bind, ['**be**', '**st**', Expression], '**in**', Expression

Def Expression

'**def**', Pattern Bind, '=', Expression, {';', Pattern Bind, '=', Expression},
'**in**', Expression

If Expression

'**if**', Expression, '**then**', Expression,
{Elseif Expression},
'**else**', Expression

Elseif Expression

'**elseif**', Expression, '**then**', Expression

Cases Expression

'**cases**', Expression, ':', Cases Expression Alternatives,
[',', Others Expression], '**end**'

Cases Expression Alternatives

Cases Expression Alternative,
{',', Cases Expression Alternative}

Cases Expression Alternative

Pattern List, '→', Expression

Others Expression

'others', '→', Expression

Unary Expression

Prefix Expression
| Map Inverse Expression

Prefix Expression

Unary Operator, Expression

Unary Operator

'**+**' | '**-**' | '**abs**' | '**floor**' | '**¬**' | '**card**' | '$\mathcal{F}$' | '⋃' | '⋂' | '**hd**' | '**tl**' | '**len**' |
'**elems**' | '**inds**' | '**conc**' | '**dom**' | '**rng**' | '**merge**'

Map Inverse Expression

Expression, '$^{-1}$'

Binary Expression

Expression, Binary Operator, Expression

Binary Operator

'+' | '-' | '*' | '/' | '**div**' | '**rem**' | '**mod**' | '<' | '≤' | '>' | '≥' | '=' | '≠' | '∨' |
'∧' | '⇒' | '⇔' | '∈' | '∉' | '⊂' | '⊆' | '∪' | '∩' | '−' | '⌢' | '†' | 'ⓜ' | '◁' | '⩤' |
'▷' | '⩥' | '∘' | '↑'

*The infix '↑' can be replaced by a superscript: m↑n can be written as m^n.

Quantified Expression

'∀', Bind List, '•', Expression
| '∃', Bind List, '•', Expression
| '∃!', Bind, '•', Expression

Iota Expression

'ι', Bind, '•', Expression

Set Enumeration

'{', [Expression List], '}'

Set Comprehension

'{', Expression, '|', Bind List, ['•', Expression], '}'

Set Range Expression

'{', Expression, ',', '...', ',', Expression, '}'

Sequence Enumeration

'[', [Expression List], ']'

Sequence Comprehension

'[', Expression, '|', Set Bind, ['•', Expression], ']'

Subsequence

Expression, '(', Expression, ',', '...', ',', Expression, ')'

Map Enumeration

'{', Maplet, {',', Maplet}, '}'
| '{', '↦', '}'

Maplet

Expression, '↦', Expression

Map Comprehension

'{', Maplet, ' | ', Bind List, ['•', Expression], '}'

Tuple Constructor

'*mk_*', '(', Expression, ',', Expression List, ')'

Record Constructor

Name, '(', [Expression List], ')'

Record Modifier

'μ', '(', Expression, ',', Record Modification, {',', Record Modification}, ')'

Record Modification

Identifier, '↦', Expression

Apply

Expression, '(', [Expression List], ')'

Field Select

Expression, '.', Identifier

Function Type Instantiation

Name, '[', type, {',', Type}, ']'

Lambda Expression

'λ', Type Bind List, '•' Expression

Is Expression

Identifier, '(', Expression, ')'
| '*is_*', Basic Type, '(', Expression, ')'

Name

Identifier

Name List

Name, {',', Name}

Old Name

Identifier, '↼'

State Designator

Name
| Field Reference
| Map or Sequence Reference

Field Reference

State Designator, '.', Identifier

Map or Sequence Reference

State Designator, '(', Expression, ')'

Statement

Let Statement
| Let Be Statement
| Def Statement
| Block Statement
| Assign Statement
| If Statement
| Cases Statement
| Sequence For Loop
| Set For Loop
| Index For Loop
| While Loop
| Non-deterministic Statement
| Call statement
| Return Statement
| Always Statement
| Trap Statement
| Recursive Trap Statement
| Exit Statement
| Identity Statement

Let Statement

'let', Local definition, {',', Local definition}, 'in', Statement

Local Definition

Value Definition
| Function Definition

Let Be Statement

'**let**', Bind, ['**be**', '**st**', Expression], '**in**', Statement

Def Statement

'**def**', Equals Definition, {';', Equals Definition}, '**in**', Statement

Equals Definition

Pattern Bind, '=', Expression
| Pattern Bind, '=', Call Statement

Block Statement

'(', {Dcl Statement}, Statement, {';', Statement}, ')'

Dcl Statement

'**dcl**', Assignment Definition, ';'

Assignment Definition

Identifier, ':', Type, [':=', Expression]
| Identifier, ':', Type, [':=', Call Statement]

Assign Statement

State Designator, ':=', Expression
| State Designator, ':=', Call Statement

If Statement

'**if**', Expression, '**then**', Statement, {Elseif Statement}, '**else**', Statement

Elseif Statement

'**elseif**', Expression, '**then**', Statement

Cases Statement

'**cases**', Expression, ':', Cases Statement Alternatives,
[',', Others Statement], '**end**'

Cases Statement Alternatives

Cases Statement Alternative, {',', Cases Statement Alternative}

Cases Statement Alternative

Pattern List, '→', Statement

Others Statement

'**others**', '→', Statement

Sequence For Loop

'**for**', Pattern Bind, '**in**', ['**reverse**'], Expression, '**do**', Statement

Set For Loop

'**for**', '**all**', Pattern, '∈', Expression, '**do**', Statement

Index For Loop

'**for**', Identifier, '=', Expression, '**to**', Expression, ['**by**', Expression],
'**do**', Statement

While Loop

'**while**', Expression, '**do**', Statement

Non-deterministic Statement

'||', '(', Statement, {',', Statement}, ')'

Call Statement

Name, '(', [Expression List], ')', ['**using**', State Designator]

Return Statement

'**return**', [Expression]

Always Statement

'**always**', Statement, '**in**', Statement

Trap Statement

'**trap**', Pattern Bind, '**with**', Statement, '**in**', Statement

Recursive Trap Statement

'**tixe**', Traps, '**in**', Statement

Traps

'{', Pattern Bind, '↦', Statement, {',', Pattern Bind, '↦', Statement}, '}'

Exit Statement

'**exit**', [Expression]

Identity Statement

'**skip**'

Pattern

Pattern Identifier
| Match Value
| Set Enumeration Pattern
| Set Union Pattern
| Sequence Enumeration Pattern
| Sequence Concatenation Pattern
| Tuple Pattern
| Record Pattern

Pattern Identifier

Identifier
| '-'

Match Value

'(', Expression, ')'
| Symbolic Literal

Set Enumeration Pattern

'{', Pattern List, '}'

Set Union Pattern

Pattern, '∪', Pattern

Sequence Enumeration Pattern

'[', Pattern List, ']'

Sequence Concatenation Pattern

Pattern, '⌢', Pattern

Tuple Pattern

'*mk_*', '(', Pattern, ',', Pattern List, ')'

Record Pattern

Name, '(', [Pattern List], ')'

Pattern List

Pattern, {',', Pattern}

Pattern Bind

Pattern
| Bind

Bind

Set Bind
| Type Bind

Set Bind

Pattern, '∈', Expression

Type Bind

Pattern, ':', Type

Bind List

Multiple Bind, {',', Multiple Bind}

Multiple Bind

Multiple Set Bind
| Multiple Type Bind

Multiple Set Bind

Pattern List, '∈', Expression

Multiple Type Bind

Pattern List, ':', Type

Type Bind List

Type Bind, {',', Type Bind}

Idenifier

(Plain Letter | Greek Letter), {(Plain Letter | Greek Letter) | Digit | ''' | '_'}

Type Variable Identifier

'@', Identifier

Symbolic Literal

Numeric Literal
| Boolean Literal
| Nil Literal
| Character Literal
| Text Literal
| Quote Literal

Numeral

Digit, {Digit}

Numeric Literal

Numeral, ['.', Digit, {Digit}], [Exponent]

Exponent

'x10↑', ['+' | '-'], numeral

Boolean Literal

'true' | 'false'

Nil Literal

'nil'

Character Literal

''', Character - Newline, '''

Text Literal

'"', {'""' | Character - ('"' | Newline)},'"'

Quote Literal

Distinguished Letter, {'-' | Distinguished Letter}

Comment

'--' {Character - Newline}, Newline

Plain Letter

Alphabetic capital or lower case letter A...Za...z

Distingushed Letter

Capital letter A...Z in distinguished typeface

Greek Letter

'α' | 'β' | 'γ' | 'δ' | 'ε' | 'ζ' | 'η' | 'Θ' | 'ι' | 'κ' | 'λ' | 'μ' | 'ν' | 'ξ' | 'ο' | 'π' | 'ρ' | 'σ' | 'τ' | 'ν' | 'φ' | 'χ' | 'ψ' | 'ω' | 'Α' | 'Β' | 'Γ' | 'Δ' | 'Ε' | 'Ζ' | 'Η' | 'Θ' | 'Ι' | 'Κ' | 'Λ' | 'Μ' | 'Ν' | 'Ξ' | 'Ο' | 'Π' | 'Ρ' | 'Σ' | 'Τ' | 'Υ' | 'φ' | 'Χ' | 'Ψ' | 'Ω'

Digit

0 | 1 | 2 | 3 | 4 | 5 | 6 | 7 | 8 | 9

Newline

Text following this character starts on the next line. Multiple newlines in succession are considered as a single newline token in the syntax.

White Space

Characters having no normal graphical form such as tabs, blank spaces etc.

Appendix C

Z collected notation

The following pages gives a quick reference to the constructs of Z. The shorthand used is:
S = Set, Sc = Schema, B = Bag, M = Map, Sq = Sequence, P = Predicate,
R = Relation, N = Integer value, F = Finite Function, E = Expression,
T = Type.

Where two of these letters are placed together this infers a construct made up of the two, for example 'SS' represents a set of sets. lower-case f represents a function name, and lower-case x and y represent single elements or variable names.

Schema definition

```
 ___ Schema Name[Parameters] ______________
| Declarations
|__________________________
| Predicates
|__________________________________________
```

or

Schema Name ≙ [*Declarations* | *Predicates*]

Generic definition

```
 ===== [Parameters] ========================
| Declarations
|__________________________
| Predicates
|__________________________________________
```

Axiomatic description

Declarations
Predicates

Fixity paragraph

fixity rel
fixity leftfun
fixity rightfun
fixity leftfun N
fixity rightfun N

Predefined types and sets

$\mathbb{Z}$	Integers
$\mathbb{N}$	Natural numbers
$\mathbb{N}_1$	Positive integers

Basic Type

[X, Y]

Free type definition

FreeType ::= element_1 | ... | element_n

Abbreviation definition

X == Y

Logic and schema calculus

true, false	Logical constants
$\neg P$	Negation
$P \land Q$	Conjunction
$P \lor Q$	Disjunction
$P \Rightarrow Q$	Implication
$P \Leftrightarrow Q$	Equivalence
$\forall x : T \mid P \bullet Q$	Universal quantifier
$\exists x : T \mid P \bullet Q$	Existential quantifier
$\exists_1 x : T \mid P \bullet Q$	Unique quantifier

Schema operators

$Sc[y_1/x_1,...,y_n/x_n]$	Renaming
$Sc \setminus (x_1, ..., x_n)$	Hiding
$Sc_1 \upharpoonright Sc_2$	Projection
pre Sc	Pre-condition
$Sc_1 \mathbin{;} Sc_2$	Sequential composition
$Sc_1 >> Sc_2$	Piping

* *Note the last three operators can only be used on operations, not functions.*

Sets

$x \in S$	Membership
$x \notin S$	Non-membership
$\{x_1,..,x_n\}$	Set enumeration
$\{x : T \mid P \bullet E\}$	Set comprehension
$\varnothing$	Empty set
$S \subseteq T$	Subset relation
$S \subset T$	Proper subset relation
$\mathbb{P}S$	Power set
$\mathbb{P}_1S$	Non-empty subsets
$\mathbb{F}S$	Finite sets
$\mathbb{F}_1S$	Non-empty finite sets
$S \times T$	Cartesian product
(x, y)	Tuple
first (x, y)	First of pair
second (x, y)	Second of pair
$t.n$	Tuple selection
$S \cup T$	Set union
$S \cap T$	Set intersection
$S \setminus T$	Set difference
$\#S$	Cardinality
$\bigcup SS$	Distributed union
$\bigcap SS$	Distributed intersection

Bags

bag T	Bag type
$[\![x_1,..,x_n]\!]$	Bag enumeration
count B *x*	Count of element
n ⊗ B	Bag scaling
x in B	Bag membership
$B_1 \sqsubseteq B_2$	Sub-bag relation
$B_1 \uplus B_2$	Bag union
B_1 ⩁ B_2	Bag difference

Sequences

seq T	Finite sequence
seq_1 T	Non-empty sequence
iseq T	Injective sequence
$\langle x_1,..,x_n \rangle$	Sequence enumeration
$Sq_1 \frown Sq_2$	Concatenation
rev Sq	Reverse
head Sq	First element
last Sq	Last element
tail Sq	Sequence of all but first element
front Sq	Sequence of all but last element
Sq ↾ S	Filter
squash Sq	Compaction
Sq_1 prefix Sq_2	Prefix relation
Sq_1 suffix Sq_2	Suffix relation
Sq_1 in Sq_2	Segment relation
⁀/SqSq	Distributed concatenation
disjoint SqSq	Disjoint
Sq_1 partition Sq_2	Partition relation

Relations

$X \leftrightarrow Y$	Binary relations
$x \mapsto y$	Maplet
dom R	Domain
ran R	Range
id X	Identity relation
$R_1 \mathbin{;} R_2$	Composition
$R_1 \circ R_2$	Backward composition
$S \lhd R$	Domain restriction
$R \rhd S$	Range restriction
$S \ntriangleleft R$	Domain subtraction
$R \ntriangleright S$	Range subtraction
$R^{\sim}$	Relational inverse
$R ⦇ S ⦈$	Relational image
$R_1 \oplus R_2$	Overriding
R^k	Iteration
R^+	Transitive closure
R^*	Reflexive transitive closure

Functions

$f(x)$	Function application
$\lambda x : T \mid P \bullet E$	Lambda expression
$X \pfun Y$	Partial function
$X \rightarrow Y$	Total function
$X \pinj Y$	Partial injection
$X \rightarrowtail Y$	Total injection
$X \psurj Y$	Partial surjection
$X \twoheadrightarrow Y$	Total surjection
$X \bij Y$	Bijection
$X \ffun Y$	Finite partial function
$X \finj Y$	Finite partial injection

Arithmetic and numbers

+	Addition
-	Subtraction
div	Integer division
mod	Integer modulus
succ N	Successor function
$N_1 .. N_2$	Number range
min SN	Minimum of integer set
max SN	Maximum of integer set

Basic expressions

$x = y$	Equality
$x \neq y$	Inequality
if P **then** E_1 **else** E_2	Conditional
$\mu\, x : T \mid P \bullet E$	Mu expression
θSc	Theta expression
E.x	Selection
(**let** x== $E_1 \bullet E_2$)	Let expression
$\langle\!\langle v_1{:=}E_1,\ldots, v_n{:=}E_n \rangle\!\rangle \odot Sc$	Schema substitution
$\langle\!\langle v_1{:=}E_1,\ldots, v_n{:=}E_n \rangle\!\rangle \odot E$	Expression substitution
$\langle\!\langle v_1{:=}E_1,\ldots, v_n{:=}E_n \rangle\!\rangle \odot P$	Predicate substitution
$\langle\!\langle v_1{:=}E_1,\ldots, v_n{:=}E_n \rangle\!\rangle \odot D$	Declaration substitution

Appendix D

Z syntax

This appendix gives a representational syntax for **Z**. Though based on the concrete syntax given in the **Z** draft standards the interpretation given here is a somewhat loose one in that it also includes some, though not all, of the operators defined within the **Z** toolkit. These would not, in reality, form part of the base syntax in a more rigid specification of the notation as such operators would be defined only within the toolkit.

Because the syntax was still under development at the time of publication the syntax is necessarily incomplete as regards some of the operators and there may still be some inconsistencies within the syntactic framework. However, it does form a fair guide to the layout of **Z** specifications.

Z Specification

[Paragraph], {NarrativeText, Paragraph}, [Narrative Text]

Paragraph

Given Set Definition
| Structured Set Definition
| Axiomatic Definition
| Abbreviation Definition
| Schema Definition
| Generic Definition
| Constraint

Given Set Definition

'['Word,{','Word},']'

Structured Set Definition

Word '::=', Branch, {' | ', Branch}

Branch

Word
| Identifier,'⟨⟨', Expression, '⟩⟩'

Constraint

Predicate

Axiomatic Definition

| Declaration Part

|

| Declaration Part
|———————
| Axiom Part

Predicate is optional in an axiomatic definition.

Generic Definition

══ Generic Formal Parameters ══
Declaration Part
———————
Axiom Part
———————

|

══ Generic Formal Parameters ══
Declaration Part
———————

Axiom part of generic definition is optional.

Abbreviation Definition

Variable Abbreviation
| Prefix General Abbreviation
| Infix General Abbreviation

Variable Abbreviation

Identifier, [Generic Formal Parameters] '==' Expression

Prefix General Abbreviation

Prefix Generic Symbol, Word '==', Expression

Infix General Abbreviation

Word, Infix Generic Symbol , Word '==', Expression

Schema Definition

SchemaName,[Generic Formal Parameters],'≙',Schema

|

```
┌── SchemaName,[Generic Formal Parameters] ──────
│ Declaration Part
├─────────────────────────
│ Axiom Part
└────────────────────────────────────────────────
```

|

```
┌── SchemaName,[Generic Formal Parameters] ──────
│ Declaration Part
└────────────────────────────────────────────────
```

Predicate part of schema is optional.

Declaration Part

Declaration, {Newline, Declaration}

Declaration

Basic Declaration
| Compound Declaration

Compound Declaration

Basic Declaration, ';', Basic Declaration, {';', Basic Declaration}

Basic Declaration

Simple Declaration
| Schema

Simple Declaration

Declaration Name,{',', Declaration Name}, ':', Expression

Schema Text

Declaration, ['|', Predicate]
| Schema Text Substitution

Schema Text Substitution

Expression, '⊙', Schema Text

Schema

Quantified Schema
| Logic Schema

Quantified schema

'∀', Schema Text,'•', Schema
| '∃', Schema Text,'•', Schema
| '$\exists_1$', Schema Text,'•', Schema

Logic Schema

Schema Equivalence
| Schema Implication

Schema Equivalence

Logic Schema, '⇔', Schema Equivalence

Schema Implication

Schema Disjunction, ['⇒', Schema Implication]

Schema Disjunction

[Schema Disjunction, '∨'], Schema Conjunction

Schema Conjunction

[Schema Conjunction, '∧'], Schema Negation

Schema Negation

'¬', Schema Negation
| Compound Schema

Compound Schema

Schema Composition
| Schema Operation1

Schema Composition

Compound Schema,.' ⨾', Schema Operation1

Schema Operation1

Schema Renaming
| Schema Hiding
| Schema Operation2

Schema Operation2

Schema Projection
| Schema Operation3

Schema Operation3

Pre Schema
| Schema Operation4

Schema Operation4

Schema Decoration
| Basic Schema

Schema Renaming

Compound Schema, Rename List

Schema Hiding

Compound Schema, '\', '(', Variable Name List, ')'

Schema Projection

Schema Operation2, '↾', Logic Schema

Pre Schema

'pre', Schema Operation3

Schema Decoration

Schema, Decoration

Basic Schema

Schema Construction
| Schema Reference
| Generic Schema Reference
| Schema Substitution
| '(', Schema, ')'

Schema Construction

'[' Declaration, ['|', Predicate], ']'

Schema Reference

Schema Name

Generic Schema Reference

Schema Name, '[', Expression, {',', Expression}, ']'

Schema Substitution

Expression, '⊙', Schema

Axiom Part

Predicate, {Separator, Predicate}

Separator

';'
| Newline

Predicate

Quantified Predicate
| Logic Predicate
| '(', '**let**', Let Definition, {';', Let Definition}, '•', Predicate, ')'

Quantified Predicate

'∀', Schema Text, '•', Predicate
| '∃', Schema Text, '•', Predicate
| '$\exists_1$', Schema Text, '•', Predicate

Logic Predicate

Equivalence
| Implication

Equivalence

Logic Predicate, '⇔', Implication

Implication

Disjunction ['⇒', Implication]

Disjunction

[Disjunction, '∨'], Conjunction

Conjunction

[Conjunction, '∧'], Basic Predicate

Negation

'¬', Basic Predicate

Basic Predicate

Prefix Relation Predicate
| Infix Relation Predicate
| Compound Relation Predicate
| Schema Predicate - '(', Schema, ')'
| Truth
| Falsehood
| Predicate Substitution
| '(', Predicate, ')'
| Negation
| Membership
| Equality

Prefix Relation Predicate

Prefix Relation Symbol, Expression

Infix Relation Predicate

Expression, Infix Relation Symbol, Expression

Compound Relation Predicate

Infix Relation Predicate, Relation Symbol, Expression,
{Relation, Expression}

Predicate Substitution

Expression, '⊙', Predicate

Relation Symbol

'∈' | '='
| Infix Relation Symbol

Infix Relation Symbol

'≠' | '∉' | '⊂' | '⊆' | '<' | '>' | '≤' | '≥' | '⊑' | 'partition' | 'prefix'
| 'suffix' | 'in'

Schema Predicate

Compound Schema

Truth

'*true*'

Falsehood

'*false*'

Membership

Expression, '∈', Expression

Equality

Expression, '=', Expression

Expression0

Definition Description
| Expression

Expression

Infix General Expression
| Cartesian Product

Expression1

Definition Declaration
| Expression

Cartesian Product

Infix Function Expression , ['×', Infix Function Expression,
{'×', Infix Function Expression}]

Infix Function Expression

[Infix Function Expression, Infix Function Symbol], Expression2

Expression2

Powerset
| Prefix General Expression
| Function Application

Powerset

'ℙ', Expression3

Prefix General Relation Expression

Prefix Generic Symbol, Expression3

Function Application

[Function Application], Expression3

Expression3

Postfix Function Expression
| Superscript
| Bind Selection
| Tuple Selection
| Identifier
| Generic Instantiation
| Schema Expression
| Set Extension
| Binding Extension
| Tuple
| Sequence
| Bag
| Theta Expression
| Set Composition - '{', Schema Expression, '}'
| Lambda Expression
| Number
| If Then Else
| '(', Expression1, ')'
| Expression Substitution
| Let Expression

* *Note that the let expression may not be available in later versions of* **Z**.

Postfix Function Expression

Expression3, Postfix Function Symbol

Superscript

Expression, $^{\text{Expression1}}$

Bind Selection

Expression3, '.', Variable Name

Tuple Selection

Expression3, '.', Number

Generic Instantiation

Variable Name, '[', Expression, {',', Expression}, ']'

Schema Expression

Schema

Set Extension

'{', Expression1, {',', Expression1}, '}'

Binding Extension

'⦉', Variable Name,'', Expression0,
{',', Variable Name, '', Expression0}, '⦊'

Tuple

'(', Expression1, ',', Expression1, {',', Expression1}, ')'

Sequence

'⟨', Expression1, {',', Expression1},' ⟩'

Bag

'⟦', Expression1, {',', Expression1}, ' ⟧'

Theta Expression

'θ', Basic Schema, [Decoration]

Set Comprehension

'{', Schema Text, ['•', Expression1], '}'

Lambda Expression

'λ', Schema Text, '•', Expression

Definition Description

'μ', Schema Text, ['•', Expression]

If Then Else

'**if**', Predicate, '**then**', Expression, '**else**', Expression

Expression Substitution

Expression, '⊙', Expression

Let Expression

'(', '**let**', Let Definition, {';', Let Definition}, '•', Expression, ')'

Let Definition

Variable Name, '==', Expression

Infix Generic Symbol

'⇸' | '→' | '⤔' | '⤗' | '↣' | '⤀' | '↠' | '⤖' | '↔' | '⇻'

Infix Function Symbol

'↦' | '+' | '..' | '-' | '∪' | '\' | '⁀' | '⊎' | '⩁' | '*' | 'div' | 'mod'
| '∩' | '↾' | '⨾' | '∘' | '⊕' | '⊗' | '⩤' | '⩥' | '◁' | '▷'

Prefix Generic Symbol

'$\mathbb{P}_1$' | 'id' | '$\mathbb{F}$' | '$\mathbb{F}_1$' | 'seq' | 'seq_1' | 'iseq' | 'bag'

Prefix Relation Symbol

'disjoint'

Postfix Function Symbol

'~' | '*' | '+'

Rename List

'[', Variable Name, '/', Variable Name,
{ ',', Variable Name, '/', Variable Name}, ']'

Generic Formal Parameters

'[', Identifier, {',', Identifier}, ']'

Schema Name

Word

Identifier

Variable Name

Declaration Name

Name
| Operation Name

Variable Name

Name
| '(', Operation Name, ')'

Operation Name

'_', Infix Function Symbol, [Decoration], '_'
| '_', Infix Generic Symbol, '_'
| '_', Infix Relation Symbol, [Decoration], '_'
| Prefix Generic Symbol, '_'
| Prefix Relation Symbol, [Decoration], '_'
| '_' Postfix Function Symbol, [Decoration]
| '_', '⦇', '_', '⦈'
| '-'

Fixity Paragraph

'fixity', [Category], Template

Category

'rel'
| **'leftfun'** [Precedence]
| **'rightfun'** [Precedence]

Precedence

Number

Template

[Argument] Name {SeqArg, Name} [Argument]

SeqArg

Argument
| '...', '(', Expression, ',', Expression',', Expression, ')'

Argument

'_'

Name

Word, [Decoration]

Word

Alphanumeric
| Greek
| Symbolic

Decoration

Stroke Character, {Stroke Character}

Stroke Character

'′' | '?' | '!'
| Subscript Digit

Alphanumeric

Letter, {Letter | Digit | ('_', (Letter | Digit)}), {Subscript}

Number

Digit, {Digit}

Symbolic

Symbol, {Symbol}, {Subscript}
| Punctuation, Subscript, {Subscript}

Punctuation

',' | ';' | ':' | '(' | ')' | '𝔽' | 'ℕ' | 'ℙ' | 'ℕ'

Symbol

'∩' | '∪' | '∅' | '⦇' | '⦈' | '⁀/' | '≠' | '.' | '~' | '⟦' | '⟧' | '[' | ']' | '{' | '}'
| '⟨' | '⟩' | '/' | '¬' | '∧' | '∨' | '⇒' | '⇔' | '=' | '∈' | '::=' | '∀' | '∃'
| '•' | '×' | '≙' | '&'

Letter

Is an alphabetic letter, upper or lowercase.

Digit

'0' | '1' | '2' | '3' | '4' | '5' | '6' | '7' | '8' | '9'

Subscript Digit

Unsigned Subscripted Digit

Greek

Greek Letter, {Subscript}

Greek Letter

'α' | 'β' | 'γ' | 'δ' | 'ε' | 'ζ' | 'η' | 'θ' | 'ι' | 'κ' | 'λ' | 'μ' | 'ν'
| 'ξ' | 'π' | 'ρ' | 'σ' | 'τ' | 'υ' | 'φ' | 'χ' | 'ψ' | 'ω' | 'Γ' | 'Δ'
| 'Θ' | 'Λ' | 'Ξ' | 'Π' | 'Σ' | 'Υ' | 'Φ' | 'ψ' | 'Ω'

Newline

Text following this character starts on the next line. Multiple newlines in succession are considered as a single newline token in the syntax.

Whitespace

Although not defined in the syntax itself, a number of characters are ignored: for example, newline characters preceding or succeeding characters in the sets; Infix Function Symbols, Infix Relation Symbols, Infix Generic Symbols and Symbols.

Solutions to VDM exercises

Exercise 5.1:

$$Dollar: \mathbb{R} = 100 * Yen;$$
$$UK\_pound: \mathbb{R} = 2.4 * Dollar$$

The use of the type is optional.

Exercise 5.2:

$$T\_type = \mathbb{R}$$
$$\textbf{inv } T\_type \triangleq t \leq 200$$

Exercise 5.3:

a) Since each portable has a unique serial number we can use these as the identifier. A single computer could thus be represented as a natural number:

$$portable : \mathbb{N}$$

and the set of available portables as a set of natural numbers:

$$available : \mathbb{N}\textbf{-set}$$

We might declare this as a state variable:

state *portables* **of**
  available : ℕ**-set**
end

a) We use set difference to remove the portable from the list:

$$available - \{portable\}$$

b) We would need to state the pre-condition that the portable is available:

$$portable \in available$$

We shall see later that we can use these to declare the complete implicit operation:

OBTAIN(*portable* : $\mathbb{N}$)
ext wr *available* : $\mathbb{N}$**-set**
pre *portable* $\in$ *available*
post *available* $= \overleftarrow{available} - \{portable\}$;

c) We can use set union to return a machine to the set of available portables:

$$available \cup \{portable\}$$

We shall see later that we can use this to declare the complete operation:

RELEASE(*portable* : $\mathbb{N}$)
ext wr *available* : $\mathbb{N}$**-set**
post *available* $= \overleftarrow{available} \cup \{portable\}$;

d) We could obtain the number of elements of the set:

card *available*

We shall see later that we can use this to declare the complete operation

PORTABLES_AVAILABLE () *r* : $\mathbb{N}$
ext rd *available* : $\mathbb{N}$**-set**
post *r* = **card** *available*

Exercise 5.4:

a) We could represent the relationship between the plain text and cipher text as an injective mapping:

type

CIPHER = **char** $\overset{m}{\leftrightarrow}$ **char**

values

cipher : CIPHER =
{'A' ↦'Z', 'B'↦'H' ,'C'↦'X', 'D'↦'I' ,'E'↦'G' ,'F'↦'M',
'G'↦'A', 'H'↦'L', 'I'↦'K', 'J'↦'V', 'K'↦'E' ,'L'↦'J',
'M'↦'T', 'N'↦'S', 'O'↦'W', 'P'↦'R', 'Q'↦'D', 'R'↦'P',
'S'↦'B', 'T'↦'C', 'U'↦'N', 'V'↦'U', 'W'↦'O', 'X'↦'Y',
'Y'↦'Q', 'Z'↦'F'};

If we had intended to change the cipher during the operation we would have had to describe it in terms of a state variable, rather than a value.

b) We would use map selection to obtain the enciphered equivalent:

enciphered_letter = *cipher*(*plain_letter*).

which as we shall see later could be defined as an explicit function:

encode_character: **char** × CIPHER $\xrightarrow{\sim}$ **char**
encode_character(*ch*, *code*) $\triangleq$
code(*ch*)
pre *ch* ∈ **dom** *code*;

c) To decode we merely take the inverse mapping:

plain_letter = $cipher^{-1}$(*enciphered_letter*)

which as we shall see later could be placed in an explicit function:

decode_character: **char** × CIPHER $\xrightarrow{\sim}$ **char**
decode_character(*ch*, *code*) $\triangleq$
$code^{-1}$ (*ch*)
pre *ch* ∈ **rng** *code*;

Exercise 5.5:
We could record each *movement* as a sequence of characters[1], and the entire record of moves as a sequence of this type. Assuming we had a type *Movement* which consists of a text string:

$$Movement = \mathbf{char}^{+};$$
$$Moves = Movement^{*}$$

a) We would start with an initial state in which no movements have been made:

$$route = []$$

which as we shall see later could be described in the state as:

state *robot* **of**
route : *Moves*
init *mk-robot*(*n*) $\triangleq$ *n* = []
end

b) We could add a new move by concatenating it to the list of moves:

$$route \frown [new\_move]$$

which we shall see later could give the operation:

ADD_NEW_MOVE(*new_move* : *Movement*)
ext wr *route* :*Moves*
post $route = \overleftarrow{route} \frown [new\_move]$;

Note that we need to turn the *new_move* into a sequence in order to concatenate it to the list.

c) The total number of moves could be determined by taking the length of the sequence and subtracting one:

$$\mathbf{len}(route) - 1$$

This does not count the 'stop' command which is not a movement. The definition also does not take into account an empty sequence, but this could be covered by a separate condition or a pre-condition on the operation.

---

[1] In fact a better way would be to use an enumerated type for these movements which we shall see later in the chapter.

As we shall see later the operation could be represented as:

$$\begin{aligned}&number\_of\_moves : Moves \xrightarrow{\sim} \mathbb{N}\\&number\_of\_moves(m) \triangleq \mathbf{len}(m) - 1\\&\mathbf{pre\ len}\ m > 0;\end{aligned}$$

d) We could see if the backward movement was one of the elements of the sequence:

$$\text{“backward”} \in \mathbf{elems}\ route$$

which as we shall see later can be stated in a more general function:

$$\begin{aligned}&in\_list : \text{Movement} \times \text{Moves} \xrightarrow{\sim} \mathbb{B}\\&in\_list(move, moves\_made) \triangleq\\&\qquad move \in \mathbf{elems}\ moves\_made\end{aligned}$$

e) Since we know ‘stop’ to be the last element of the list we can use the length of the list and sequence modification to replace the last command with the new one:

$$route \dagger \{\mathbf{len}\ route \mapsto \text{“switch off”}\}$$

which could also be stated in the operation:

$$\begin{aligned}&UPDATE\_LAST\_ELEMENT(new\_command : Movement)\\&\mathbf{ext\ wr}\ route : Moves\\&\mathbf{post}\ \ route = \overleftharpoon{route} \dagger \{\mathbf{len}\ \overleftharpoon{route} \mapsto new\_command\}\end{aligned}$$

f) To convert we could write a function which extracts the first element of the list and translates this, and then recursively calls itself with the remainder of the list, concatenating the result of this to the translated element. We would need a terminating condition, which could be if the list consists of a single element. The function would require use of the head **hd** and tail **tl** operators, as well as the concatenation operator. We could define the operation as:

$$\begin{aligned}&convert : Moves \xrightarrow{\sim} \mathbb{Z}^*\\&convert(r) \triangleq\\&\qquad \mathbf{if\ len}\ r = 1\ \mathbf{then}\ [translate(r)]\\&\qquad \mathbf{else}\ [translate(\mathbf{hd}\ r)] \frown convert(\mathbf{tl}\ r)\\&\ \ \mathbf{pre\ len}\ r > 0\end{aligned}$$

which we shall see later in the chapter.

Exercise 5.6:
Firstly we define a single record:

$$\begin{aligned} \textit{Stock\_Item} :: \; & \textit{product\_name} && : \mathbf{char}^+ \\ & \textit{supplier\_name} && : \mathbf{char}^+ \\ & \textit{unit\_price} && : \mathbb{R} \\ & \textit{units\_in\_stock} && : \mathbb{N} \\ & \textit{units\_on\_order} && : \mathbb{N}; \end{aligned}$$

and a key:

$$\textit{Product\_Identifier} = \mathbb{N}_1;$$

Our stock consists of a set of mappings from Product_Identifier to Stock item:

$$\textit{Stock} = \textit{Product\_Identifier} \xrightarrow{m} \textit{Stock\_Item}$$

We now define a state variable of this type to represent our stock:

$$\begin{aligned} & \mathbf{state}\ \textit{stores}\ \mathbf{of} \\ & \quad \textit{stock} : \textit{Stock} \\ & \mathbf{init}\ \textit{mk-stores}(n) \triangleq n = \{\mapsto\} \\ & \mathbf{end} \end{aligned}$$

a) We would use the mk function to add a new item. For example:

$$\textit{stock} = \overleftarrow{\textit{stock}} \dagger \textit{mk-Stock\_Item}(\text{“Spanner”}, \text{"ACME"}, 2.50, 10, 12)$$

which as we will see can be placed in an operation:

$$\begin{aligned} & \textit{ADD}(\textit{pid} : \mathbb{N}_1, \textit{pd} : \mathbf{char}^+, \textit{sp} : \mathbf{char}^+, \textit{pc} : \mathbb{R}, \textit{stk} : \mathbb{N}, \textit{od} : \mathbb{N}) \\ & \mathbf{ext\ wr}\ \textit{stock} : \textit{Stock} \\ & \mathbf{post}\ \textit{stock} = \overleftarrow{\textit{stock}} \dagger \{\textit{pid} \mapsto \textit{mk-Stock\_Item}(\textit{pd}, \textit{sp}, \textit{pc}, \textit{stk}, \textit{od})\}\ ; \end{aligned}$$

b) We use record modification to change the price:

$$\mu(\textit{stock}(\textit{product\_identifier}), \textit{unit\_price} \mapsto \textit{new\_price})$$

which as we shall see later can be placed in an operation:

$$\begin{aligned} & \textit{CHANGE\_PRICE}(\textit{pid} : \mathbb{N}_1,\ \textit{new\_price} : \mathbb{R}) \\ & \mathbf{ext\ wr}\ \textit{stock} : \textit{Stock} \\ & \mathbf{pre}\ \textit{pid} \in \mathbf{dom}\ \textit{stock} \\ & \mathbf{post}\ \textit{stock} = \overleftarrow{\textit{stock}} \dagger \{\textit{pid} \mapsto \mu(\textit{stock}(\textit{pid}), \textit{unit\_price} \mapsto \textit{new\_price})\ \}; \end{aligned}$$

c) We would use record selection to find the number of items in stock

$$stock(product\_identifier).units\_in\_stock$$

which we could describe in the operation:

NUMBER_IN_STOCK(*pid* : *Product_Identifier*) *r* : ℕ
ext rd *stock* : *Stock*
pre *pid* ∈ **dom** *stock*
post *r* = *stock*(*pid*).*units_in_stock*;

Exercise 5.7:

Movement = LEFT | RIGHT | FORWARD | BACKWARD

Exercise 5.8:

a) See answer in cipher exercise.

b)

-- number of occurrences of a number in a sequence
no_occurences: ℕ × ℕ* ⥲ ℕ
no_occurences(*n*, *s*) ≙
  card {i | *i* ∈ **inds** s • *s*(*i*) = *n*};

c)

-- returns the number that occurs most frequently in the list
most_frequent_number(*s*: ℕ*) *x* : ℕ
pre s ≠ []
post ∃*x* ∈ elems(s) •
  (¬∃*y* ∈ elems(s) • *no_occurences*(*x*, s) < *no_occurences*(*y*, s))

Exercise 5.9:

a) Look at the answer given in the stock control system in exercise 5.6.

b)

READ_TEMP() *r* : ℝ
ext rd *probetemp* : ℝ
post *r* = *probetemp*;

SET_TEMP : ℝ ⥲ ()
SET_TEMP(*temp*) ≙
probetemp := *temp*

```
state system of
   probetemp : ℝ
end
```

Note the use of equality and assignment in these operations.

Exercise 5.10:

a)

```
merge_adjacent_moves: Moves → Moves
merge_adjacent_moves(moves) ≜
if len moves < 2 then moves
elseif moves(1) = moves(2) then
     merge_adjacent_moves(tl moves)
else [moves(1)] ⁀ merge_adjacent_moves(tl moves);
```

b)

```
report_error: ℕ → Message
report_error(err) ≜
cases err:
    1 → "Internal arithmetic fault in the processor",
    2 → "Battery power low, or failing",
    3 → "Motor stuck",
    4 → "Sensor has failed, or is damaged",
others → "Unspecified error"
end;
```

Exercise 5.11:

```
REPLACE : WORD ×WORD ⥲ ()
REPLACE(oldword, newword) ≜
    for i = 1 to len wordfile do
       if wordfile(i) = oldword then
          wordfile(i) := newword
       else skip;
```

Exercise 5.12:

$REPLACE : \text{WORD} \times \text{WORD} \xrightarrow{o} \mathbb{N}$
$REPLACE(oldword, newword) \triangleq$
(**dcl** *count* : $\mathbb{N}$:= 0;
 for *i* = 1 **to len** *wordfile* **do**
  if *wordfile*(i) = *oldword* **then**
   (*wordfile*(i) := *newword*;
    count:= *count* + 1)
  else skip;
 return *count*);

Exercise 5.13:

types
  $Button = \text{INCREASE} \mid \text{DECREASE}$
values
  $Button\text{-}map : Button \xrightarrow{m} (\mathbb{Z} \to \mathbb{Z}) =$
   $\{\text{INCREMENT} \mapsto \lambda x : \mathbb{Z} \bullet x + 1$
   $\text{DECREMENT} \mapsto \lambda x : \mathbb{Z} \bullet x - 1\}$
operations
  $BUTTON\_ACTION : Button \xrightarrow{o} ()$
  $BUTTON\_ACTION(b) \triangleq i := button\text{-}map(b)(i)$

state *system* **of**
  $i : \mathbb{Z}$
end

Solutions to Z exercises

Exercise 6.1: The first five names are all legitimate identifiers, but of the remaining names *1st_field* and *_data* are illegal because they do not start with an alphabetic character and *last-name* is invalid because it uses a dash, rather than an underscore. *b_3* whilst a legal identifier is not particularly useful as it does not express any property of what the variable is, or does. It is best to use more meaningful names.

Exercise 6.2: One way of defining this would be to define a free type:

REPORT ::= 'name in list' | 'name not in list'

which could then be used in a schema such as:

```
── InDir ──────────────────────────────
│ ΞDIR
│ name? : NAME
│ status!: REPORT
├──────────────────────────
│ name? ∈ dom(dir) ∧ status! = 'name in list'
│ ∨ name? ∉ dom(dir) ∧ status! = 'name not in list'
└───────────────────────────────────────
```

This type definition uses the convention of enclosing text in single quotes; there is some contention about this, and although it is used in many books there is reasonable doubt that it constitutes syntactically correct **Z**. Though there have been attempts to introduce string literals into the **Z** standard the semantics of such objects have not yet been clearly defined and are probably best avoided. A better method is simply to use identifiers with meaningful names for the messages, leaving the messages themselves abstract:

REPORT ::= in_list | not_in_list

This is often considered more appropriate as it does not elaborate too deeply on the exact contents of the message, and how they are represented.

```
    InDir ___________________________________________
┌───
│ ΞDIR
│ name? : NAME
│ status!: REPORT
├──────────────────────
│ name? ∈ dom(dir) ∧ status! = in_list
│ ∨ name? ∉ dom(dir) ∧ status! = not_in_list
└──────────────────────────────────────────────────
```

Finally, a rarely used way is to define your own type CHAR containing all the individual characters required and a type TEXT consisting of a sequence of that type. Whilst more general, this solution is unnecessarily complex for most uses since we will have only a fixed set of messages. It is also less clear since we would not be able to see the set of all messages in a specification as we can in the former method.

Exercise 6.3:

a).

[NAME]
$people\_in\_roomA : \mathbb{P}NAME$
$people\_in\_roomB : \mathbb{P}NAME$

b)

$allowed\_people : \mathbb{P}NAME$
$people\_in\_roomA \subseteq allowed\_people$

c)

$$people\_in\_roomA \cap people\_in\_roomB = \varnothing$$

d):

$$no\_of\_people = \#(people\_in\_roomA \cup people\_in\_roomB)$$

Exercise 6.4: We can describe flight details as a set of tuples consisting of airport names and associated destinations:

$$HasFlightsTo : \mathbb{P}\,(\text{AIRPORT} \times \text{DESTINATION})$$

and then assign values:

$$HasFlightsTo = \{(Heathrow, Paris), (Heathrow, New\_York), (Charles\_de\_Gaulle, London)\}$$

We shall see later in the chapter another way of describing this.

Exercise 6.5: Firstly, we might define two variables *service* representing the current process being used and *services_used* which is a bag containing all those processes used so far:

$$service : \mathbb{N}$$
$$services\_used : \mathsf{bag}\ \mathbb{N}$$

At the beginning of the day services used would be set to empty:

$$services\_used = [\![\,]\!]$$

Each time a service is used its number is added to the list:

$$services\_used \uplus [\![service]\!]$$

At the end of the day we can determine if a particular item was used by setting *service* to the appropriate service value and then seeing if it is in the bag:

$$service \sqsubset services\_used$$

and if so, we can find out how many times it was used:

$$count\ services\_used\ service$$

Exercise 6.6:

[ASCII]

```
┌── FILE ─────────────────────────────
│ file: seq ASCII
└─────────────────────────────────────
```

a)

Init

FILE

$file = \langle\rangle$

b)

Append

ΔFILE
$text? : \mathbf{seq}\ ASCII$

$file' = file \frown text$

c).

Insert

ΔFILE
$text? : \mathbf{seq}\ ASCII$
$position? : \mathbb{N}$

$position? \leq \#file$
$(\exists\, x,y : \mathbf{seq}\ ASCII \mid \#x = position? \bullet file = x \frown y \land file' = x \frown text? \frown y)$

d)

Delete

ΔFILE
$start\_pos?, end\_pos? : \mathbb{N}_1$

$start\_pos? \leq end\_pos? \land end\_pos? \leq \#file$
$(\exists x, text, y : \mathbf{seq}\ ASCII \mid \#x = start\_pos? - 1 \land$
$\#text = end\_pos? - (start\_pos? + 1) \bullet$
$file = x \frown text \frown y \land$
$file' = x \frown y)$

Exercise 6.7:

Insert

$\Delta FILE$
$newtext? : TEXT$
$position? : \mathbb{N}$

$position? \leq \#file$
$(\exists x,y : TEXT \mid \#x = position? \bullet file = x \frown y \ \wedge file' = x \frown text? \frown y)$

Exercise 6.8:

[X]

$add\_element : X \times \mathbf{seq}\ X \rightarrow \mathbf{seq}\ X$

$\forall x: X; s: \mathbf{seq}\ X \bullet add\_element\ (x, s) = \langle x \rangle \frown s$

[X]

$occurrences : X \times \mathrm{seq}\ X \rightarrow \mathbb{N}$

$\forall x: X; s: \mathbf{seq}\ X \bullet occurrences(x, s) = \#(s \upharpoonright \{x\})$

Exercise 6.9:

$| \ digit : 1 \mathrel{..} 9$

or

$digit : \mathbb{N}_1$

$digit \leq 9$

are two possible definitions.

Exercise 6.10:

a) First, we define the user type:

[ELEM]

And the queue as sequence of these elements:

```
  Queue ____________________________________
| queue: seq ELEM
|___________________________________________
```

b)

```
  Init _____________________________________
| Queue
|______________________
| queue = ⟨⟩
|___________________________________________
```

c)

```
  Enqueue __________________________________
| ΔQueue
| x?:ELEM
|______________________
| queue' = queue ⁀ ⟨x?⟩
|___________________________________________
```

```
  Dequeue __________________________________
| ΔQueue
| x!:ELEM
|______________________
| queue ≠ ⟨⟩
| queue = ⟨x!⟩ ⁀ queue'
|___________________________________________
```

Trying to extract an element from an empty queue would give an error, so we need to state that the queue must not be empty for this operation to work.

Exercise 6.11:

```
___ PreLogon ________________________
| SYSTEM
| name?: NAME
|____________________
| name? ∈ allowed
| name? ∉ logged_on
| #logged_on < max_capacity
|_____________________________________
```

Exercise 6.12:

a) Firstly, require a type to return a message stating what the error condition is. We can define this as:

REPORT ::= queue_empty

We now write the schema to interrogate the queue to see if it is empty and return a message if this is the case. This operation does not affect the state of the queue so we use the 'Ξ' before the Queue schema.

```
___ IsEmpty! ________________________
| ΞQueue
| message! : REPORT
|____________________
| queue = ⟨⟩ ∧ message! = queue_empty
|_____________________________________
```

IsEmpty! has an exclamation mark after it to show that its purpose is to report an error. By convention schema names ending in '!' denote errors.

b) We can now define a new Dequeue operation which will either get the next element in the list or return an error message:

NewDequeue ≙ IsEmpty! ∨ Dequeue

Exercise 6.13:
Given:

```
Prime
─────────────────────────────
x : ℕ
─────────────────────────────
¬(∃ y, z: ℕ | x ∉ {y, z} • x = y * z)
─────────────────────────────
```

we could state:

$$\exists x : \mathbb{N} \bullet \text{Prime}$$

Exercise 6.14:
a)

```
HSchema
─────────────────────────────
a : ℤ
─────────────────────────────
∃ b, c: ℤ • a = (b + c)
─────────────────────────────
```

b) The result would be identical.

Exercise 6.15:

$$\text{Coordinates} \mathrel{\widehat{=}} \text{Position}[column/\ x, row/y]$$

which would give the new schema:

```
RSchema
─────────────────────────────
column, row : ℕ
─────────────────────────────
```

Exercise 6.16:

$$\text{Diagonal} \mathrel{\widehat{=}} \text{IncX} \mathbin{;} \text{IncY}$$

Exercise 6.17:

a)

Time24hr

$minutes? : \mathbb{N}$
$minutes!, \ hours! : \mathbb{N}$

$hours! = minutes? \ \mathbf{div} \ 60$
$minutes! = minutes? \ \mathbf{mod} \ 60$

b)

Time12hr

$hours? : \mathbb{N}$
$hours! : \mathbb{N}$

$hours! = hours? \ \mathbf{mod} \ 12$

c)

$$Time \mathrel{\widehat=} Time24hr >> Time12hr$$

Exercise 6.18:

$\_ \ \text{DividesInto} \ \_ : \mathbb{N} \leftrightarrow \mathbb{N}$

$\forall x, y : \mathbb{N} \bullet x \ \text{DividesInto} \ y \Leftrightarrow (\exists z : \mathbb{N} \bullet x \ * z = y)$

Exercise 6.19: We can do this with a recursive definition:

$sum : \text{seq} \ \mathbb{N} \rightarrow \mathbb{N}$

$\forall n : \mathbb{N}; \text{s}, \text{t} : \mathbf{seq} \ \mathbb{N} \bullet$
$sum\langle\rangle = 0$
$sum\langle n\rangle = n$
$sum \ s \frown t = sum \ (s) + sum \ (t)$

Exercise 6.20:

$$decrement \triangleq (\lambda n: \mathbb{N} \mid n > 0 \bullet n - 1)$$

Note that we constrain the values to those above zero, as the predecessor for values equal to or below zero would be undefined for the natural numbers. The equivalent set comprehension is:

$$\{n: \mathbb{N} \mid n > 0 \bullet n \mapsto (n - 1)\}$$

Exercise 6.21:

```
── Difference ──────────────────────────
│ x?, y? : N
│ variation! : N
├────────────────
│ variation! = if x? > y? then x? - y? else y? - x?
└────────────────────────────────────────
```

Exercise 6.22:

```
── SquareTop ───────────────────────────
│ numlist, numlist':seq N
├────────────────
│ (let hd == head numlist •
│    (let square == hd + hd •
│       numlist' = ⟨square⟩ ⁀ tail numlist
│ ))
└────────────────────────────────────────
```

Recommended reading

The following list of books covers in greater detail many of the subjects described in this book:

Baber L. R. *Error-Free Software: Know-how and Know-why of Program Correctness*. Wiley series in software engineering practice, 1991.
A highly readable and concise guide to proof analysis. It forms a good comprehensive introduction to the area.

Dawes J. *The VDM-SL Reference Guide*. Pitman, 1991
The principal guide to **VDM-SL** giving the complete syntax of the language and numerous examples of use. A new version of the book is due soon to cope with changes brought about by standardisation work in the area. It remains one of the best reference guides to the language. It is also more readable than the standards papers and has a number of excellent examples of specifications in the language.

Dromey G. *Program Derivation: The development of programs from Specifications*. Addison Wesley, International computer science series, 1989.
A comprehensive and detailed guide to the derivation of programs from formal specifications. The book explains everything from mathematical induction to loop invariants with hundreds of useful examples. Although a large book and difficult to read in parts, it serves as an excellent source of reference. There are very few areas not covered in its many pages.

Spivey J. M. *The Z Notation: A reference manual,* 2nd edition. Prentice Hall, International series on computer science, 1992.
As the definitive reference book for **Z**, it probably represents the best guide available. Much of the current standardisation work in **Z** being based, at least in part, upon it.

As well as these books it is also recommended that the reader look at current standardisation work in the area of formal methods. At the time of writing draft standards documents for both **VDM-SL** and **Z** were in circulation. Information on the **Z** standard is available from the Oxford University Computing Laboratory, Programming Research Group.

Another source of reference to both **Z** and **VDM** is the comp.specification newsgroups available through the Internet, as well as a number of Web sites dedicated to different formal notations. At the time of writing the Web site:

http://www.comlab.ox.ac.uk/archive/formal-methods.html#notations

provided a good index to these.

Glossary

Abstract data type: A data type in which the details of its implementation are hidden from its users, enhancing modularity and security. This means that one representation can be replaced by another without changing the external behaviour of the operations. They are defined by a set of valid values and the operations on these values.
Abstract type: A type containing no predefined operators for generating, manipulating or collating its values apart from testing for equality (see also Sort).
Associative: An operator '$\underline{o}$' is associative if $(a \ \underline{o} \ b) \ \underline{o} \ c = a \ \underline{o} \ (b \ \underline{o} \ c)$. The order of evaluation with such an operator is of no consequence and the operator binds equally on both of it's arguments. For example, 1 + 3 + 5 would give the same result whether we add the one and the three first, or the three and the five. Operators can also be left and right associative in which case the expression $a \ \underline{o} \ b \ \underline{o} \ c$ would be taken as meaning $(a \ \underline{o} \ b) \ \underline{o} \ c$ if the operator is left associative, and $a \ \underline{o} \ (b \ \underline{o} \ c)$ if right associative. In these cases the precedence of one of the arguments is higher.
Binding: Bindings associate values with a collection of variable names. They consist of a collection of named variables each with an associated type and a typed value.
Canonical expression: An expression (or value) that cannot be reduced further. For example, the numeral 9 cannot be reduced further, whereas (4 + 5) can, and is therefore not a canonical value.
Commutative: An operator '$\underline{o}$' is commutative if $a \ \underline{o} \ b = b \ \underline{o} \ a$. The operator for set union is therefore associative since the order of its arguments is unimportant.

Composite type: A type made up a number of component types. For example, a record consisting of a number of fields each of which is a type.
Compound types: Types constructed from other types, normally by the use of type constructors.
Comprehension: The definition of sets and lists by some property common to all the elements of them, rather than explicitly defining each element individually. For example, $\{x \mid x > 5\}$ would be the set of all numbers having a value greater than 5.
Consistency: Having the property that a derivation does not contradict that from which it is derived.
CSP (Communicating Sequential Processes): A formal specification language allowing specification of concurrency and communications. CSP formed the basis of the formal description language LOTOS.
Denotational semantics: A way of specifying the meaning of a language by defining a mapping from the language into a set of objects constructable in a set of expressions in a calculus.
Dialogue Specification: The specification of the user interface. The form in which the system will interact with the user.
Equivalence: Equal in value, quantity etc. In computing showing the equivalence of two functions is computationally intractable.
Estelle: A specification language partly formally defined for describing distributed or concurrent processing systems. Based on the programming language Pascal, with extensions, an Estelle specification defines a system of hierarchical state machines communicating via bi-directional channels.
Exception handler: A piece of code that is activated when an error, such as under- or over-flow, occurs during run-time and which is designed to recover or report the error.
Explicit definition: Where the definition is given in a form that shows how the operation will be carried out. These are more concrete than implicit definitions.
Flat type: A type which cannot contain function types (see below).
Function types: Types used to show the type parameters of a function, usually of the form $T_1 \rightarrow T_2$ or $() \rightarrow T_2$ (where T is a type). Such types are sometimes referred to as non-flat types, and as function signatures.
Higher-order functions: Functions that take other functions as arguments and produce functions as results.
Imperative language: A language consisting of a sequence of commands that express how an initial state is transformed to a final state, where state changes are either changes to the contents of memory cells or I/O operations (side effects).
Implicit definition: Where the definition is given in terms of what the operation is required to accomplish, without any consideration as to how the task is to be carried out. Operations in this form usually consist of a pre- and post-condition and are considered abstract.

Infix notation: Occurring in the middle. For example, the plus sign is placed between two numbers _ + _.
LOTOS (Language of Temporal Ordering Specification): A mathematically defined formal definition language that allows modelling of synchronous and asynchronous communication and is therefore ideally suited to specifying protocols.
Maximal type: A type which is not a subtype of any other type apart from itself. The maximal type of a type is the largest type of which it is a subset. For example, in the specification language **Z** two sets of the form $A = \{2, 4, 6\}$ and $B = \{1, 2, 3\}$, although different, would share the same maximal type $\mathbb{P}\mathbb{Z}$. Type checking in a number of formal languages involves ignoring any subtype predicates placed on types thereby checking only their maximal types.
Model-orientated specification languages: The specification is an abstract model of the system being specified.
Named type: A type that has a unique identifier representing or denoting the type. For example, natural $\mathbb{N}$, real $\mathbb{R}$ and integer $\mathbb{Z}$. The name or symbol represents a unique type and when it is referred to represents the type with its associated properties.
Non-determinism: A property whereby an event or value cannot be determined beforehand, such as the allowing of more than one possible state after execution of an operation for a single state before the operation, or being unable to determine which of a series of commands is executed next.
Object-orientated: A programming paradigm in which a program is viewed as a collection of discrete objects, abstract data types, that are self-contained sets of data structures and routines that interact with other objects. A program is thus seen as the interaction of a collection of objects.

The fundamental idea behind object-orientated methods is that the structure of programs represents the structure of the real world. Using this method you devise a set of classes that represents some class in the world, for example people, dogs etc. Classes inherit properties from other classes. Within classes you have instances; for example, each person is an instance of the class people. A class describes a set of properties, for example name, address etc. Each instance describes a specific property, for example that of being called 'Fred'.

Objects communicate by messages sent between them. A class will specify what messages it will respond to. Different objects will respond to the same message in ways appropriate to themselves. Thus a string, a real number and a picture will respond to the message 'print yourself' differently. Unlike normal programming an object-orientated program does not proceed by following a set of instructions, but by the sending of messages. For example, an object can be sent a message telling it to multiply itself by three and will respond with a message containing the result. An object can also make calls to other objects in order to respond to a message.

Other concepts encapsulated within the object-orientated paradigm include inheritance (the ability of objects to inherit properties from each other) and generics (the parameterising of types). Object-orientated methodologies make abstraction easier and encourage security (since objects can be manipulated only by their own set of operations).

Operational semantics: A way of specifying the meaning of a program by specifying the effect at run-time of statement execution.

Overloading: An operation or a variable is overloaded when it can operate on many different sorts (or types). For example, the operation *add* could be overloaded to allow addition of integers, reals, matrices etc.

Polymorphic function: A function that operates on some type, where the type is arbitrary; for example a sort that can take numbers, characters, words etc. Thus the same function can be used on many different types.

Postfix notation: Occurring after. For example the inverse symbol x^{-1}.

Prefix: Occurring before. For example, the successor operator succ(x).

RAISE (Rigorous Approach to Industrial Software Engineering): A specification method with functional, concurrent and imperative attributes all covered by a single semantic base and a well-defined set of proof rules. The RAISE language (RSL) is based on VDM with a number of enhancements, including facilities for modularisation, modelling of concurrency and possibilities for using algebraic specification styles.

Referential transparency: A notation is referentially transparent if the only thing that matters about an expression is its value. Within a part of a program with a fixed set of bindings, the value of a subexpression is the same whenever it occurs and the subexpression can be replaced by its value without changing the value of the whole expression. Languages with side effects, such as I/O operations or storing values in memory cells are *not* referentially transparent.

SDL (Specification and Description Language): Based on an extended finite state machine model supplemented by capabilities for abstract data types. SDL provides constructs to represent structures, behaviours, interfaces and communication links as well as for module encapsulation and refinement useful for the representation of a variety of telecommunications systems.

Semantics: A system of rules according to which the meanings of constructs in a language are determined.

Sequent: In logic, a sequent is a pair consisting of a set of premises and a conclusion which forms a well-formed formula.

Side effect: Many languages have notations that resemble expressions syntactically but in addition to yielding values the evaluation of the expressions has side effects such as storing new values in memory or outputting values.

Signature: A declaration indicating an object's type.

Sort: A type with no predefined value literals or operators apart from equality. Also termed an abstract type. Sometimes used more liberally to simply mean a type. In algebraic languages it is often used to mean the symbol representing a type.

Under-determination: Specifying a system in such a way that it is not constrained to a particular method. For example, a function may have a post-condition that is general enough that a whole class (or set) of algorithms would fulfil it rather than there being only one possible way of obtaining the required post-condition.

Under-specification: Where some property of the specification is left undefined and therefore cannot be determined.

Validation: A test to determine whether an implemented system fulfils or complies with its specified requirements. It is concerned with checking that the product matches the original requirements.

VDM (Vienna Development Method): A formal development method with three components: a notation for expressing software specifications, design and development; an inference system for constructing formal proofs of correctness; and a methodological framework for developing software from a specification in a formally verifiable manner.

Verification: A test to demonstrate consistency and completeness showing that one description bears the correct relationship to another. If a formal specification system is used, mathematical techniques, including theorem proving, can be used to accomplish this. Verification is concerned with checking that one phase of a software project accurately reflects the intentions of the previous phase. It is concerned with determining if the product is being developed correctly.

Wide-spectrum: Wide-spectrum languages contain both high-level abstract and low-level concrete structures. The motivation behind this being that the abstract specification can be refined to a highly concrete form whilst still remaining within the specification language's semantic environment. The translation process to the programming languages environment is thus minimised and this has advantages in that refinement can be proved by the use of mathematical induction. Minimising the translation process makes it easier to provide a correspondence since it is more likely that the lower-level constructs of the specification language resemble those of the programming language.

In a normal refinement the specification becomes more concrete. At the same time the choices of implementation become narrower; for example, at the top level we may specify that we wish a list to be sorted, lower down we would have to define how it is sorted. There are, however, still quite a few choices left when we reach the translation stage. A lot of translation is therefore still necessary to convert the program into an implementable piece of software.

With wide-spectrum specification languages there is far more refinement and so the number of alternatives is reduced to a point where there is almost a one-to-one correspondence between the specification language and constructs in the programming language. Only minor translation is therefore necessary and this leads to easier correspondence between the constructs in the two environments.

Z: Specification language using a combination of logic and elementary set theory. Texts describing programs are structured by means of schemas, together with a schema calculus. A graphical representation for schemas is provided by boxes.

Index